Ghost Warriors

Long Range Patrol
Airborne Rangers

Lt. Bob Stein

© Copyright 2016 by Robert G. Stein
All Rights Reserved

The author welcomes your thoughts and stories at
comments@ghostwarriorsbook.com

ISBN-13: 978-1534851450

ABOUT THE COVER

The ghost warrior on the cover is Milt Hendrickson (Vietnam, 1968). The book's title, *Ghost Warriors*, is attributed to the original commander of E-Company, 20th Infantry Long Range Patrol (Airborne), Major Dandridge M. Malone, who said,

"The advantage our patrol teams will enjoy is enemy confusion as to the size, strength, and intentions of the *ghost-like American warriors*."

While 2,600,000 U.S. military served in Vietnam, only 5,300 saw action as Army Long Range Patrol, Long Range Reconnaissance Patrol, or Rangers.

Major Malone is signing the first company order authorizing the Table of Organization and Equipment to activate E-Company on October 15, 1967. The rest is a part of American military history.

DEDICATION

This book is dedicated to E-Company, Long Range Patrol, and to all the Long Range Patrol and Long Range Reconnaissance Patrol teams that fought and died in the Vietnam War. I am indebted to the bravery, camaraderie, and spirit of E-Company's Long Range Patrol's 4th Platoon, whose experiences shape this story. This document recognizes these combatants, most of whom received neither recognition nor medals from the Army, all of whom deserved both. This book is also dedicated to the children, grandchildren, and descendants of these warriors and their families and friends, who watched them change, adapt, grow, and persevere. Every Long Range Patrol soldier should be forever proud of his part of history and the heritage of today's 75th Ranger Regiment.

TABLE OF CONTENTS

Foreword	1
Two Sergeants Major	5
Long Range Patrol: Dream, Concept, Reality	13
Chippergate 4-4	21
Four and a Wake-Up	37
Starlight Patrol	41
Brains for Lunch	57
Pterodactyl 22, Double Deuce	97
The Selection Process	105
Lt. Stein Meets Lt. Mayer	115
Major Malone in the Field	135
Night Combat Jump	139
Marine Force Recon	143
U.S. Army Rangers	151
Three Unique Patrols	157
Christmas Patrol	165
Wolf Pack Three-Niner: Death On Call	169
Mayer's Second Tour	173
Grins and Guffaws	181
Why This Book?	193
Why America Lost the War	217
3rd US. Infantry: The Old Guard	239
Off We Go Into the Wild Blue Yonder	249
After All, War is Hell, And Grief Is Collateral Damage: Reminiscences from Wives and Loved Ones in the States	257
What Did We Learn from the Vietnam Experience?	275

Appendix I: History of E-Company (LRP) 20th Infantry IFFV and
   C-Company (RGR) 75th Infantry IFFV 309
Appendix II: Recondo School, E-20 4th Platoon LRP Roster 315
Appendix III: Long Range Patrol and Rangers of the Vietnam Era
   Killed in Action 317
Appendix IV: First Brigade, 101st Airborne Division 319
Appendix V: Army Orders for Combat Infantry Badge.........................321

Foreword

Ghost Warriors is about a Long Range Patrol (Airborne) Company formed in Vietnam in late 1967 and reflagged into today's modern Army Rangers fifteen months later. As the official paperwork stated, their mission was, "to provide long range reconnaissance, surveillance, and target acquisition patrol capabilities to 1st Field Force Vietnam." The volunteers selected for this company were, for the most part, American teenage paratroopers, average age only nineteen, going into the lion's den to struggle with combat veterans of the North Vietnamese army averaging twenty-three years old. No forces in Vietnam had more close-up contact with the enemy than these soldiers.

Small patrol teams of five or six soldiers were inserted usually by helicopters, sometimes by Navy boats or parachute, into dense, typically triple-canopy jungle areas well beyond existing artillery fans. Communications could be hit or miss via mountaintop or airborne radio relays. The LRP soldiers' lives were dependent on their jungle survival and fighting skills, supported by six helicopters plus a Bird Dog aircraft assigned to the team.

There were four unifying threads for the men of the LRP Company and the 4th Platoon:

- All had volunteered multiple times.
- All were airborne and had earned their jump wings.
- All would graduate from Special Forces Recondo School authorizing them to wear the Recondo insignia.
- All returned from Vietnam as Rangers.

Decisions regarding the content of this book are the author's. The *Ghost Warriors'* true stories belong to the soldiers of the Long Range Patrol.

Ghost Warrior Geography
Vietnam - II Corps

During the Vietnam War, South Vietnam was divided into four Corps tactical zones for military operations. E-Company's twenty-eight combat teams patrolled exclusively within II Corps, the largest of the four areas, with headquarters in Nha Trang on the zone's southeastern coast. The U.S. military activated II Corps Command on March 15, 1966. It became the largest corps command in Vietnam and one of the largest in U.S. Army history.

CHAPTER 1

Four brave men who do not know each other will not dare to attack a lion. Four less brave, but knowing each other well, sure of their reliability and consequently of mutual aid, will attack resolutely.

Charles Ardant du Picq (1821-1870)

TWO SERGEANTS MAJOR

At first light S. Sgt. Tom Workman[1], leader of Team 4-3, met Capt. Don Williams and his 0-1 Bird Dog on the An Khe flight line to prep for a visual reconnaissance (VR) of their assigned area of operation (AO). After agreeing on the flight path and coordinating their maps, Tom scrambled up behind Don and they were off, climbing to several thousand feet above the beauty of Vietnam and an ocean of green jungle. Tom looked down, knowing that he and his team would be under that canopy the next morning, and thought of the adventures and dangers tomorrow would bring. Don broke squelch (turned on voice communication) and reported, "There's a small opening adjacent to deep jungle cover that might work for the insertion."

Tom scanned his map, found the field, and marked it. He wanted another look flying both lower and nearer that landing zone (LZ), but he knew any additional air reconnaissance could alert the watching enemy eyes about the Americans' intentions. With a last glance over his right shoulder, Tom showed Don where to fly the plane to mark their extraction LZ plus two alternate LZs should onsite enemy or unseen obstacles such as water or tree stumps require the primary sites to be abandoned. The men agreed on their selections and returned to An Khe.

Tom had a long list of things to do when he landed. He found S. Sgt. Ray Bohrer, his trusted assistant team leader.[1] He showed Ray the selected primary, alternates, and extraction LZs and they developed a recon route based on the intelligence 1st Field Force had given to Major Malone, E-

---

[1] S. Sgt. is the abbreviation (AP style) for the Army title, Staff Sergeant (SSG). Team 4-3 probably had the finest leadership of any Long Range Patrol team in Vietnam. Later in their careers both Ray and Tom became sergeants major.

Company commander, through platoon leader, Lt. Stein and provided to Team 4-3 at their briefing. Frequent enemy activity had been reported in their AO.

Team 4-3 was involved with their Long Range Patrol Company's assignment to screen the South Vietnam population centers of II Corps for North Vietnamese troops coming off the Ho Chi Minh trail. The team's mission was to patrol for four days with extraction scheduled for first light on Sunday. Temperatures were in the lower 100s and the always high humidity meant water was a critical consideration for the men.

Depending on the availability of surface water in the AO, each team member would normally carry four canteens of water on web belts plus two two-quart canteens in their rucksack. However, the patrol weight restrictions issued by Tom for this mission dictated the team would only carry limited amounts of water, and vital replenishment would come from small streams. All infantry soldiers carried iodine water purification pills (Halazone tablets) in bottles of fifty in the pockets of their canteen covers or in their survival kits. They could drop one tablet per quart of water into a canteen and the water would be safe to drink within a few minutes.

Team leaders could determine the weapons and loads for their soldiers. Lt. Stein knew that these brave men would choose weapons and ammunition that would best support their mission, which would include engaging the enemy in close combat. If they wanted a specific weapon, they carried it. Tom carried his M-16 rifle and a .45 caliber pistol. Ray Bohrer's piece was a chopped M-79 grenade launcher; he wore a vest of 40mm gas grenades, shotgun shells, and high explosive (HE) rounds. The minimum basic ammo per man was 400 to 800 rounds per rifle, fourteen to twenty-six twenty-round magazines, four frags (grenades), two smokes (smoke grenades of various colors), a Claymore mine, plus one "Willy Pete" (white phosphorus grenade).

The radio telephone operator (RTO) carried fewer rounds because of the PRC-25 radio's heavy twenty-six pound weight. The RTO also carried two radio batteries and an extra handset since moisture often disabled the radio, plus a second flexible longer antenna. In addition, each team member carried one radio battery to ensure clear communication throughout their patrol, one meal (Long Range Patrol or Long Range

Reconnaissance Patrol ration)[2] per day in the field, and an infrared (IR) strobe light. Ray carried the Olympus Pen Double E issue 35mm half frame recon camera.[3] Tom, as team leader, carried a URC emergency radio with an extra battery. Finally, each team member carried a morphine syrette in case of severe wounds and a container of serum albumin in a canister for immediate first aid (blood replacement and treatment for shock), plus bug juice (mosquito repellant), camouflage sticks, and malaria pills—a white pill daily, an orange pill weekly. (Darrell Presley, Tom Workman, Ray Bohrer, Del Ayers and Jerry Shankle took all the pills, but still came down with malaria. Each man was hospitalized for two to four weeks.)

Six combat medics were attached to the platoon; one of their duties was to dispense medicine to help the soldiers stay awake and suppress coughs. A medic distributed the capsules and pills, or if a medic was not a part of a particular team, the team leader would distribute them. Green and black plastic capsules containing amphetamines, commonly called Green Hornets or Yellow Jackets by the troops, helped them maintain a constant level of alertness.[4] Codeine in the form of 30 mg white tablets was a cough suppressant.

Once Tom and Ray checked the team's supplies, they reviewed patrol responsibilities with the men to ensure everyone knew the playbook should someone go down; during the four-day patrol there would be little or no talking. After the team was finally locked and loaded each member slept, but not well; they knew many missions lasted less than a day or so ending in a nasty gunfight. Don Kinton (point), Darrell Presley (RTO), Richard Gosnell (rear security), and their team leaders all wondered how long it

---

[2] Natick Labs designed ration packets for long-range reconnaissance troops, who found the standard C-Ration to be too heavy. The packets weighted 11 ounces, approximately a third of the weight of the C-rations, and were available in eight different menus. The rations, which were first issued in 1964, consisted of a pre-cooked freeze-dried meal in a reconstitution package and contained approximately 1,100 calories. Though they were intended to be hydrated, the meals could be eaten dry if necessary.

[3] Ray still has the camera and occasionally snaps pictures with it.

[4] Some research has shown people engaged in attention-intensive duty coupled with monotonous tasks find it almost impossible to retain a constant level of alertness without stimulus. This was the thinking behind disseminating the meds.

would be before they were spotted. They didn't know that five would depart, but only four would return alive.

Before first light each man headed to the waiting chopper, and then jumped up and down in a final noise check for the team leaders to ensure all their equipment was buttoned down. Noise discipline was critical to team success. With the team aboard and with the sound of the Huey warming up, the five Rangers were ready for infiltration. Tom made eye contact with the men, giving each a reassuring look. Nothing else needed to be said. Tom took his place between the two pilots and showed them the exact corner of the LZ where he wanted the bird to drop them.

They took off; quickly three other troop-carrying helicopters (slicks) plus two gunships joined Tom's Huey. The Command and Control chopper was Lt. Stein's, and the two additional slicks were there to pull out the team and chopper crew should the insertion helicopter be shot down. In addition, the choppers would carry on several ruses, faking landings to confuse the enemy ground troops and buy time for the team to land before the "bad guys" detected them. When Tom's Huey was within three to four feet off the ground, Team 4-3 pushed off the struts and ran fifty meters into the jungle to lay dog (be silent and observe at a 360-degree angle). It was very quiet.

After a quick communication check, they began their four-day mission. The men worked their way up the low hills, crossing game trails and foot paths which were not marked on their normally accurate maps. They encountered two small hooches (thatched huts) with still-burning fires, live chickens, and a pig; these were probably the homes of an extended South Vietnamese family. The team's maps showed this area was a free-fire zone and any individuals in the zone were assumed to be enemies. Team 4-3 took their knives, killed the animals, and moved back into the safety of the jungle.

Early the next day the team sighted numerous small groups of North Vietnamese army (NVA) soldiers and reported them to headquarters. Ray wanted a picture of the NVA to allow HQ to better understand the quality and physical condition of the enemy, but getting photos without being seen was tricky since some line-of-sight was necessary. Ray was able to take several photos when NVA soldiers crossed openings in the jungle. Later the team encountered—and noted on their maps—a high-speed trail capable of allowing passage for two soldiers side by side.

HQ delayed their pick-up by six hours because the team's choppers were on other missions, but the men discovered something interesting that Sunday morning while working their way to the LZ. Approximately a half-mile west of the extraction LZ, under triple canopy, they found a locked bamboo hooch. Tom was boosted onto Ray's shoulders so he could peer under the thatched roof. He saw boxes of ammunition, rocket-propelled-grenades (RPGs) and other military supplies. Tom thought for a moment, remembering that his mission was to gather intelligence, but knew the operation was already a success. The team would be in base camp in two hours and he didn't want to leave this weapons cache to the enemy.

Tom and the team debated strategy. It was not possible to call for artillery strikes since they were outside of any artillery fans, and airstrikes without ground observers would be ineffective. Immediate air support was not available since destroying this small hooch would not rank high on the military target list. They pried open the bamboo walls of the ammunition hooch with their Ka-Bar knives and considered how to destroy the cache: white phosphorus grenades? No, the explosions would immediately alert the NVA. Tom directed his team to sprinkle all their flammable bug juice on top of the ammo stores, thinking the burning repellant would burn through the entire stack. The men lit the fluid and headed for the LZ.

As the hooch burned, with multiple ammo explosions coupled with black smoke, the patrol neared the designated LZ to await pickup. When they got within fifty meters of the clearly marked LZ, the vegetation became less dense and they took on ineffective small arms fire. Tom told Darrell Presley, his RTO, to call for extraction under fire and a flight of Australian slicks and gunships, not familiar with LRP procedures, were diverted in air to Team 4-3's position. (Lt. Stein's six helicopters were still on the ground at the An Khe airfield, forty-five miles from the team.)

Sgt. Workman directed his team to begin returning fire to keep separation from the NVA and to allow an Aussie slick to dip down and recover his team. Workman contacted the incoming slicks and gunships and told them where his team was located along with the assumed location of the enemy. The team moved to the open field for pickup, but continued to receive fire. Presley popped a purple smoke grenade to serve as a benchmark and direct the gunship fire. Tom gave a compass bearing and directed the guns to fire on an azimuth[5] 100 to 125 meters from the purple smoke. The gunship pilot answered, "Roger that, rolling in hot," just as the enemy set up a machine gun and began to increase their rate of fire.

Tom was on the radio when a bullet severed the cord between his handset and the radio carried by Presley. Don Kinton took a shot in the chest with a massive exit wound in his back. A slick dropped down to pick up the team, but hovered six feet above the ground. Workman, Presley, and Gosnell had the wounded, 150-pound, equipment-loaded Kinton above their shoulders, but were unable to lift him into the chopper. Massive amounts of Kinton's blood and bone rained on the men. At the front of the chopper, Ray Bohrer pointed down to the ground directing the pilot to go lower, but the pilot rapidly shook his head—no, no, no! He wanted to keep some space between the ground and his bird to enable him to dip the nose, quickly gather speed and be off the hot LZ. Ray was limping because his ankle had been pierced by a punji stick.[6] With one hand he pointed his M-79 at the reluctant pilot's head and pointed to the ground with his other hand.[7] The pilot lowered the helicopter and Team 4-3 quickly climbed aboard.

Tom Workman held Don's head and hand and Ray heard him say, "It's getting real grey." Ray told him, "We'll be at the hospital soon." Don looked at Ray and said his final words, "I'll catch you later." Don was dead when they arrived at the 71st Evacuation Hospital in Pleiku.[8] No one knew for sure if it was enemy fire or fire from the gunships, but when Lt. Stein

---

[5] Azimuth: horizontal direction of an object from a fixed point expressed as an angle.
[6] Punji stick: a type of simple booby trapped stake made of wood or bamboo and generally placed upright in the ground.
[7] Sgt. Maj. Ray Bohrer stayed with the action; early in his career he attended the JFK Special Warfare School and served in reconnaissance units of the 82nd Airborne Division and in Germany with Recon in the 1st Battalion of the 509th Airborne. Ray requested a second Vietnam tour in 1969 and returned to E-Company, which by then had been reflagged to Charlie Company 75th Airborne Rangers. During the last three months of his second tour, Ray was in the 173rd Airborne Brigade's recon unit. He served in the Army twenty-seven years.
[8] Donald Ray Kinton is honored on the Vietnam Memorial Wall in Washington, D.C., panel 46E, Line 19.

met the chopper at the hospital Tom Workman told him, "It was our own damn gunships that killed Don."

CHAPTER 2

The battlefield is a tough place. Danger is everywhere. Who wins is determined by which side can best put together the skill, will and teamwork of soldiers.

Col. Dandridge M. Malone

LONG RANGE PATROL: DREAM, CONCEPT, REALITY

The summer of 1965 saw thirty Recondo School cadre from the 101st Airborne Division travel to West Point. Their mission was to instruct cadets in patrolling, survival skills, map reading, field medicine, jungle penetration, McGuire Rig, Slide for Life, log walk, hand-to-hand combat, and other competencies from the Recondo School at Ft. Campbell, Kentucky. Maj. Malone, a professor at the Point, took the opportunity to introduce his vision and concept of a Long Range Patrol (LRP) Company to these airborne trainers.

One evening after Recondo training was over, Maj. Malone invited the airborne trainers to his home and shared the plan he was going to present to the United States Army. He told the assembled cadre he would be proud and honored, should his dream be accepted, if they would volunteer for the new LRP Company. The LRP would be different from existing Long Range Reconnaissance Patrols (LRRP) in that LRPs would go much farther into enemy territory—far beyond any artillery support and outside the range of an infantry battalion's radio network. LRPs would need to rely on their skills, four slicks, two gunships, and an O-1 Bird Dog aircraft should they run into trouble. Sgt. Regis Murphy, a Ranger School graduate remembers thinking, I want to follow this man. The Army approved the major's plan and Malone was designated as the Officer in Charge (OIC).

Malone began his Army career as a private and ended as a colonel almost thirty years later. During that time, he received a Bachelor of Science degree from Vanderbilt University, a Master of Science degree from Purdue, and graduated from the Army's Command and General Staff College as well as the Army War College. Renowned as the Army's leading expert on leadership both in garrison and combat, he taught the subject to noncommissioned officers, West Point cadets, and students at various Army service schools including the Army War College. In 1980, Malone developed an audiotape on military leadership titled, *Soldier*. In 1983, he authored a book, *Small Unit Leadership: A Commonsense Approach*. The cover quote by Gen. S.L.A. Marshall summarizes Malone's philosophy, "Platoons seal the fate of armies."

Malone's LRP Company was formed in Vietnam on October 15, 1967 mainly from 101st troops in I Corps. Maj. Malone remembered Regis Murphy from the West Point airborne trainers' meeting and sought him out; Malone found Murphy with the 5th Special Forces Group just completing his first tour in Vietnam. While Murphy was with the 5th, their Special Forces camp in the dangerous A Shau Valley was being assaulted by several NVA regiments in February and March 1966. Part of Sgt. Murphy's MIKE (Mobile Strike Force Command) battalion comprised of fourteen American Special Forces and 550 Chinese Nung mercenaries was sent to aid the camp's defense.

The following is Sgt. Regis Murphy's description of a patrol mission designed to gather information and then, when the mission was completed, to ambush targets of opportunity as choppers from the famous 281st Assault Helicopter Company extracted them. Three weeks after his patrol, the Special Forces camp at A Shau was overrun; half of the Americans and most of their Chinese Nung troops were killed. Sgt. Murphy's account begins:

We were inserted into the A Shau at 0730 on a Wednesday, I believe. As usual, we knew the NVA were there and they knew we were coming. The sound of a fast-approaching Huey was a dead giveaway to the enemy that we were there. While the thickness of the jungle kept our whereabouts a secret, it also did theirs. We were even up so far.

In the late afternoon, we observed three groups of undetermined size moving from northwest to the southeast. They were North Vietnamese regulars, well-equipped and moving rather fast, apparently with little fear of being observed and certainly not believing they would be attacked, at least not from the ground. We always appreciated their confidence as it worked to our advantage more often than not. Since our initial mission was to Observe and Report, we remained in the vicinity of a junction of three trails and a small stream, and maintained our status of Stealth and Security until nightfall. Unlike American forces, which could be resupplied with water, the NVA would almost always stay close to a water supply and usually were found not far from lakes or streams. At dusk, we moved closer to the trail junction and set up our electric Claymore mines to cover the largest portion of open ground, which in this terrain wasn't much. We also taped one white phosphorous grenade in a tree alongside the trail or in a position where we believed the enemy, when fired upon, would take cover or attempt to maneuver to us. Every one of our men carried about four feet by one inch of Army issue green tape wrapped around the handle of his sharp knife. Tape was used for taping mines or grenades in trees where they would be more effective, taping the hands and mouths of prisoners, marking aiming points, taping one's collar up at night, quieting anything that made noise, and hundreds of other uses.

At night, the sounds of the jungle animals gave us a slight feeling of security since we knew that the enemy moved at night only when it was mission essential to do so, and the animal noises (or lack thereof) would keep us informed of any movement in the area. The idea that they, the enemy, were better at night travel or fighting than us was a myth purported by some fiction writer or newspaper reporters attempting to create a story! The truth of the matter was, even though this was their backyard, they did not like to move through the jungle after nightfall. Since the majority of the North Vietnamese army was made up of conscripts, with many being city boys, even though they were well-trained and motivated they were still human. Most hadn't overcome the basic instinct, for example, of attempting to stay dry when it rained or to sleep when they stopped for the night or after they ate. These habits worked to our advantage on several occasions.

The quieting of the jungle animals at night announced one of two things: either there was human movement in the area or it was about to rain. An underestimated characteristic of rain is that it rains equally on everyone on whom it falls. Simple and true however, soldiers react differently to it depending on their training and mission. Rookies tend to futilely attempt to protect themselves from it and stay dry, a ridiculous act to experienced soldiers especially in the A Shau Valley.

This was the big league. This place was like no other on the face of the earth. It was a green purgatory, a place of suffering, perhaps to atone for one's sins, but a prelude to hell where only the dead are excused. And in this soil there were plenty of dead, who for years attempted to survive its wrath. Bones of Chinese, Mongols, Japanese, French, British, Laotians, Cambodians, Vietnamese, and now Americans fertilized the evil growing and forever present here in this valley of death and lost souls.

Tonight we could hear rain above us filtering through the darkness and finally falling softly on us. The humidity increased and breathing in the wet, heavy air added to our discomfort. Nights in the A Shau Valley were experienced moment by moment where anticipation of pain and suffering were excruciatingly savored by the level of weakness—or preparedness—or madness of each soldier's mind. Nights there were often referred to as *lifetimes in darkness* by many of those who survived them. When the rain fell silent, we knew the silence announced the arrival of malaria-carrying mosquitoes. These tiny devils had the ability to, in effect, add to one's madness. They seemed to attack in coordinated waves on the most unprotected body parts, and even when driven off would only temporarily halt their vicious assault. Our men however, at this level of training and experience, would remain still and silently take the pain of these insect enemies until their feeding was satisfied or slim rays of daylight cut through the dark jungle.

By now our wet bodies began to feel the congealing of the jungle floor or the mud where we lay. It felt like our clothes were stiffening and we could smell the drying foliage. The smell would often signal the brain to come back to full alertness as the jungle animals would begin to greet the new day. Just before daylight, we'd pass around a canteen of water, drinking it until it was empty and preparing for whatever the shades of light might bring.

After an early morning communications check, hopefully with good results, we'd tap each other to confirm that we each were fully awake and alert. We knew the habits of the enemy well; we sniffed the air for the aroma of cooking rice or garlic—the Vietnamese soldiers' favorite way to spice up their military rations. Listening for movement at this time of day was much more effective than looking for it; if we saw movement this early in the day, chances are we'd be forced into contact due to the proximate location of our night halt position to a road or trail. Therefore, when sufficient light became available, the team would back deeper into the jungle to avoid such contact unless an order to force contact was received.

When such a change of mission was issued, the team used everything at its disposal to its advantage. We would plan artillery fire, alert tactical aircraft to determine its availability, and then estimate and confirm a time and location for extraction. We would also confirm the location where a reaction force would be inserted. Finally, we would disseminate the plans among the team.

The *point* of an enemy formation usually consisted of three men. We could determine their level of training and experience by the way they moved and how they carried their weapons. Rookies moved rather nonchalantly and carried their weapons over their shoulders or with one hand, whereas veterans moved cautiously, looking all around and carrying their weapons at-the-ready. Today, we saw rookies coming down the trail directly into the kill zone of our Claymores. As our mission had now changed, everyone was poised to initiate action as soon as the mines were set off. After immediately notifying the rear of our situation via preplanned code words and alerting the artillery, we all were tense. We were holding for that moment when the memory of our suffering during the last twelve hours would be unleashed on the poor souls now walking, unaware of our presence, down range from us.

When possible we would allow the point of the enemy unit to pass, assigning their fate to the two men on that side. The two men on the other side of our line would be responsible for the detonation of the second Claymore mine whenever they decided it best to do so. The initial Claymore blast directed at the lead element of the unit (once the point had passed) would be activated by the team leader as the radio operator fired one magazine, and then turned to cover our rear and confirm via the radio that we were in contact. We would call for artillery fire knowing that slicks and gunships were now on the way. In this situation, the enemy's usual reaction was to counterattack on our left, their right. It was in this area that we located a white phosphorus grenade and placed fire from our grenade launcher. When faced with a phosphorus explosion, the enemy would often believe that the area was marked by the artillery, and the sounds of the exploding shells from the grenade launcher, sounding similar to the report of a small mortar, would direct them to attempt to assault on the other side of our line. Usually, there would be a respite of a few seconds as they attempted to evaluate the situation and reorganize. This was when we would retreat either directly to the pickup zone or to a fallback position where we prepared the light antitank weapons for firing. These weapons fired an anti-tank rocket that, when used in the jungle, would penetrate through several layers of jungle growth before exploding and sounding like a crew-served weapon. The idea was to add to the confusion of the enemy commander as well as to mark our position for the incoming aircraft.

We were hopeful—*very* hopeful—that our wait would be short and the gunships were already on-station. Shifting the artillery fire to suspected locations from which the enemy may have come and using the gunships for local targets, the team would set up a tight three-sixty defensive position and hope the exfiltration slicks would get there before the enemy regrouped and decided to attempt another assault. There was and remains to this day nothing—absolutely nothing like the sound of a Huey coming to rescue you from a place like the A Shau Valley under the circumstances just described. The anticipation accompanied by the hope that you may get out of here without being killed or wounded is almost unbearable. You have a moment to think about it and the realization of your situation sets in. Your breathing and heart rate increase and for a second you feel the pounding in your temples and chest. You find yourself attempting to pierce the jungle rooftop and see your salvation coming directly for you. Unfortunately, as your rescuers get closer, so often your enemy does, as well.

Boarding the ship in times like this changes your concern from the enemy's fire to the fire of our helicopter door gunners. This friendly fire was probably the most common danger to patrols in this war. As the pickup chopper would flair back to land, one or more of us, depending upon the enemy situation, would slowly stand up with our rifle above our head and wave to the pilot and door gunners of the landing ship.

As soon as the helicopter's crew recognized us, we would run to board in twos. The first two to board would go to the opposite side and cover that area. The next two would split with one sitting between the pilots and the other in the middle of the troop compartment so the front of the ship could be covered. The last two to board, usually the team leader and radio telephone operator, once aboard would yell and signal with thumbs up to go. Usually by this time, the aircraft was already lifting off and rapidly attempting to get out of the area while maintaining a low altitude until well clear of the landing zone.

The flight back was as quiet as the one out. There was no gleeful yelling or patting teammates' backs. It was a time of coming back to the other side of the abnormal environment in which these men found themselves. The team counted at least nine confirmed NVA dead or wounded, but thought there were possibly more.

Awaiting them upon landing were friends who had been monitoring their activities out there. When possible, those friends would have a cold beer or some ice water for the returning team, and they always gave them a welcome hug of understanding and congratulations for surviving the A Shau. Those friends knew that every day in that valley was the same but different regardless of how many times you went into it. Coming out in one piece was something to celebrate. After a debriefing, the team would immediately rearm, refit, and prepare to do it again when called.

CHAPTER 3

Bravery is the capacity to perform properly even when scared half to death.

Gen. Omar Bradley

CHIPPERGATE 4-4

Oscar Caraway was the assistant team leader of Patrol Team 4-4, call sign Chippergate. The following are his reflections on one of the 4th Platoon's most dangerous missions. All of the men were wounded, all would survive, two with over a year in U.S. military hospitals. Two were awarded Silver Stars, three received Bronze Stars with "V" (Valor) device, and five were awarded Purple Hearts.[9] In addition, a Distinguished Flying Cross was awarded to Wolf-pack gunship commander, Jim Fisher. Oscar recalls:

It was early morning on February 18, 1968. Our team was on downtime when S. Sgt. Bob Johnston got a call. He wondered who was in trouble this time. Wisheart was the usual suspect; he was eighteen years old and full of energy. Sgt. Johnston thought it must be something serious to be called in to see Maj. O'Conner, our new company commander; he was right—dead right. The major needed our team to cover some very dangerous territory. We were aggressive and always wanted to be in the field. We were the perfect men for the job.

While I began to ready the team, Sgt. Johnston went up in the O-1 Bird Dog aircraft piloted by Capt. Don Williams, to conduct a VR (visual reconnaissance) to look over the terrain. He needed to look for LZs and pickup locations. He knew this one was going to be difficult since all he could see was the dense canopy of the jungle. It was nothing but extremely steep slopes. He picked some spots that he thought might work.

---

[9] **Silver Star:** a military combat award for gallantry in action against an enemy of the U.S. **Bronze Star:** awarded for heroism or meritorious service in a combat zone; the "V" device is awarded for valor in combat. **Purple Heart:** awarded for wounds suffered in in combat against an enemy of the U.S.; it is the nation's oldest military award. **Distinguished Flying Cross:** awarded for heroism or extraordinary achievement while participating in aerial flight.

By afternoon it was hot and sticky. Sgt. Johnston came to the team to brief us on the mission. We were anxious, but always ready for whatever mission our team leader said was next. Sgt. Johnston looked as serious as I'd ever seen him as we waited for him to speak. My team included Del Ayers (medic and radio operator), Lieuan Hansen (scout rifleman), John Wisheart (medic and rifleman), and me, Oscar Caraway (assistant team leader).

Sgt. Johnston started the briefing by telling us, "Take only a small ration of food but pack double ammo and grenades." He said to bring water, but don't expect to eat. I could tell this mission was going to be different and knew by the look in his eyes that he had a bad feeling about it. I knew this meant we were going into a *hot* area and were sure to get into a firefight. The normal 20-round magazines for our M-16 were switched out to thirties. We were accustomed to hard missions and danger was part of our job description. Any of us would follow Sgt. Johnston anytime, anywhere, and under any circumstances. We were ready to do our duty.

On that day, February 18, all our attention was focused on being prepared for this mission. That night no one on the team slept much. February 19 began as another hot day and we woke up sweating. As we loaded on the Huey for first light insertion, I paused and relived a moment of the Tet Offensive from only about a month earlier. Now I had to focus on this day, this mission. Today the objective was to locate and identify NVA troops and look for battalion-sized bivouac sites west of Plei Djereng. There had been reports of large groups of enemy troops throughout the area and along the Cambodian border.

As we lifted off the tarmac, we all looked at each other and I wondered what we were going to face. We were all young and proud, all Army Airborne and we always led the way. We were a seamless team with complete trust and confidence in each other and in everyone's ability to perform. Not one of us knew this would be our last mission together and for some of us our last mission ever.

After a ride that seemed to take a lifetime, we finally arrived at the first insertion point, but the chopper could not get us low enough to allow us to exit the bird. The second insertion point was the same. Our third and last insertion point put us miles into the jungle, deep beyond the Cambodian border, a place no American soldier was supposed to be. We didn't hesitate, though; we were ready to do the job.

The jungle was very dense with trees and vegetation; our only way to ground level was with rope ladders, our bodies hanging almost parallel to the ground, hand over hand, a foot to the next rung, muscles straining with a seventy-pound ruck, anxiety building with each step closer to the ground and our brains screaming commands to muscles. We had to get to the ground. We must do the mission and then, my team and God willing, come back alive.

After penetrating the triple canopy of trees, the helicopter disappeared. All was quiet. We waited for our leader to give the order to proceed, ready for anything. We talked in whispers and used hand signals to organize our team. We began to move through the jungle, following our LRP (Long Range Patrol) team's marching order: PFC Wisheart (point), S. Sgt. Johnston (team leader), SPC4 Ayers (RTO), SPC4 Hansen (rifleman) and me, Sgt. Caraway (assistant team leader and rear security).

We moved through the jungle like a well-oiled machine. Few words were spoken. We set out to complete the mission, resolved in spirit and secure in our experience as a LRP combat-team. Stealth was our protection, training our confidence, duty our motivation, and brotherhood our salvation. Within an hour we were able to locate a bivouac area. The jungle floor was clean and well-kept under triple canopy camouflage to prevent aerial detection. This was a large enemy base camp, well-hidden and obviously being used. It consisted of many bunkers, a tunnel complex, an aid station, and troop quarters.

Our team had been on many missions and seen many villages and NVA camps, but this one was unlike any other. We knew the enemy had just been there. Their smell lingered and the cooking pots were still warm. We saw a barber station with hair on the ground, not yet swept up. Also, there was a grave site, the dirt fresh and moist. The NVA soldier buried there could hold valuable information. Did we take the time and the risk to dig him up? The team decided that he must be exhumed, but we would wait until extraction day so as not to be detected. We would come back for him.

We quickly inspected the bunker/tunnel complex to determine what, if any supplies were available to the NVA upon their return from the Tet assault that could support other enemy missions. We moved through the area to gather as much intelligence as we could. With the mission complete and the NVA bivouac area scouted, we had no reason to stay. We needed to get out of there and later call in air strikes.

The entire team was nervous and on edge. We could feel the presence of the NVA all around us, and then the jungle sounds changed to silence. The hairs on the back of our necks were up and we knew we had to get out of their bivouac area. We left no trace as we went through the jungle, staying away from the trails, doing what LRPs do best.

After locating the NVA base camp, which was estimated to hold between eight hundred and nine hundred enemies, we called in the exact location through the aid of Capt. Don Williams' Bird Dog O-1 acting as a relay station. Then we sent a late afternoon position fix. We confirmed the azimuth to a landing zone for extraction on 20 February. The end of the mission was now in our grasp. Our team needed only to cross a heavily used and well-traveled high-speed trail to get to the planned go-to-ground night site. We moved parallel with the trail which was on a steep slope with heavy foliage. It was very windy. Suddenly, Sgt. Johnston's hand went up—Stop! We instinctively followed our training and immediately crouched down. Our eyes were peeled. He had heard something; a clank—what was it? Was it only in our minds or was it NVA?

We waited about five minutes but heard nothing; Sgt. Johnston motioned for Wisheart (who was on point) to fall back. Being team leader, Johnston was now going to lead. This was not protocol, but Johnston knew we were in trouble and he would protect his men even if it meant his life. He did not turn around to check our positions; he trusted our performance as a team. Controlled fear was our courage and a plan was in place. There was no choice; we knew we must cross the trail. Just ten more feet and we would be safe, back in the thick foliage.

Sgt. Johnston waited until the trail looked clear to cross. He then stepped out carefully with his left foot. The ground hid a low damp spot and his foot slid onto the trail. He regained his balance and looked up from the ground only to make eye contact with three NVA soldiers. They were caught off guard; we were alert and ready. They knew we were not supposed to be there. Sgt. Johnston's left side was exposed. Immediately a firefight began. The first enemy round penetrated low into the sergeant's torso, breaking his rib and puncturing his lung. His body spun around from the force of the bullet, only to catch a second round that took out his spleen. He went down with bullets finding his right arm and leg. Wisheart, farther back at the trail's edge, was hit in the leg next and he fell to the ground. The two of them were exposed with Johnston out on the trail and Wisheart at its edge.

As quickly as their feet hit the trail, a column of NVA soldiers appeared right on top of us. They apparently heard the helicopter looking for a place to drop us and went to recon the area. We were in full camo; they wore gray fatigues. Apparently the enemy column had been heading back to their bivouac area. Wisheart tried to put out fire with his M-16, but it jammed. Sgt. Johnston's CAR-15 (a smaller version of the M-16) was within his grasp, so he reached over and secured it. Both men were immobilized and still lying in the open. Ayers immediately called in coordinates. I could see him next to Wisheart, but now Ayers was shot through the arm. He continued to treat their wounds with one hand and fire his weapon with the other as if he was not injured. All three men were in a terrible crossfire.

Hansen and I, still fifteen feet back, instinctively began giving cover fire and I headed to high ground. My position was perfect so I could cover any one of the men. I had to hold the NVA back until my team could be pulled back to a safer position. Hansen fired his M-79 grenade launcher, taking out two NVA directly in front of Ayers and Wisheart. I could see Sgt. Johnston and Wisheart, although injured, were not out of this fight and never stopped firing. The sergeant was putting out fire using his .45.

Hansen took a position next to the trail behind a small boulder. Chaos began to lose its grip. We were gaining back control and we were going to keep fighting. The NVA might kill us, but we refused to submit! Hansen became targeted by an NVA. As I looked to my left, I could see he was still behind the boulder, but he was pinned down and shot through the hand.

I could see the NVA through the foliage. Hansen yelled out, "Get 'em!" and with the squeeze of my trigger, that enemy was no longer a threat. My attention shifted back to the trail. In horror, I could see an NVA soldier standing above Sgt. Johnston who was covered with blood. As I turned my gun, Johnston raised his .45 caliber pistol with his left arm and put another enemy down with a shot in the forehead.

That guy shouldn't have underestimated my sergeant. That NVA saw there were only a few of us, but Bob Johnston was not going to let any enemy soldier expose our one weakness. Even though shot through the hand, Hansen sounded like an army all by himself spraying fire and grenades 360 degrees.

We had to move forward—the gap between us had to be closed. The enemy was trying to outflank us rather than rush us; this mistake saved our lives. We could hear them scrambling. Apparently they thought there were a lot of us this deep into Cambodia and this close to their base, so they decided not to overrun us. They were confused and had no idea how many of us there were, only how fierce we were.

No one quits, no one folds! We all knew this was the fight of our lives and a fight for life itself. We had to pour out firepower. Hansen and I continued to cover our fallen teammates. Sgt. Johnston, almost fatally wounded, was still barking orders. What a leader! We were all returning fire. Sgt. Johnston was shot in the chest, the side, the leg, and twice in the right arm.

The world was moving in slow motion as I maneuvered through the broken falling branches and jungle leaves to get to my sergeant's side; Hansen covered me so I could make it. All I could think about was that I had to retrieve my fallen friends, my team. As a team, we worked together and helped drag Sgt. Johnston back to a sheltered position.

Hansen readied two bottles of serum albumin that he and Johnston used as a substitute for plasma and treatment of shock. Ayers, a medic by training, injected the 500ccs of albumin into Sgt. Johnston's left arm. Sgt. Johnston switched his .45 caliber pistol to his right hand, reloaded and continued firing at the enemy. He didn't realize his arm was broken with two bullet holes in it. With every shot his arm was flailing violently, so I grabbed the .45 fearing he would shoot himself or one of us. He wasn't ready to stop fighting.

Ayers ordered Wisheart to call for an extraction and threw him the radio. Not fifteen minutes earlier, we had called in our location. LRP teams are skilled in reading maps and compasses correctly and Sgt. Johnston had a practice of regularly calculating our location and marking our maps. Wisheart, surrounded by chaos, radioed the incoming pilot, but didn't use his proper call sign. He gave our position and the pilot replied, "Please use proper radio procedure." We really loved those guys, but this was no time for proper radio procedure. Wisheart yelled, "Get your ass down here now and get us out!"

At this point we were only ten to fifteen feet from the faces of the NVA troops. They were everywhere—their faces seemed to be never-ending. The more we shot, the more the NVA came out of nowhere, it seemed. I realized we were in a no-win situation. There was nowhere to retreat and we were surrounded. We five men were too shot up to get away and only three of us could run.

We were Chippergate 4-4. A commitment made long ago required that either all of us made it or no one would be saved. All that was left to do was to fight to the end together as a team. We looked at each other; we knew we were going to fight to the last bullet, the last breath, taking no prisoners. The minutes began to blur and one by one the NVA continued to fall. I yelled to the team each time I eliminated another threat. I thought, I may not get them all, but I'm going to make sure that some of them are not around to kill another day.

The whole thing was surreal—and then I saw the purple smoke. It was a miracle! The wind had stopped and the smoke stayed directly above us. The gunships had arrived. Three or four of them began blistering the entire area surrounding us with rockets and machine gun support. The gunships continually fired, almost directly upon us, and the enemy was being forced back. NVA were scattering in every open space. Suddenly a Huey was hovering over us and a jungle penetrator was lowered, first for the ones who were the worst wounded. The penetrator was not always carried by the ships, but in Sgt. Johnston's foresight, he told the helicopter crew to have it aboard that day.

Wisheart pulled Sgt. Johnston onto the rig which was not much more than cables and a small plank. As the penetrator lifted him up and away, Sgt. Johnston began to slip. Wisheart grabbed him and held onto him as if he was holding on to life itself. The two reached the helicopter, but didn't have the strength to climb in. The helicopter was under heavy fire and the door gunner climbed out onto the strut to pull the men to safety. They were finally secure, but the gunner took a hit to his leg. Half our team was out of the battle. In spite of leg wounds that had shattered his ankle and foot, Wisheart, showing great dedication to his team leader, continued to apply pressure to Sgt. Johnston's sucking chest wound.

Sustaining six serious wounds, Sgt. Johnston's odds in his race with death worsened after he was aboard the helicopter. It was a combat chopper with two pilots and two door gunners that supported the 4th Platoon's patrol teams. They did not have medical training and with Johnston's huge loss of blood covering his entire body, the door gunner assumed he was in great pain (he wasn't) and gave him an unrequested shot of morphine into his leg. Johnston remembered from his Recondo School training that morphine should *not* be administered if there is a serious chest wound, because it stops the ability to breathe. Johnston knew he had a chest wound because his mouth kept re-filling with blood; he mumbled a request to attach the empty morphine bottle to his shirt to alert the medical staff. As breathing became almost impossible, Johnston struggled to get to the open chopper doorway for additional oxygen. He stuck his head out of the helicopter and into the 80 to 100 mph wind. This allowed him to breathe just a bit and kept him alive.

The pilots had called for a Dust-Off (an acronym for Dedicated Unhesitating Service To Our Fighting Forces) chopper to meet them at the nearest fire base. When both choppers landed, the medics from the Dust-Off triaged the three wounded men: Wisheart, his ankle and foot shattered by two rounds, the door gunner needed care for his leg wound, and Johnston was touch-and-go between life and death. The Dust-Off chopper flew at maximum speed to the Pleiku hospital where medical doctors waited. Johnston was hand-carried by stretcher directly into surgery and his prognosis was grim. All his AK-47 wounds were serious and two were life-threatening—the first shot had hit and broken a rib and lodged in his spleen. The surgeon removed it. The second shot had broken another rib and entered his lung, which caused the sucking chest wound. That bullet was also removed. Normally, these powerful rounds would enter and exit, but because they hit his ribs and perhaps some equipment he carried, both rounds lodged in his body. (Sgt. Johnston always wanted those two rounds as Vietnam souvenirs, but that never happened.)

Next, the doctors looked at his wounded right arm, which could not function. (Johnston had transferred his .45 caliber pistol from his right hand to his left hand and had shot and killed an NVA soldier only ninety minutes earlier.) The first NVA bullet in his arm hit and broke his wrist and the second shattered his radius and ulna. The Pleiku medical staff placed a straight cast on that arm and it awaited surgery in Japan. The gunshot wound to his leg was only a flesh wound so it was just cleaned and bandaged. Johnston remembered receiving the leg wound; that round had felt like a bee sting, but when he looked down his pant leg was smoking. His last wound had been caused by an exploding grenade, unknown if friendly or enemy, but it caused his face to swell and turn black. Finally, he was stabilized.

Meanwhile back on the ground, Ayers was doing all the coordinating while Hansen and I laid down fire with our next to last mags of ammo. The steady firing of the gunships was able to push the NVA's point of attack force back a bit. At last, a second extraction helicopter was able to feed a McGuire Rig (three nylon ropes with three seats attached) through the trees. I remembered practicing that technique with live choppers and McGuire Rigs at Special Forces Recondo School in Nha Trang and it had been great fun. Not so now.

Small arms fire continued as the McGuire Rig was dropped. Now was our chance to get out! Hansen and I fired our last mags at the NVA troops that were still close by. Ayers gathered all our weapons and prepared to leave. As we secured ourselves in the McGuire Rig, I continued to fire at the enemy until I emptied my last mag. I had no ammo left. At that point, I was the only one not wounded. We sat on the rig, held on tightly, and looked up trying to see the blue sky beyond the canopy. The helicopter was taking too many hits and the pilot had to pull forward with full power before we were clear of the treetops.

As we were dragged through the trees, the thick branches pummeled me causing a severe head concussion, lacerations, and neck trauma. The only thing that kept me in the rig was the efforts of my two wounded teammates who refused to let the jungle take me back. Hansen was yelling up to the pilot to slow down. We were flying at 80 mph for what was to be a forty-mile ride. As we were ripped through the canopy, the rig began to spin violently under the chopper. It spun at such high speeds that our grip on our weapons broke and our guns fell 1200 feet back into the jungle.

At last, we made it back to base and to safety! We were deposited on the ground in a tangled heap without strength to move, exhausted, and nearly dead. At this point, base medics split us up for specific medical care. Chippergate 4-4 was no more.

I guess I was transferred to a Dust-Off chopper for transport to Pleiku Hospital, because the last thing I remember seeing before fading out was the jungle. I woke up in the intensive care unit at Pleiku. I opened my eyes and saw Sgt. Johnston in the bed across from me. Both of us were bandaged and could hardly move. I looked at him knowing how badly he'd been wounded, and watched him raise his hand as best he could to acknowledge me. I raised mine back and then the nurses wheeled him away. Was that our goodbye? I wondered how he could survive. He had been through so much. This was how it happened in war—so many of our teammates were suddenly gone. We would go forward to whatever the Army said to do next, not knowing the other's condition, whether dead or alive.

There was to be one more Chippergate 4-4 "casualty." S. Sgt. Swift, leader of Team 4-1 and a veteran of the Korean War, and S. Sgt. Brokaw his assistant team leader, were visiting Sgt. Johnston in the intensive care unit. The doctor came in and told them he was going to pull a large tube out of Johnston's body "like a garden hose." The doc pulled and pulled the long tube that was covered with blood and mucus. Swift fainted, hitting his head on the metal corner of the adjacent bed, and was knocked unconscious. He was admitted to the hospital overnight and released the next day. Sgt. Johnston recovered at Pleiku until he was stable enough to endure the six-hour flight to Japan for more surgery.

On February 19, 1968, each member of Chippergate 4-4 performed his job to survive an experience only a combat soldier can fully grasp. Others struggle to understand, but only those who experience it can comprehend. Our need to protect each other and prevent an overwhelming NVA force from overpowering us saved our lives. I am alive today because of my team. Their heroic deeds made survival possible. We lived and breathed and thought and worked as one, without question. Each of us was an airborne volunteer; we could have no lag time and no indecisiveness. We were adaptable, systematic, and eerily calm.

In time I recovered from my wounds and returned to the 4th Platoon of E-Company LRP 20th Infantry. I was awarded my own team and never again had the opportunity or privilege to patrol with those fine troopers of Chippergate 4-4. As a team we experienced what only those who serve know. My friend Del Ayers (SPC4/Medic and RTO) survived that day as well. As a sergeant, he was awarded his own team until he was DEROSed (Date Eligible for Return from Overseas) back to the U.S. Then Del began another mission, one that continued for thirty-nine years until April 3, 2007. That mission was to find the whereabouts of team Chippergate 4-4, each and every one of us.

Del retrieved the following team stats for that day, February 19, 1968: we were awarded two Silver Stars, three Bronze Stars, and five Purple Hearts, but our biggest reward was this—we all survived.

Chippergate Aftermath

Sgt. Johnston was in Pleiku hospital's intensive care unit for two weeks and in intermediate care for four more weeks awaiting sufficient recovery to allow medical transfer to Camp Zama in Japan. On the medical plane ride to Japan, he was seated on a lower bed and a box lunch was set on his lap. Even then, he was unable to open the lunch container until a nurse assisted with the sandwich and punched the straw into his milk carton.

At Camp Zama, Johnston went back into intensive care for an additional two weeks. The medical team focused on the shattered bones up and down his arm. With pins plus a wrist-to-shoulder elbow cast, he partially recovered and was able to transfer to medical facilities in the United States. After several long flights, Johnston arrived at the Valley Forge military hospital in Phoenixville, Pennsylvania, where he was admitted for four months. Upon release from Valley Forge, he was transferred to Ft. Bragg, North Carolina and assigned to the 82nd Airborne Division, but his medical condition prohibited him from regaining jump status. He was then transferred to Ft. Lewis, Washington where, as an airborne recruiter, he gave presentations about the Army airborne experience to potential soldiers in Washington State.

Three troopers from the 82nd Airborne Division (a handful were at Ft. Lewis receiving special training) were planning a night jump to maintain their airborne status. They asked Sgt. Johnston if he'd like to join them. Of course he said, "affirmative" and the men boarded a C141 Starlifter at McCord Air Force Base near Ft. Lewis. The plane was on a three-hour Air Force mission, but the pilots had agreed to fly over the Jones Lake drop zone on their way back to McCord. Johnston thought it was cool that four guys were jumping out of a plane designed to hold 123 heavily equipped combat paratroopers. That's when he got the urge to get back to Vietnam.

His medical records dictated that he should *not* be allowed to return to Vietnam, particularly with jump status, but he knew the clerk who had his records—the records that would deny him orders to Vietnam. The clerk said, "You must be crazy wanting back to Vietnam for a third tour," but after a few beers at the NCO club, the clerk approved Johnston's transfer as airborne unassigned stationed in Bien Hoa outside of Saigon. Johnston still doesn't know if the clerk didn't read his 1049 (a form requesting an Army action) and personnel records or let him slide as a favor to his request.

At the Bien Hoa replacement center, a captain called Johnston into his office and asked if he would be interested in interviewing for a special assignment. He thought that nothing could be quite as special as the LRP 4th Platoon but said, "Okay." That special assignment turned out to be on the security detail for Four-Star Gen. Creighton Abrams,[10] who had just

---

[10] Gen. Creighton Abrams led Patton's armored forces in WWII to relieve the 101st Airborne Division at Bastogne. Patton said of him, "I'm supposed to be the Army's best

taken Gen. Westmoreland's position, and who eventually became Army Chief of Staff, the top officer in the United States Army. When Johnston entered the general's headquarters, several warrant officers and enlisted men introduced themselves and said they were the general's security team. After his interview, Bob was designated the NCOIC (Non-commissioned Officer in Charge) of Abrams security team replacing the warrant officers. Bob enjoyed his time with Gen. Abrams and the two became good friends.

Sgt. Johnston normally rode in the front seat of a Jeep with a mounted M-60 machine gun following Abram's only lightly armored Chrysler. (It was nothing like today's VIP cars.) The Chrysler always flew an impressive red flag with four white general stars. Johnston regularly coordinated with the South Vietnamese army, navy and marines, as well as National Security police, CIA, Secret Service (U.S. Vice President Agnew visited South Vietnam during this time), and troops from all major commands. Johnston also assisted in the development of safe houses for Vietnamese and U.S. spies, defensible bunkers in the event of another Tet, and security plans for multiple contingencies.

Johnston served the general for a year. He then spent the last eight months of his Army career in Stuttgart, Germany as NCOIC of the Patch security detail. Patch Barracks was the U.S. European "Pentagon" and required a top-secret clearance to enter. Patch tracked all U.S. and NATO forces, including the location of submarines, current deployment of naval combat ships, SAC (Strategic Air Command) bombers, Army and Marine combat brigades, and all other defense forces. After leaving the Army, Johnston applied to the U.S. Marshals Service and became a deputy U.S. Marshal. In 1983 he was promoted to inspector in the federal witness protection program.

As a marshal, one of Johnston's long-term assignments was to protect a witness who was testifying against a terrorist mastermind, Mohammed Rasheed, who had overseen the hijacking of multiple airplanes and killings in the '80s including TWA's flight 847 on June 15, 1985. One passenger, Robert Stethem, an unarmed U.S. sailor, was tortured (his body could only

---

tank commander, but I have one peer: Abe Abrams. He's the world champion." The M1 Abrams tank (named for Gen. Abrams) is still America's main battle tank.

be identified through fingerprints) and dumped on the tarmac in Beirut, Lebanon. Rasheed's trial was in a Greek court at a women's prison in Athens because Greece refused to extradite the terrorist to the United States. Each day Johnston and his security detail would take a key witness, a Palestinian, from an Athens safe house to the prison; the detail varied the route for the safety of the witness.

Among the most dangerous trials for which Johnston had witness protection responsibility was that of Carlos Lehder, co-founder of the Medellin Cartel headed by Pablo Escobar. The trial took place in federal court in Jacksonville, Florida. Lehder revolutionized the cocaine trade by transporting the drug to the U.S. using small aircraft. Today, he's in a maximum-security prison serving life without parole plus 135 years.

During the Cold War with the Soviet Union, Johnston assisted (four times) in the exchange of spies at the Glienicke Bridge[11] over the Havel River in Berlin. Perhaps the most public exchange took place on February 1, 1986 when the human rights campaigner and political prisoner, Anatoly Sharansky, plus three Western agents were exchanged for Karl Koecher and four Eastern bloc agents.

Bob Johnston retired in 1994 after thirty-two years as an Army sergeant and a U.S. Marshal, Senior Inspector. Although retired, he sometimes carries his badge and pistol and does background investigations. He is a great American and has successfully fought the enemies of the United States his entire life. In the spring 2009 issue of the 75th Ranger Regiment Association's *Patrolling* magazine, Bob commented on his LRP missions:

Looking back on my different careers, I feel the one that stands out the most was the one with the 4th Platoon of E-Company LRP. There's something about LRP missions that cannot be found in any other profession. I guess maybe that's the way it should be. There has never been anything like it, before or since. With the LRP Platoon, I met and walked the boonies with some of the finest men I have ever been associated with. I

---

[11] The Glienicke Bridge was featured in the 2015 movie, *Bridge of Spies*, which was directed by Steven Spielberg and starred Tom Hanks.

will always remember those of you I have had the honor to serve with. You are truly above the rest.

Phoenix Gunfight

"Gunfight at Drugstore" was the headline in *The Arizona Republic*, Phoenix's major newspaper. The article included a picture of Del Ayers. All LRPs in Vietnam were warriors itching to damage their enemies. After the war most of them settled down, but not everyone. Del Ayers, a member of Chippergate Team 4-4, was shot while on patrol and every man of his five-man team was seriously wounded. As described previously, he escaped death or capture by a fairy-tale ending to his mission.

Del returned to the States and took a position as a police officer with the Phoenix police department. He later requested to go undercover with a primary mission of discovering and prosecuting drug dealers. He thought his last major gunfight occurred in Vietnam. But no, he was wrong!

On April 4, 1978, Del was on a stakeout at the Revco store on McDowell Street in Phoenix. His assignment was to catch the criminals who had robbed fourteen drugstores during the prior two months. As he stood behind the pharmacy counter in a white coat playing pharmacist, two gunmen entered wearing ski masks and rubber gloves. The first, (David M. Howell, 25, of Cleveland) carried two drawn pistols, a stolen .357 magnum revolver and a 9mm semi-automatic. He walked to the counter and demanded, "Are you the pharmacist?"

Del said, "Yeah, what do you want?"

Before the gunman could answer, Del fired off five quick rounds from his pistol and hit the gunman three times. Howell fired four rounds at Del's head, but all shot high. As Howell fell to the floor his accomplice ran out to their car. Del crouched behind an aisle endcap and reloaded. Two customers in the store were on their hands and knees; Del got them into the back room and locked the door.

Meanwhile, the second robber (James Nuggent, 24, of Parma, Ohio) came back into the drugstore and dragged Howell out. They were almost to their car when Nuggent spotted Del at the store's front door. Nuggent fired four shots from his 9mm semi-automatic pistol, one round shattering the glass window next to Del. Del then fired just one round which parked Nuggent on the ground with a gunshot in his chest. By that time multiple police patrol cars arrived; the robbers were cuffed and put into an ambulance. Both men were listed in serious condition at area hospitals. Later in the day, a couple of police buddies came over to Del's house. They raised their beers and gave this toast, "Good guy two, bad guys zero."

At trial the two robbers were given sentences of seven years to life. One died in prison and the other was released after serving his sentence. When Del was asked if he was worried that the guy he shot would come looking for him, Del replied, "No. One bullet ended up in his back and he always had a hard time walking."

The City of Phoenix gave Del a Medal of Valor as well as recognizing him as Phoenix Police Officer of the Year, but he was not yet done. When he was sixty-five years old, Del saw a nineteen-year-old robbing a liquor store and pushing the proprietor to the ground. Unarmed, Del ran and tackled the thief and then held him on the ground until patrol cars arrived. Again, it was "Good guy one, bad guy zero!"

CHAPTER 4

Men acquainted with the battlefield will not be found among the numbers that glibly talk of another war.

Dwight D. Eisenhower

FOUR AND A WAKE-UP

Randy Mills probably had as many near-death experiences as anyone in the platoon. Three times the soldier next to him was killed by an enemy aimed shot. Randy's nerves were still raw when he joined the 4th Platoon.

September 1967 found Mills as the second squad leader, 4th Platoon, A-Company, 502nd Infantry, 1st Brigade of the 101st Airborne Division. A series of battles took place in I Corps at the beginning of October 1967. Randy's company was conducting Search and Destroy missions near Chui Lai. Strong NVA forces were all around, and he fought daily in small gunfights for over thirty days. On October 1, 1967, his platoon was fighting their way to a small hilltop and taking many casualties on the way. Randy's platoon leader, 1st Lt. James Peake, told Randy, "Keep your head down!" just as Peake was shot. Randy's platoon took the hilltop and called for a Medevac helicopter and more gunships. Many helicopters arrived, one bringing in a 106mm recoilless rifle, and Dust-Offs taking Peake and the other wounded to field hospitals.[12]

Four days later, as A-Company was being resupplied with replacements and ammunition and taking on incoming rifle fire, SFC McDaniels pointed to where the fire was coming from and asked Randy if he saw the enemy. Randy had seen twelve NVA run into the treeline and McDaniels told him, "That's where we're going in the morning." Sgt. McDaniels and Randy were the only two sergeants left in his platoon.

---

[12] Peake, a West Point graduate, was awarded the Silver and Bronze Stars. After returning from his tour in Vietnam, he received his medical doctorate from Cornell University in 1972. He served as a cardiac surgeon and commander in several medical posts culminating in his appointment as U.S. Army Surgeon General from 2000 to 2004. President George W. Bush nominated Peake to be Secretary of Veterans Affairs; he was unanimously confirmed by the United States Senate in 2007 and served for two years.

The next morning, Randy's depleted squad of five soldiers was still the company's point squad, and they came across several small hooches. An old man stood next to them and, through the interpreter, told the squad that NVA soldiers were there earlier. The NVA told the old man to let the Americans know they'd be on the other side of the river waiting for them. Mills told his company commander there was a treeline that would provide cover to the river. "Lead the way," the Commanding Officer (CO) directed him. Mills located the shallow river and his squad waded through it. Rader was walking squad point with Howard next, just ahead of Randy. The NVA opened fire, hitting Howard four times in the neck; Randy heard him say, "I can't breathe." That was it for Howard. Lynch, the machine gunner behind Randy, was also hit.

"Are you okay?" Randy asked.

"I can't move either leg," Lynch answered.

Immediately two more NVA were killed trying to move behind Randy's squad. The platoon sergeant told Randy that the 3rd Platoon was going to hook up tight to Randy's squad. After a few minutes they did and everything calmed down. About 2300 hours, the 3rd Platoon received on-target mortar rounds killing seven and wounding thirteen men. Randy and his squad retrieved the men who'd been killed in the mortar attack and placed them with Howard's body.

The company commander came by with his 1st sergeant and told Randy he anticipated a human wave attack that night, but it didn't happen. At that point, the strength of A-Company was just forty-nine able-bodied soldiers. Ham and lima beans hot meals had been sent to the front, but because of the constant combat the food wasn't eaten for two days. Unfortunately, the 100-degree outdoor temperature caused the meals to spoil, but the men were unaware of that and ate them. Randy suffered severe food poisoning; he and nine other soldiers of A-Company were evacuated to the field hospital.

While he was recuperating, Randy heard that volunteers were being accepted for a Long Range Patrol Company being formed in Vietnam from 101st troopers with combat experience. He requested an interview and met Capt. Leaptrott, the new executive officer of E-Company, 20th Infantry

LRP. After their talk, Randy quickly said, "Sign me up." The next morning, he was on a twin engine Caribou C-7 flight to Phan Rang.

In Phan Rang, Randy became assistant team leader of Team 4-1. In one of many memorable missions, he flew out of An Khe in the Central Highlands with Jim Brokaw (team leader), Jerry Shankle (RTO), Steve Woodson, (slack), Richard McKenzie (rifleman/scout), and John Higgens (rear security). Their LZ was on a dry rice paddy adjacent to a double canopy jungle; this was to be their patrol's Area of Operation. Dashing to the jungle, they lay dog for about fifteen minutes. Then the team started to receive fire from both the east and west. The surprised but refocused enemy had figured out where the team entered the jungle and started to hunt them. Team 4-1 made a 180 degree turn and ran through the dry rice paddy into a stand of elephant grass the size of an enlarged football field; it was completely surrounded by the rice paddy. They were trapped.

The seven-foot high grasses allowed Team 4-1 to see the legs of the enemy troops now on the dry rice paddy, hear them talking excitedly, and watch them begin reconnaissance by gunfire. Randy and his men held their nerve and gunfire while Jerry Shankle, their RTO, was attempting to contact headquarters and request extraction under fire. Jerry couldn't make radio contact. While bullets whistled through the high grasses, he calmly switched to a longer antenna, which sometimes doubled the range and proved more effective. At last Jerry had communication; he was told helicopters were being scrambled and to hang on because four Bandit slicks and two Wolf Pack gunships were on the way.

When the choppers arrived on-station, Randy told Jerry to verbally identify their location to the pilots and tell them we couldn't pop smoke because it might start a fire in the dry grass. Randy wanted the enemy to be unsure of their exact location. Brokaw and Mills hoped the downwash from the helicopters' blades would push the grass down far enough to allow Team 4-1 to board the Huey. It appeared that tactic might be the men's best chance for exfiltration. Gunships were told to cover the pickup; they flew in a circle around the tall elephant grass firing rockets and machine guns to keep the enemy pinned down so they couldn't accurately shoot at the incoming slick. Just like the parting of the Red Sea for Moses, the elephant grass opened up, allowing the slick to recover Team 4-1.

It was mid-March and the 4th Platoon had been operating out of An Khe a little over a month. In this particular AO, all patrols had traded gunfire on every mission. Admittedly some were minor skirmishes, but any exchange of gunfire takes an emotional toll. Each clash required an assessment of the danger, enemy strength, geography, and the possibility of utilizing additional friendly forces. At that point, team members and helicopter crews were drained and fatigued, but First Field Force Headquarters continued to push for and demand reports on enemy activities. It was just weeks after the Tet attack and with all the carnage and political grief, Headquarters wanted no second surprise attack.

Randy Mills was in my (Lt. Stein's) GP medium tent to discuss his team's next mission. Randy had only four days and a wake-up until he would be rotating back to the United States. He was telling me his nerves were gone, he was suffering battle fatigue, and was not able to lead another team in the field. I said I could understand his state of mind, but no one on the seven teams was receiving stand-down time due to ongoing enemy actions. The only way Randy could get out of this mission was to find his replacement. Just like an actor following a movie cue, into the tent walked Oscar Caraway (who'd recently been released from the hospital). Randy looked at him and said, "There's your leader, Sir! Oscar can take my place to lead the mission."

Oscar's team had taken a beating three weeks prior. All five members were wounded, two seriously enough to require nearly a year to recuperate in a U.S. military hospital, but Oscar Caraway accepted the responsibility of leading Team 4-5, his first time as team leader.

CHAPTER 5

Nothing is more exhilarating than to be shot at without result.

Winston Churchill

STARLIGHT PATROL

The NVA were looking for us—they knew we were there. Their lanterns glowed through the jungle's triple canopy. We held our position. If they were to take us out, so be it, but it would not be before we first took some of them down. In this moment we became brothers, not a brotherhood that just anyone knows, but one that is known only by those in it.

Let me explain. I am Sgt. Oscar Caraway, LRP team leader of the 4th Platoon's Team 4-5. After Tet (beginning January 31, 1968), I was a member of Team 4-4 and was tasked with the mission of developing intelligence on the strengths, intentions, and capabilities of the North Vietnamese army from the west of Pleiku and into Cambodia. Our team's mission on February 19, 1968 had decimated our entire five-man patrol. (Every team member received a Purple Heart with two men needing nearly a year to recuperate in U.S. military hospitals.)

It was the middle of March and I had just been released from the ICU unit in Pleiku. I entered Lt. Stein's headquarters tent to report back to duty. The lieutenant was having a heated conversation with Sgt. Randy Mills, leader of Team 4-5. Randy had only four days until he rotated back to the States and the lieutenant was telling him he must lead his last mission unless he found his replacement. I walked in and Randy pointed at me, saying, "There's your leader; he'll do it."

My 4th Platoon had been in Camp Enari and Ban Me Thuot during the Tet Offensive. Three weeks later, we were still using Enari as a base to launch patrols so we could discover the enemy's military intentions near the Cambodian border. Gen. Weyland of II Corps and the 4th Infantry Division requested this reconnaissance. We were ordered to determine enemy strength and intentions in a specific mountainous area adjacent to a river serving as the border between Vietnam and Cambodia.

41

I had the honor of being an assistant to Sgt. Bob Johnston so I was trained by the best. He taught me the most important objectives: 1) accomplish the mission and 2) stay alive—in that order. I was ready to serve again in mind and heart, even if still recovering from a head wound suffered on my last mission with Sgt. Johnston, and not quite "all there." Still, I was as well-prepared as any young man could be for what was about to happen.

In Camp Enari I was awarded my own team; I faced all new men and all new missions. The team included Sgt. Haney (assistant team leader), Milt Hendrickson (point), John Higgens (slack), Bob Shaffer (RTO), and me. This team was solid, tough, and ready to fight, but I was the new man on this already established team. My question was: how do I prove myself and gain their respect?

As the team leader, I knew I had to be very confident and show them I was someone they could trust and follow, just as I had felt about my team leader Sgt. Bob Johnston. I had all the credentials I needed, but the only way to build team confidence is during action. Having as many missions under my belt as any other team leader, I was primed for my next encounter with the NVA.

I loved the jungle. I loved moving through it undetected, proving I had what it took to stay alive. It was time to revenge the Chippergate mission four weeks earlier and deal it out in spades to the NVA. The platoon calling card I left on enemy bodies conveyed my motto: *We kill for fun in the true Airborne tradition.* That motto is *not* politically correct today—and perhaps wasn't in 1968 either.

This was an especially solemn time. My mentor, Sgt. Johnston, the man I looked up to, the man I saw as invincible, I now *thought* was dead. We didn't know each other's fate, which was not unusual. That's was how it was—you get up and keep going with no looking back, but could I live up to Sgt. Johnston's expectations? Could I make him proud and honor him? Everything he taught me would now be on the line. Success on the next mission was in my hands and I would not allow myself to fail.

My orders meant life or death for myself and the men under me. There would be no time to panic or time to think. You had to *do* what you were told and *know* what you were supposed to do. That's how day-to-day life was in the LRP. I was ready and would proudly lead the way. These men would follow me and, if necessary, obey orders to fight and die. There would be no questions asked and no quarter given.

When we'd been together about a week, we started to bond and Team 4-5 was born. On the firing range and during practice drills, we had the chance to see each other and appreciate the strengths of our team. Overseeing our practice was Lt. Stein. He was responsible for coordinating teams and we answered to him. He was the judge and would assign us to teams. He would evaluate our skills and abilities and was in control of our immediate future missions. Lt. Stein was the backbone of all the teams and we looked to him with utmost respect and trust.

How good was my team? Sgt. Haney was an excellent assistant team leader and I knew he would lead if I went down. Shaffer was big, muscular and tough, a good RTO. Higgens had our backs and was the right man to cover our rear security. What about our point man, Milt Hendrickson? This was the most important position so I needed to be sure he was well qualified.

I questioned other team leaders and found out that Milt was *one* of the best, if not our *best* point man. His experience in combat was solid; he was a man's man, mature in action and a man to follow in and out of the jungle. Even though our team was a group of young men, all around eighteen to nineteen years of age, (the average age of our NVA enemy was twenty-three), our time in battle proved us to be seasoned veterans. With the team strong in all aspects, it was time to go hunting NVA.

Our first mission as Team 4-5 was forming in the jungle outside Ban Me Thuot. The 33rd NVA Regiment had begun grouping and was causing pain and death for farmers, the townspeople and any South Vietnamese they would encounter. Not only were they looting, torturing, burning, attacking, and killing them, but they were also killing our own brothers, U.S. troops, at any and every chance they could. The 4th Infantry needed us to gather information. We needed to be their eyes on the ground beyond the enemy lines.

This would not be easy. Five separate teams had been shot out of the jungle immediately after insertion into that particular AO. Their touchdown point had been compromised as soon as they hit the ground.

Daylight insertions did not work, so we devised a new plan. The Airborne LRPs would be the only ones qualified for a mission this dangerous.

Lt. Stein was at LRP mission control headquarters. He would be the one to finalize the mission and make all the technical decisions. He was our only lifeline if anything went wrong. The stakes were high and everyone knew it. If we called for help and Lt. Stein didn't make the right call, we would all die on the ground. We never had any doubts. We knew he would protect our team; he was our protection from the sky. My team and all teams of the 4th Platoon appreciated everything he did for us. Lt. Stein always held strong under extreme pressure and had our backs.

I received the call to go to headquarters for a briefing; it was hot and sticky with a heavy air of anticipation for the "what ifs" of the day. After the briefing, the message was clear—this was a different day and this mission was going to be different. We were going to be spotting the enemy at night in the dark and we would be executing a night insertion, the most dangerous patrol technique known at the time. This would give the team no chance to retreat, no assistance, no gunships, no one. We knew this: if our team were seen going in, we'd be found and eliminated. We knew the risks, and although we had reservations, we would go willingly. We had been trained and we had confidence in each other and ourselves. We were Team 4-5 Airborne Rangers. We led the way and we were one.

Our only question was this: how would we see at night? Getting in would be one thing. Watching the NVA and gathering information in the dark was another. Headquarters had the answer: the eight pound, handheld AN/PVS-1 Starlight Scope. It was top secret. It gathered light from where there seemed to be none, and the scope's advanced technology allowed it to intensify light up to 30,000 times. Although images tended to blur and ghost if someone moved the scope, it was a remarkable device. For centuries darkness ended an army's battle, but an army that's able to see at night has a tremendous tactical advantage over an enemy enveloped in darkness. Our enemy usually used oil lanterns or flashlights while moving at night and was easy to spot.

This mission was now even more exciting than we'd imagined. We had a plan and we were ready to deploy. Everything had been set in motion. The day before this mission, Sgt. Haney and I did a chopper over-flight of the patrol zone of operation. We selected a suitable landing zone, alternative LZs, and finally the extraction LZ. We briefed the patrol and let them know that we were to be inserted at last light the following day. The morning of the mission, the team tested our weapons and checked all equipment, including our new secret weapon the Starlight Scope. We practiced immediate action drills and camoed up. Milt made sure everyone was ready; he checked and double-checked all the equipment and our team. He was very aware of the dangers that lay before us and would not allow any oversights. I knew then why he was ranked the top LRP point man.

It was approximately 1930 hours—just before dark, and time to go. Platoon leader Stein was at the tarmac when we arrived. We were nervous, but ready. Lt. Stein was going to fly in the CC (Command and Control) ship. He would manage the load-up and insertion. We took off with four slicks and two gunships. We needed to confuse the enemy, so we were going to land slicks all over the countryside to cover our actual touchdown. My team thought this tactic would work. We had to get in without detection and then we needed time to disappear into the thick foliage.

As we were descending toward the LZ, I saw Milt looking forward. He would be first out and he knew if things went wrong he was the NVA's first target. Milt didn't look afraid; he looked strong and ready to face anything. As soon as I was out of the slick, my feet hit the ground and I was running and maneuvering through the branches heading for the thick jungle canopy. My mind and body instinctively knew I had to get to cover; I could not stop moving and I needed to be set up. I could hear the choppers roaring above us—the blades popping and air moving in every direction. That sound represented safety, but then the engines began to strain as they were pulling up. Moments later all was quiet and still, and the only thing I could hear was my heart beating. This was a sound I wanted to hear—it meant I'd made it.

We needed to lay dog, listen to the jungle noises and let them tell us our next move, so we did. We listened about ten minutes, communicating only by hand signals. We'd done it! We were on the ground and undetected. After a quick commo check with Lt. Stein, our mission began.

Milt turned and looked at me. I signaled him forward and he knew exactly what to do. Our team would follow him. As we began moving up the side of a mountain on steep, treacherous terrain, I went forward with all my gear and the Starlight Scope loaded on my back. The scope I held was invaluable. It would be our eyes at night and during daylight hours we would lay dog. This was the plan: we would be there three days and then Lt. Stein would come to take us "home," our mission completed.

Milt was moving slowly up the mountainside and we were following, each of us as quiet and stealthy as the man in front of us. Our goal was to secure a position near a trail or opening so we could observe the NVA as they moved at night. We needed to gather information on their weapons, strength, and anything else we could glean from their movements. Milt was trying to find cover so we could recon the area and set up a perimeter. It was almost completely dark now as we moved through the Kunai grass under first double, then triple canopy of tree cover.

About three quarters up the mountainside and to our dog site, Milt froze. When his feet stopped, ours stopped, too. He signaled the team and we all dropped down. With every one of my senses surging, I moved ever so carefully to Milt. He very quietly told me he'd heard voices directly in front of us about ten feet away. It was dark now and the area was thick with overgrowth. We couldn't see them—we just listened. Then, these voices were not only in front of us; they were to the right—and to the left. I immediately had the team reverse. This was *not* where we wanted to be. We were way too close to the enemy.

We'd walked right into a group of NVA soldiers. As we were moving carefully back down the hill, I was trying to call in a situation report, but using only whispers I couldn't be sure anyone heard me. However, I was positive Lt. Stein was listening for *any* communication. At this point, I didn't know if my team's location was compromised, and I had no choice but to assume the NVA knew we were on that mountain. There could be no mistakes, no wrong moves, not one fall; even the crack of a stick under our feet could bring NVA troops on top of us.

We kept moving down and to the side of the hill since it was too dark to see below us. I knew there was still a chance we could find a safe location. We just needed a little time to develop a new plan, but the enemy wouldn't let up. We were being pursued—they were hunting for us. We had no other option but to find cover and stop moving. Milt reached a large tree that was encircled by thick brush. We immediately became one with the ground and invisible forming a 360-degree perimeter around the tree so we could make our stand and hold our ground. If we were going to be taken out, we would face the enemy and take some of them with us. Team 4-5 was in position.

Milt had his weapon pointed in the direction of the enemy. We all had each other's back, the sweat dripping down the sides of our faces and our adrenaline pumping. I could hear my heart beat again, but this time it signified something very different. I was convinced that if this were it, we would fight and protect each other until the last heartbeat. We were brothers. We all felt it and we all knew it.

What we didn't know was the extent of the danger we were in. Because of the darkness, we were not aware that we'd crossed a high-speed trail (one that allowed two or three soldiers to walk abreast and move miles in a short period of time) and were located right beside it. All we knew was we had to be 100 percent alert and we were. We waited without even looking at each other, our eyes focused and straining to see into the pitch-black night. My Starlight Scope was of no use because of the thick vegetation surrounding the team.

About thirty minutes passed and we heard the NVA coming toward us. We could see lights, oil lanterns, and flashlights. We all held our breath and didn't move. We could hear them passing not more than five feet away and we counted at least seventy-five enemy lights in the initial group on the trail. They were so close I could smell them. It was now completely obvious; the entire area was full of NVA. They were not only looking for us on the mountainside, but this was a main thoroughfare.

The night was long. We saw and heard more troops and more lights. The hills were covered with the enemy. The hardcore NVA was also on a mission—to find us and kill us if they could. We knew each of us had a bounty on our heads since we were the hated Long Range Patrol.

The NVA's noise and equipment discipline was excellent, but not as good as ours. We were right there and they didn't know it. This gave me a sense of pride and determination, and it reminded me who I was, where I was from, and not only the things I'd been taught, but the men who taught me. I held onto these facts, but faced another. Daylight was coming and when the sun came up they would find us. In daylight, Team 4-5 had no chance. The NVA were looking for us; every one of them had weapons and there were so many of them. The jungle crawled with them. In my mind, I could see their dark eyes—I still can. It was time to make a decision and I was in charge; before first light we would be moving out. We could take a stand in the night, but I would not allow us to be sitting ducks come morning. Men's lives were in my hands and I would not let them down.

The plan was simple: drop rucks and all unnecessary gear and keep only weapons, ammo, and the radio. We would try to get past and through the enemy. Milt thought he could punch a hole in the jungle and through the NVA. We would follow, giving him our complete trust.

As I began unloading my gear, I hesitated. What about the Starlight Scope? It had been entrusted to me. It was top secret and our officers expected it to return with us, but it was heavy and bulky and our lives were worth more. I could not take it with us; it had to stay. I was sure survival was possible, but I knew our chances were slim. Still, I had survived odds like this before.

The sun's first light told me it was time to move. I signaled my men forward and we were on our hands and knees for hundreds of yards as the hours passed. Then there it was! Milt found an opening for escape. We stood up, but with our first movements we were spotted. We had to run! Everyone had to run! We made contact and both sides began firing. There were glimpses of NVA moving through the jungle everywhere. We were shooting at anything that moved. Our training was paying off. We knew where to fire (aiming low), how to move forward, and how to hold the enemy back for a moment. This would be our one chance to call for an emergency extraction. It would be up to Lt. Stein to save us. His experience and expertise was now our only hope.

Shaffer hit the ground and called in our situation report, making it clear we'd made contact and were being pursued; while he was reporting, we continued to cover him. Just as we expected, Lt. Stein had four slicks and two gunships on quick reaction status. His choppers were warmed up and in the air in minutes. They were on the way.

Lt. Stein and I negotiated an open LZ for extraction. Next we had to get there. We needed to move farther downhill through heavy jungle vegetation. The dense bamboo thicket slowed us down; as we broke through, the noise continued to alert the NVA where we were and which way we were heading. They continued in hot pursuit and we five continued holding off dozens or more, not to mention the large number we were facing on the entire mountainside. Then we heard the beautiful sound of six helicopters coming to our rescue. They were there! Lt. Stein was in the Command and Control chopper ready to aid us in getting down to the LZ. The lieutenant and I were in communication. His gunships were going to make a pass. The lieutenant requested we pop smoke to mark our position. The red smoke was put out and the color identified. Lt. Stein directed his gunships to fire between the ridge above us and the smoke. He was careful to fire parallel to the smoke and the ridgeline so we wouldn't be on the gun target line. The gunships opened fire with rockets and machine guns.

We kept popping smoke; each time the gunships were firing closer to us than they had on the previous run. This was a very risky maneuver, but we had to slow the NVA. We had to keep moving or die trying. After breaking through the last of the bamboo, we found ourselves at the bottom of the mountain next to an old rice paddy. This was just where we needed to be. Team 4-5 positioned a defensive line facing uphill, ready to fight anyone who followed us. The last pass from the gunships was so close that the hot brass from the cartridges hit us and we dropped for cover. Lt. Stein informed me that with the next pass-by, the slick would be coming to pick up the team.

I told Milt to go out and guide the chopper—the most dangerous part of any extraction. The incoming door gunners were nervous coming into a hot LZ and when a camouflaged soldier popped up like a jungle ghost, it required superb fire discipline not to have friendly fire casualties. As Milt was motioning the chopper down for extraction, a gunship was firing constantly on each side of the chopper. We turned and ran toward it. As we ran, my mind silenced and I took note: we were all there. We were running for the chopper—all of us were alive! Then I heard the rushing sound of bullets. Bullets were flying everywhere. The sound was deafening. We couldn't hear anything but the machine guns, not even our own heart beats. We were not loaded yet and I wondered if we would really make it or be shot while loading. There was no looking back—you just go forward. If anyone was hit, we would grab him and get him to the chopper, but we must keep loading. We had to get out.

Team 4-5 was loaded. We were holding on tightly and screaming, "We're in! Go, go, go!" The chopper lifted at full throttle with rotors popping and we were heading out. Both door gunners fired their M60s until we found the safety of the blue sky. "Safe"—that was a word I hadn't used for a while, but we *were* safe, with no one even wounded. After we pulled up, Lt. Stein had his gunships expend their remaining ammunition on the enemy's suspected locations. The door gunners and Lt. Stein fired into the jungle at the unseen enemy. This eighteen-hour mission to go only one-half mile in and one-half mile out was as intense as any I ever experienced.

We returned to camp and I immediately rushed to headquarters to debrief the colonel and his team. I was excited and proud to let them know about the strength of the NVA, the high-speed trail, and that my men made it out safely. We were ready for our next mission. A major asked about the secret scope. I explained the seriousness of the situation and told him we had to leave it with the rest of the gear. I tried to make the colonel and his team understand that we had to drop all unnecessary equipment and get out. That was the standard operating procedure on high-speed evasions from large enemy forces—you drop and go. But this was not standard to them; this was their Starlight Scope. No one was interested in *why* the scope was left behind. They just wanted it back—and quickly. They explained to me that a Starlight had never been lost in Vietnam and I would not be the first to lose one, especially on their watch.

Lt. Stein was ordered to bring back that scope with no questions and no excuses. Since his dedication to following orders was unwavering, he began planning a recovery mission. He knew we could accomplish any task. He had complete confidence in our training, our skills, and us. This was a team he had personally mentored. We'd made it in once and we could do it again. We could and would complete this mission.

That afternoon Lt. Stein contacted the 1st Battalion of the 22nd Infantry 4th Division and found a 4th Division Company about a three-day tactical march from the mountainside where we'd left the scope and equipment. This company had approximately 110 men plus air support and

I felt secure with them. They would provide cover so we could locate the Starlight Scope. I thought we probably could find the place I'd dropped it, but usually when gear was left the NVA retrieved it. Would it really still be there?

I went back to my men. They were ready and willing to turn around and head back into the jungle, to the mountainside we had just left, to recover our gear and the top-secret scope. We immediately began to regroup, preparing ourselves. We knew what was out there and we would be ready this time. Lt. Stein pulled me aside, looked me right in the eyes and asked, "Can you find that scope?" I looked back at him, and although not entirely sure I knew I *had* to find it, so with all the confidence in me I replied, "Yes, Sir."

The next thing the lieutenant said was a surprise. I would be the *only* team member going. I would lead the troops of the 4th Division to the scope; it would be totally up to me to navigate through the jungle back to that tree where we'd found protection during the night. Team 4-5 would not go in together.

We all looked at each other, but no words were spoken. I would go without my brothers and they'd have to let me go alone. We all were disappointed, but there was nothing to say—orders were orders. At least they would get some rest and be safe for about a week. They went back to the barracks. I went forward and followed Lt. Stein to the chopper. We jumped on and we were off

As we lifted off the tarmac and flew toward the jungle, I sat on the outer door of the slick. I peered down at the trees watching the beautiful landscape pass beneath me. How could it be so peaceful looking from above, and just below be filled with death and war? I contemplated the mission that I was now on ... no team ... just my mission. I realized I was probably the only one-man mission the 4th Platoon or any other LRP Company had ever sent out. Now I had even more to prove to everyone, but mostly to myself.

Since I was the team leader, I would be expected to lead an infantry company (officers included) on a three-day march to a mountainside to find a single most important large tree and locate the Starlight Scope. I thought about the tree. In my mind, I could see its outline and the branches as they looked above me, but I had only seen the tree in the dark, and I hadn't made a position mark on our map that would be of any value. Not to mention that the mountainside was full of NVA soldiers who would not be happy to have us there. It was all daunting—it would be for anyone. I would have to rely on my training for this to be successful. I thought of Sgt. Johnston and the other three men I had served with in Chippergate 4-4. I would do this mission for them.

The popping of the chopper's blades brought me back to reality. The chopper was descending toward green signal smoke that was floating up from a jungle opening. I arrived to meet a new group of brave men so we could go on this mission together. I was a squad leader with the 101st Airborne Infantry 1/327 A-Company "The Assassins" 2nd Platoon. I had been through three major battles with the Screaming Eagles prior to joining my Long Range Patrol Company. These experiences would all be to my advantage. I knew I would fit into any infantry company perfectly. Now it was time to find that scope!

There I was getting off the slick by myself; it was the strangest feeling. My feet hit the ground running. I could hear my boots pounding the ground because I was alone without my team. Never had an insertion felt this way. To *feel* alone and to *be* alone on the jungle floor of Vietnam was a moment I will never forget.

I saw the company commander and wondered how this mission would end. Would these men fight as hard as the other men I'd served with? The 4th Infantry Division had a reputation of being strong and fearless, but what about this company? Time would tell.

Before dark I received a situation report and devised a plan of action with the officers. An artillery battery with six 105mm Howitzers was moved into a position to support our company. Each 105 had an eight-man crew and could fire three to eight rounds per minute with a variety of ammo and an effective range of a slightly more than seven miles. I would lead this company whose main order was keeping me alive if and when contact was made with the NVA. As much as I wanted to stay alive, I did not want anyone to risk his life for me. I quickly came to the realization that it wasn't necessarily *me* they wanted to protect, but the information I held. That Starlight Scope was important. I *had* thought about it, but at that moment I grasped the scope's true value. Because of the 4th Infantry Company's vigilant protection of me, I was not to be the *point man*, but I was to *point the way*.

The captain told me to stay with his 1st Platoon near the platoon leader and his RTO. I was toward the back of the point squad almost in the middle of eight or nine soldiers. I directed the squad and marked the trail, followed by the entire company to the mountainside and hopefully the Starlight Scope. I was instructed to stay in radio contact with the captain, so under almost any circumstances I would be kept safe whether I wanted to be or not.

Two days of marching passed with no NVA contact. We couldn't see the mountain except on the map—the triple canopy made seeing anything but what was directly in front of us impossible—but I could feel we were getting closer to it. Very soon now we would know if I was going to find that tree. We would know if I was going to be the first, and maybe the only, sergeant to lose a top-secret weapon in Vietnam. I had less than twenty-four hours before the culmination of this mission.

That night was unusually hot. I sat with the company officers going over plans to move up the mountainside. I explained to the captain the details of my mission just a few days prior. I told him I had only seen this area in the dark, and was not really sure where I was going to go once we got to the bottom of the mountain. That's when we decided I would take the point position. There was no one else who could do the job, and I had to be up front to retrace my team's steps. It was all on me; all these men were looking to me and following me. The pressure to succeed was to the max.

I was thinking about Team 4-5, wishing my point man, Milt, and the other men were there. Walking point for an infantry company was not a completely new assignment to me since I had done it before. I had been positioned as *a* point man but not *the* point man. To some degree, I knew what to expect. I knew there would not be a head-on attack and the NVA soldiers would only have small arms to fire.

I also knew that together Team 4-5 would have had a better chance of figuring this out, but that was not the way it was going to be. I would need to find one tree within a half-mile length on a mountainside, in the thick brush of the jungle. I knew there was a large trail nearby, but that was all I could be sure of. My plan was to go to the original insertion LZ and move upwards, trying to retrace our steps. That was the only thing to do, but the last time I was there things didn't go as planned. I had no idea what to expect. I would have to resort to taking this mission on the fly.

It was dawn on our *D Day*. This was it, the third day of marching, which meant it was time for me to move to the front. The whole company would be following me today. As I was moving forward and passing all these soldiers, I looked at them—so many men. I was thinking, "Follow me, trust me, I will lead the way." I tried to look at many as I possibly could right in their eyes; I wanted them to feel total confidence in me. I wanted them to know I was a man to follow.

Within two miles of the LZ, we began taking fire from snipers and the NVA began making small ambushes, the way they loved to fight. These were their standard tactics. I hoped these attacks were not a sign of bad things to come. Either way, one thing was sure, they were not happy to have us back so soon.

We were crossing through an old rice paddy before we began the incline, exactly where I'd entered before with Team 4-5. I glanced at the sky and saw gunships were holding over us. I could hear choppers landing behind us. More troops were arriving. Looking back now, I feel like it was all unbelievable.

I entered the jungle and was at point with over one hundred men behind me. It quickly became an all-out attack on that mountainside, but there was support everywhere. The gunships were firing in front and to the sides of our column. I felt untouchable. The NVA troops were scattering everywhere, but because of the great number of NVA we were taking some fire. I continued pushing up the hill in the direction I believed we had taken before. This mission was not going to be given to us. If we were to find the secret scope, the NVA were going to make us fight for it. They were going to make a stand and they did not want to be pushed off that small mountain. We didn't care. We were going to push them out and they had no idea how determined we were. The battle for that mountainside was on.

This was a massive number of men fighting. There were still many NVA soldiers, just as Team 4-5 had reported. We actually had to hold up and wait for more support, which was provided immediately. The 4th Infantry was moving in troops for our support as we were fighting our way up.

I reached a site we had not passed in the previous mission and I stopped. Within hours the territory was ours. There was a perimeter forming around the entire area and the NVA were successfully pushed back. We stopped attacking and the 4th Infantry troops continued to protect the perimeter and fight. I could hear the NVA all around me. I knew they had to be wondering why we were there, what we wanted, and what had just happened.

I couldn't think about anything except locating the tree. I had to think. Where was that tree with our packs and the Starlight? I concentrated on my mission ... find the scope. I kept moving through the jungle, the excitement of the battle all around me with the anticipation that at any moment, I may be holding the scope in my hands again. It was all very powerful.

All that I can say is that within a short period of time, I came upon the tree. I knew it was the one! I crawled into the surrounding brush and there it was. Yes, most amazingly the Starlight Scope, untouched and in perfect condition, was exactly where I had left it. It was a miracle!

A full platoon of U.S. troops surrounded the tree and me. The soldiers grabbed all the equipment, they grabbed me, and we headed back down to the LZ at double-time. A slick came in as I ran into the landing zone; I jumped in, placed the gear beside me, and held the Starlight Scope in my hands. It all happened so fast, there was not time to even reflect on my amazing find. As we lifted I said out loud, "Mission complete."

While in the air returning to base, I considered the massive coordination and thought that was put into this mission. A lot of brass made it work. They wanted that scope at any cost. I knew the only thing that saved my stripes and me that day was that the NVA did not find that scope. It still boggles the mind. What were the odds they didn't find it? A million to one, the way I figure it.

As we landed and I got off the chopper there he was, Lt. Stein, smiling. He placed his hand on my shoulder and said, "Great job! All that's left is to sign the Starlight Scope back in." It was as if he never doubted me. I felt so much pride in knowing this man and I trusted he felt the same about me. As we walked, Sgt. Johnston came to my mind—he and my entire Team Chippergate 4-4.

I have never heard of any other one-man mission on any recon team in Vietnam, so I consider it a first and only. I believe it to be the only time a Starlight Scope was lost and recovered under heavy fire in only five days. This specific mission's success goes to the bravery and determination of my Team 4-5, the men of the 4th Infantry Division, and to Lt. Stein for allowing me to redeem myself, believing in me, and trusting I could get the job done—which I did. I was in shock then, and when I think about it today, I still am.

CHAPTER 6

Going to war is its own reward. Don't expect anything more.

James Worth

Brains for Lunch

My name is James Worth. I live outside of Brownsville, Oregon in the middle of private forest. I am a retired building contractor. I was born in Berkeley, California in 1948 and grew up in the San Francisco East Bay. I am from a large family; my dad had eight kids, of which I am the second. My parents were divorced when I was eight and I, along with three brothers, were raised by my mom. I was in the high school Class of '66, but being a troublemaker didn't graduate and later got my GED in the Army.

My role models—my dad and my uncle—were combat vets; my dad was an infantry officer in Europe and my uncle was a Marine in the Pacific. I always assumed I would be in the military and I wanted to see what war was like. I wound up spending more time in combat than both my role models put together.

In April 1966 at age seventeen, I enlisted in the Army for Airborne Infantry. Looking back, this seems to have been based on nothing more than youthful bravado, a desire for adventure, and an overdeveloped zeal for civic duty. I knew nothing of the politics behind the war; I only knew there was a shooting war and I wanted to be in it. I was highly impressed with the film *The Longest Day* and that's where I got the idea to be a paratrooper. I wanted to jump into combat, slay dozens, get the pretty girl, and live happily ever after while bands played inspiring music.

Like every other young GI of the time, my illusions started to be shattered on the first day at the reception center in Ft. Ord, California. The Army wasn't at all like I thought it would be. They were mean to us! I never thought about not completing my enlistment; as far as I was concerned for the next three years, the only way home for me was straight ahead.

I made it through Infantry School (Basic and Advanced Infantry Training) in a breeze; I ate that kind of stuff up when I was a kid. I'd always seen myself as a soldier. Jump School was a lot tougher but I found those hidden resources I needed and made it through. I never thought about quitting; it was what I was determined to do.

I graduated from Jump School a full-fledged paratrooper, still only seventeen. Looking back from the safety of old age, I can say I'm glad I did it. I showed up for the Vietnam War dressed up as a U.S. Army paratrooper. I'm still proud of that. That wasn't re-enactment, it was *actment*. Not being content to just read American history, I set off to make some of my own. Being still seventeen, I was sent to Panama instead of Vietnam. With the exception of a few other seventeen-year-olds like me, half of whom went to Germany, all the rest of my Jump School class, a couple of hundred guys, went to Vietnam. I didn't realize how good I had it in Panama 'til later in Vietnam.

In Panama, I was in the 3rd Battalion of the 508th PIR, a detached battalion of the 82nd, which was the U.S. Army's permanent reaction force for Latin America. We jumped a lot, which I liked and trained a lot, mostly in the jungle. This was the best training you could get for Vietnam, especially compared to the people who trained in Ft. Dix, New Jersey and Ft. Ord, California. We jumped all over Panama and humped the Panamanian jungle. I thought it was tough, but didn't realize until later just how good I had it in Panama.

One day they dropped us close to the huge Gatun Locks and marched us over to a train. We rode the train in boxcars and gondolas back to Panama City where trucks picked us up. The tracks ran right alongside the canal and sometimes out on causeways. Not many people can say they went across the Panama Canal in a gondola, but I can. They ran us through an abbreviated version of the Jungle School, and then we served as AIs (Assistant Instructors), mostly setting up equipment, serving as aggressors and looking for lost Jungle School trainees on the Escape and Evasion Course. By the time I got to Vietnam, I knew all about moving silently through the jungle. I still practice moving silently through the forest.

But just *playing* war wasn't enough for me. I wanted to see real war so I volunteered for Vietnam shortly after I turned eighteen in December

1966. Five months later, after a month's leave, I got my wish: an all-expense paid trip to Vietnam. When I arrived in April 1967, I was assigned to the 1st Brigade of the 101st Airborne Division. At that time there was only one brigade of the 101st in Vietnam. The 1st Brigade had three battalions: the 1st and 2nd Battalions of the 327th and the 2nd Battalion of the 502nd (known respectively as the 1st Batt, 2nd Batt, and the Oh Deuce). After a week of P Training (Acclimatization and Familiarization), I was sent out into the field with the 2nd Platoon, A-Company/1st Battalion/327PIR.

And thus commenced the worst five months of my life. Some men called the 101st Airborne the *Jail Without Walls*; you could run away, but there was nowhere to go. You realized very shortly that you'd been sentenced to a year of this, and that's how they treated you, too. I started out as an ammo bearer, the same as everyone else. After a few weeks of that, I was a rifleman, still carrying a box of machine gun ammo, though. After a couple of months, I volunteered to carry the radio for the platoon leader after the previous RTO was wounded.

I did this primarily to get away from a racist black squad leader. He would send the white guys out on all the really dangerous stuff while he and his friends laughed. Dan, a close friend from that squad, had the same experience with the guy and Dan volunteered to carry the machine gun to get away. Every white guy in that squad volunteered to do something more dangerous to get out of that situation. After a couple of months carrying the radio, the squad leader's best friend threatened my life, so I punched him out and told the squad leader what I thought of him. His friend and I both threatened to kill each other and I figured I was going to have to do it, so I had motivation to move along when the opportunity came along. The way the 101st Airborne fights a war is to start with a well-trained, motivated unit, keep the unit in the field and then just keep putting in replacements until the war is over. That's the way they did it in WWII[13] and that's the way they did it in Vietnam. By the time I got there, we were all replacements with no one really knowing much at all. Command changed way too frequently: in the five-plus months I was in the First Batt, I had

---

[13] The HBO series *Band of Brothers* illustrates this style of war.

two different battalion commanding officers, two different company C.O.s and five different platoon leaders. As such, there was no unit memory and each new command kept doing the same thing over and over. Our practices were repetitive and unimaginative.

I remember only one real tactic: A- and B-Company will sweep the valley, while C-Company serves as the blocking force! You *have* to think the enemy was smart enough to figure that one out. It's what we did: sweep and patrol for days until someone shot at us. That was our main tactic: serve as targets and then fight it out with whoever shot at us.

Command could get very anarchic when no one could figure out what was happening. It often seemed like no one knew what he was doing, but after studying warfare for many years, I have concluded that all combat may be that way. You never get good at it. It's *always* a scramble, *always* about an attempt to figure out what's going on and then figure out what to do. It's important—maybe more important—to know when and where *not* to shoot as it is to know when and where *to* shoot. Your life and the lives of your friends depend on this. You come to understand this isn't practice; it's the real thing. That's when it seems most unreal, like it's not supposed to be happening, but when you're sitting there watching it and participating in it, you know this is as real as it's ever going to get.

Combat was short and nasty: they ambushed us and we ambushed them. There was no clear plan of action; when the firing started, half the problem was figuring out what to do. On one of my first night ambush patrols, I pulled the trigger on a Claymore mine that killed six people—unarmed civilians carrying a wounded man. It was horrific, like walking away from a terrible accident that I intentionally caused. And that's how I spent the "Summer of Love," 1967.

The motto of the 101st is *Rendezvous with Destiny*, but a more appropriate motto would have been *Homeless People with Guns*. I think the Army does it this way because they *know* the most effective infantryman is not a happy, contented one. The Army sort of encourages a *de rigeur* angry attitude because the truth is, you can't do what you have to do when you're happy and content. You're much more willing to risk your life in a fight when you're so miserable you think you have nothing at all to lose. Do you think the U.S. Army doesn't know that? No, the best soldiers, in my not inconsiderable experience, are always pissed off and thinking they're getting screwed. I believe that was the basis for the 101st's and other units' treatment of their men, both in Vietnam and in WWII. I really can't see any other reason why they'd treat us that way, other than indifference, incompetence, and just pure meanness—which I would definitely not rule out.

I did not sit at a table, on a chair, or on a toilet during those five months. The *showers* were showerheads attached to canvas bags that we would fill with water and then hoist with a rope up on a rack. The toilets were 55-gallon drums that were cut in half with a wooden seat on top and placed in the open out in a field. We never had hot water or beds. We never went to a PX or saw the inside of a bar. Any barracks we saw were someone else's, usually the ARVN (Army of the Republic of Vietnam), which did not endear them to us in the least. (Amazingly enough, at the 101st's base camp in Phan Rang, a set of barracks was built for everyone in the division, but were never slept in during the war and were known as the Phantom Barracks. *Your tax dollars at work!*)

We'd go out on operations as long as five weeks and eat C-rations the whole time. I can count on one hand the times I had hot meals in the field, and once we sent the hot meal back and ate Cs because it was that bad—a real insult. The joke was they'd send us clean clothes once a month whether we needed them or not, but it was no joke. People were walking around wearing muddy, bloody rags for days and weeks.

Life was tough in the 101st, but that five months I spent sleeping on the ground every night in monsoon season was sure no record. I have friends who did an entire year like that. You can imagine what that does to your attitude. We took more casualties in the time I was in that half-strength 101st Platoon (and I knew all of them) than we took in the six months I was in E-Company, a full-strength Long Range Patrol Company (and I only knew a few of them).

We had two good-sized battles involving my whole company and other units in Chu Lai. The second battle was the biggest one I was in. Our company was pinned down in the middle of rice paddies (poor leadership) in the rain when we couldn't get air support and we were almost overrun. That was the only time in the war I saw lines of enemies attacking, as scary a situation as there could be. At age eighteen, this was the day I shot my first man in the back, and I shot a few in the front that day, too. I satisfied my ambition to be in a war on that day. I knew then I'd made it to The Big Time, as big as it ever gets. After that, I was all for going home and living a quiet life, but there were still six months to go and the only way home was straight ahead.

During this time, I met my friend George "Hutch" Hutchison, who I was later to know better in the 4th Platoon, E-Company Long Range Patrol. His company of the Second Batt had been overrun at night. He and another guy had dragged a wounded man into our perimeter after shooting their way out. Typical of the 101st, Hutch didn't receive a medal for this. (They were stingy with medals except for the officers.) He stayed in my hole for a couple of days and then left for the rear. Later I met him in Phan Rang, where we were in the same platoon in E-Company and were good friends throughout.

After this battle, I was sitting in a hole in the rain, opening a can of breakfast with a bayonet. I was cursing everyone not in the hole and whatever childish, idiotic notions had gotten me there and wishing I were somewhere else, *anywhere* else. The rain stopped and a figure appeared. I looked up and there in front of me with light behind him stood a strange captain. He said, "Are you Worth?" I said, "Yeah, what the fuck do *you* want?" By that time, I didn't care what they did to me. Send me to jail, *please*; I could use a dry bed and a good night's sleep. He said he had my name on a list to go into a new Long Range Patrol Company because of my training in the jungles of Panama. I asked him if I would have to terminate airborne. I liked jumping and jump pay so I would never want to quit airborne, as mean as it was. He assured me I'd stay on jump status.

I didn't know what the Long Range Patrol was, but I looked up at him and could see that he was clean and shiny, well-fed and wearing clean clothes. I looked at the muddy hole I was sitting in. I knew if they were looking for volunteers from the Infantry, it was probably suicidal—all the good things were taken long before they got that far forward. Then I thought, fuck all this patriotism, *I'm getting screwed!* I want to be clean and well-fed, too. I want to sit at a table and eat real food again with a knife and a fork, crap on a toilet, and sleep in a bed. But most of all, right then, I just wanted to stop shaking.

I stood up, gave away everything I had to my pals (except my .45, which I put in my pocket), and flew off with the captain. It was the best choice I made in the Army; I never regretted it. My replacement as radioman was seriously wounded just two weeks later. And the captain who invited me to join the Long Range Patrol was killed the next day by a random shot while he was riding in a helicopter. As the saying goes, when your number's up, it's definitely up.

And that's how I volunteered for the Long Range Patrol. Whatever that captain was doing sure looked a whole lot better than what I was doing; it was all very simple and believable. I thought, it can't be worse than this, and I was right. That choice got me to some strange places a grunt never saw, and a view of the Vietnam War that very, very few people ever had. I got to walk point on LRP patrols on what was called the Ho Chi Minh Trail. (That's what I was doing the day I turned nineteen.) And I finally did get some clean clothes and a shower. True story: If I hadn't joined the LRP, I wouldn't have had *any* fun in Vietnam at all. Ask any 101st veteran in E-Company if he made the right choice by joining the Long Range Patrol Company and he will agree with me.

We went back to Phan Rang; I hadn't seen it since I first arrived. As I was signing out of my company, I found out all my personal stuff (along with everyone else's) had been looted in the *secure* place we'd left it. Nobody told me *not* to bring a full kit of stuff to the 'Nam so I did, and it was all gone. After five months in continuous combat, I left the 101st with a pistol in my pocket and the dirty clothes on my back feeling like a refugee from hell. (This was not the only time in the Army when I had all my stuff ripped off when left in a *secure* place.) Ciao, 101st; it's time to rendezvous with another destiny.

The Army was just forming up E-Company (LRP)/20th INF (ABN). They assembled us 101st vets together and a strange lieutenant proceeded to rage through our ranks, giving us the old Jump School harassment rant to make us know what a tough guy he was and I guess, how insignificant he thought we were. Lt. Greene was a real Green Beret tough guy and he told us he was "gonna teach us The Law of the Jungle" (which one I'm not sure).

That was the wrong tack to take with people who had just come off the front-line with the 101st after a major battle, and thought they deserved a little respect and kind treatment. We didn't need an ass-chewing or to be told we didn't know anything. We needed a pat on the back, a shower, and a cold beer. We hadn't just *read* the Law of the Jungle, we wrote it! And our reward for that was obviously going to be a ration of shit from some cherry.

Some men quit right then and I thought, if this is what I signed up for, I'm going back, too. Who needs to try to fight a war with that kind of abuse behind him? I never understood why someone would want to start a relationship with me by getting me to hate him, but that was common behavior in the U.S. Army. I think they called it *leadership.* Sometimes in Vietnam I knew for sure I had enemies in front of me *and* behind me, too, and that was not idle paranoia either. It was hard to stay motivated with people like that behind me, just itching to belittle me and fuck me over. At least the 101st showed a combat soldier a little respect (no KP for example).

I had almost determined to go back, but then Lt. "Law of the Jungle" Greene was replaced with Lt. Robert Stein, a 1st Cav. combat vet. He was a completely different type of officer; the kind who tells you what to do and ensures that you do it, but doesn't feel the need to harass or belittle you the entire time or try to make you feel like a basic trainee. I came to have a lot of respect for Lt. Stein and I still do. He was a real person, not some martinet. (Lt. Law of the Jungle was later killed, and got somebody else killed, too, on his first operation, when he stupidly led the way into a Claymore ambush. He should have left that Law of the Jungle stuff to the *real* pros such as my humble self. I hadn't just *read* it.)

My new platoon was made up of two groups; about half were guys like me who were 101st combat vets and the other half were newly arrived from the States, some of whom were combat vets on their second tour. The thinking was that we old-timers would school the cherries so when we left after a year there would be some continuity. I was assigned to the 4th Platoon, Team 4-6. My team started with five other guys: S. Sgt.

Samuelson (team leader), Sgt. Sedgwick (assistant team leader), myself (a SPC4), and three PFC FNGs (newbies, also called cherries), named Spears, Besecke, and Perry. Samuelson and Sedgwick were on their second tours and had been medics for a year in the 1st Cav.

Our new team flew to Nha Trang to go through Recondo School, but not before I went downtown to get a beer and otherwise relax. Like all other 101st combat veterans, I had long ago concluded that nobody was going to take responsibility for me enjoying any part of the war but me. Other than my R&R I never officially got to go anyplace nice that whole year, (three-day passes to Vung Tau were for REMFs,[14] not combat grunts), so I always looked for the chance to have a good time in the war on my own initiative (and they were few and far between).

The description of a good LRP includes initiative and boldness. You can't turn that on and off like a light switch. Bold people tend to be bold whenever they feel like it; it's why they're bold. That's especially true of 101st vets who figure they don't have much to lose in any event. These are the not the type of people who wait around and ask permission for what they do. When you're bold enough to go on LRP patrols on the Ho Chi Minh Trail, you think you should be able to do whatever the hell you want whenever you want as long as you show up for work on time (trust me on this). And so it was for chances to win the hearts and minds of the populace. When the opportunity presented itself, LRPs were the type to take it boldly, especially when it involved women and liquor. And especially because it was combined with the mindset that we were getting screwed anyway. I always figured: what's the worst thing they can do to me? Put me back in the infantry and send me to Vietnam?

I'm proud to say that as far as I know, LRPs developed the important military tactic of patrolling downtown. We took the line of, "Passes? We don't need no stinking passes, we're on patrol! See all these guns we got!" Here's something I learned in the Vietnam War: you can get away with a lot with personality and charm, but you can get away with a lot more with personality, charm, and a locked and loaded M-16.

---

[14] Slang, "rear-echelon motherfucker," a soldier far from the front-line.

Though still only eighteen years old when I graduated from Recondo School, I had already been on and off military bases on three continents and a major isthmus. Though but a young lad, at this time in my life I was fairly well-steeped in vice including but not limited to: drinking, gambling, carousing with loose women, smoking tobacco and pot. I found these things helpful to calm myself down after a hard day in the war. You had to find your own way to live through the day with whatever psychological quirks might become part of your personality. The Army issued an interesting variety of drugs like amphetamines, morphine, and codeine, but antidepressants hadn't yet been invented.

I reconnoitered downtown Nha Trang the night before Recondo School started. This was the first time in almost six months in Vietnam that I had the chance to get away by myself. I just stuck my .45 in my pocket and walked right out the gate past the jabbering Vietnamese guards. *"Me no tuk tuk Vietnamese!"* I came back in the same way, *"Do I look like a VC, assholes?"*

I had money to spend. Though I only took out $60 per month with the 101st, there was no place to spend it or trustworthy place to keep it, so like a lot of guys I was carrying a couple hundred bucks around. This was big money at the time. Six months into my tour, it was the first time I'd been in a bar in Vietnam and the first time I'd talked to a woman who looked and smelled good. I don't mind saying that after five months of superlative hard living I really enjoyed it, overpriced though it may have been. Those few hours cost me all the money I had, but what else did I have to spend it on?

Pot was cheap and easy to get. You could get a fat bag of Cambodian Red for ten dollars, or a couple of cartons of cigarettes for free. You couldn't buy cigarette papers, so everybody smoked pot out of Dr. Grabow pipes, which could be purchased in the PX. You could always tell a *head* because of the pipe stem sticking out of his breast pocket and a suspicious big bulge in his leg pocket. I smoked pot to calm myself down since what I did could sometimes be physically, emotionally, and spiritually draining, but it was also sort of a *Blows Against the Empire* thing. It was still a revolutionary act back then. It was one of the ways I had of telling the Army, *"FTA; I'm still myself!"* I still smoke pot now and then; it's good for PTSD. If it makes anyone feel better, I also drank to excess in Vietnam nearly every chance I could get.

Penalties for pot usage could be draconian, but there was a fairly strong little countercultural group in our platoon. They were mostly blacks and people like me who later turned out to be hippies, but still a significant minority. Many of the NCOs smoked it, too; I won't name names. There were enough the Army couldn't kick us all out for smoking pot, so they tended to look the other way.

I do hope our indulging in all that exotic vice wasn't what lost the war, and if it was I *sure* am sorry and I just *know* the rest of the guys would be, too. I don't want to imply that all LRPs were as vice-ridden as some of us more fallen Boy Scouts, either. There *were* responsible ones there, too. Golly Gee Whizarooney! There were good fathers and husbands who always said their prayers in a cold bath every night after kissing their family's picture. There were upstanding citizens, paragons of the community, someone you'd want to have for a neighbor. Some of them even went into law enforcement later or became high government officials. *And then there were the rest of us.*

Recondo School in Nha Trang was tough, but it was the kind of school EVERY grunt should have gone through. We were instructed on a whole bunch of good-to-know stuff like enemy weapons identification and various habits of the Vietnamese. There was also stuff we didn't need to know, like how to set up a field antenna. And there was stuff that was just wrong, like duct taping over the head of an M-79.

We also learned fun stuff such as rappelling off forty-foot high towers and one hundred-twenty feet out of helicopters. Eeeeyow! Zoom! There was also the Maguire Rig; it had long nylon straps with loops attached to a rope dangling down from a slick. You'd sit in the loops and away you'd go, spinning over the countryside. That was exciting and a great adventure! What an adventure! They showed us how to rig up the equipment and I remember thinking, this is some mighty technical stuff for an 11B to be doing. They wouldn't even give a grunt a screwdriver in those days!

There were long runs and forced marches, but they were doable after combat. They weren't exactly a walk on the beach, but anything's better than nights on guard in the jungle getting eaten up by mosquitoes. 101st vets thought of Recondo School as a paid vacation (Beds! Showers! Chairs! Forks!) Of especial note was The Dying Cockroach, a form of trainee torture I had not seen before or since. Basically you were forced to lie on your back with your arms and legs extended straight up. When your limbs finally started to shake, you were then derided and harassed for being a Dying Cockroach. Then they'd make you do push-ups and laugh while you groveled around with your face in the dirt. No, I'm not kidding. If the Army had any school where they treated you decently and with respect, I never saw it.

I think one of the reasons I am proud of, and why I enjoyed being in this unit, was that we all went through training together and we all drilled heavily in it. Everybody knew what to do and everybody was on the same page. Everybody knew who the dedicated ones were. Everybody knew who the bold ones were. It was a demonstration of cool I hadn't seen since Jump School. These were the gamest people I ever knew; they would do anything! I'm proud I got to be with these guys because this was some real soldiering—some real adventure.

The kind of men who joined the LRPs were extremely adventurous, aggressive individuals. I liked the idea of taking the war to the enemy instead of waiting for him to bring it to us, like we had to do in the 101st, and I know the others did, too. We took the war to the enemy and shoved it down his throat. I'm proud of that too—that's what I came to do. LRPs were sometimes called the "Poor Man's Special Forces." We did everything they did, including jumping into combat—even assault from the sea. (Not me either time, but I would have gone.) We were pulled out on Maguire Rigs and Jacob's Ladders. We went out on patrol in the area of the Ho Chi Minh Trail, so far away from help that we had to post teams midway to relay the radio messages. Nobody took greater risks than we did because you're going to get killed just so dead for your country no matter how well-trained you are.

They asked me if I wanted to carry the PRC-25 radio, knowing I'd carried it in the 101st. I told them, "No, I'd rather even walk point the whole time than carry the radio." I hated carrying the radio. I had to stand there getting shot at while someone else talked on the radio, and that made me nervous. I'd rather be shooting back or preferably shooting first; it's more my nature. That's how I got to walk point on all the patrols I went on but one. I didn't mind walking point. It was an easier job than carrying the radio, plus it paid the same. By then I was okay with pulling the trigger on people; there was no hesitation, which was the have-to, drop-dead requirement for the job. To get back home, I was ready to shoot all the Vietnamese I needed to, along with anyone else foolish enough to get in my way. I guess this was being all I could be. (The Army slogan was *"Be all that you can be,"* but it seemed like whenever we really *were* all we could be, they'd get all pissed off.)

After Recondo School, Lt. Stein sent different teams to different places to work OJT (On-the-Job Training) with various LRRP units. LRRP or Long Range Reconnaissance Patrol teams and LRP teams were organized differently, both being dangerous and usually consisting of five to six soldiers. LRRP teams were supported by their infantry battalion, were on the battalion's radio network and, if necessary, one of the battalion's companies or platoons would be sent to rescue an endangered LRRP team. Most of the time, only one or two undedicated helicopters were supporting their LRRPs and the teams were normally found operating within four miles of their battalion's area of operation. In contrast, LRP teams went far afield, sometimes fifty miles away from any American or friendly forces. LRP teams had their own radio net and direct air support from four Huey troopships, two gunships, plus an O-1 Bird Dog used for recon and radio relay.

A reaction force was identified for each team in the field; it was usually a Montagnard company led by American Special Forces or an American Infantry Company whose mission was guarding their battalion fire base headquarters. Everyone knew the truth about these reaction forces. They had no dedicated air assets and could not arrive in time to rescue endangered patrol teams. The earliest they could roll in was the next day after the team's fate was sealed. They didn't bother to tell us this; it might have lowered our morale.

Lt. Stein, 4th platoon leader, sent Team 4-6 to Bong Son to patrol with the 1st Cavalry LRRPs. We went on two patrols with a semi-legendary sergeant named Bumgarner, who was known as the Bummer. I've seen his name in a few books, like Nick Turse's *Kill Anything That Moves* (cool title). Bumgarner was the type who wore twin .45s out on patrol. On one patrol he chased after a Vietnamese while firing a .45 in each hand. I had to pursue to cover him, but was cursing him the whole time. I thought it was a fairly stupid thing for a LRRP to do because he could have run us into a trap. That's what Lt. "Law of the Jungle" did. They'd told us in Recondo School that we were there to observe, not engage, that gunfire was the last resort, the first resort being hauling ass and calling for extraction. Gunfire was supposedly only for those times when you couldn't go forward, backward, or sideways.

My team leader, Charles "Sam" Samuelson, was career Army (so was Sedgwick) and Sam knew other people in different units, like the Special Forces, so we sometimes hung out with them. We would try to get different kinds of exotic weapons. Our team had a silenced Sten gun, some Grease Guns, and a Browning Automatic Rifle (BAR) along with M1 and M2 carbines. These weapons would come and go like baseball cards. We mostly just used them for going to town; in the field we mostly carried M-16s and CAR-15s. I traded some souvenir stuff to a helicopter pilot for a .38 snub-nosed revolver and carried it everywhere.

The point of carrying exotic weapons was to differentiate us from grunts and to look different, *cool*. LRPs and LRRPs had a reputation of being psycho crazy fighters so we'd try to live up to the image. This was one of the ways we had of expressing our individuality in the world's most conforming culture. We cultivated the spook look: LRP hats, sunglasses, tiger fatigues, and exotic weapons. We'd see how long we could grow our hair and beards before eyebrows were raised. Nobody knew quite who we were and nobody would mess with us.

LRP hats were cut-down camo flop brim hats with the brim cut down to about one inch. People would individualize their hats with grenade rings and jump-wings. The tradition was never to wash the hats and they'd get fairly ripe. I sewed a bright orange patch inside mine (it was a piece of helicopter landing pad), so I could hold the hat upside down and, unseen by the enemy, use it to signal helicopters. We also wore tiger fatigues a lot because they were easiest to get. We were issued Air Force camouflage fatigues, but they were impossible to replace. A set of regular fatigues was hard enough to get out of Army Supply but a new set of Air Force camo fatigues was impossible. We bought the tiger fatigues and always had enough, but they were technically unauthorized so the word was out that the NVA would torture anyone wearing tigers. That meant wearing tiger fatigues would result in a fight to the death every time, since surrender was not an option. I never heard of anyone surviving if they were captured wearing tigers.

Part of the fun of being an LRP was to see what you could get away with; never forget these were the boldest people you'd *ever* run across and heavily armed, too. If they'd think it, they'd do it. I felt a lot like a little kid tagging after the big kids, which was technically true, and there were some mighty fearsome big kids to try and keep up with. We were an orphan outfit, newly created, so there was ample opportunity to slip between the cracks.

Our base camp, which we shared with the 4th Infantry Division, was in Camp Enari, near Pleiku. This was the only place in the Army where we had our own bar in our barracks. I never knew if we were officially attached to the 4th Division or not, but both the 4th and we acted like we weren't. They didn't like us because we stole lots of stuff from them and, being Airborne, kicking ass on straight legs (non-Airborne soldiers) just sort of came naturally. I remember more than one formation when some beat-up looking 4th Division NCO or officer came through our ranks looking for the "Usual Suspects" who had probably just gone out on patrol that morning. One of the NCO beer halls burned down after ejecting a bunch of LRPs.

There are some good things to be said about total uniformity. For example, you never have to wonder what to wear. Everybody looks exactly alike and this can be very useful at times. This is why LRPs wore regular issue jungle fatigues now and then. At times it could be advantageous to look like everyone else. We'd always try to have at least one regular fatigue shirt with a 4th Division or 1st Cavalry patch, depending on where we were. This could be considered camouflage in its own way.

We always figured that if it said U.S. Army on it then it was meant for us because we were *in* the U.S. Army and fighting a war, too. (This is also called "freelance socialism.") If you ever see a picture of LRPs in a Jeep, it's almost a dead certainty the Jeep was stolen. My team had its own Jeep for a while, parked where no one else could find it. We figured the Jeep that Congress wanted us to have probably got sent to Korea by mistake, so we borrowed that one until they could get everything all straightened out. Some no-good thieving bastard stole it from us while we were on patrol; there's just no *end* to human wickedness in this evil world.

Here's a good example of that: two of our NCOs volunteered to do KP for the 1st Cavalry. They walked right up and volunteered in the mess hall saying they just wanted to help out. The cooks gave them something to do and as soon as the cooks' backs were turned, said NCOs started walking cases of steaks out the back door to a waiting (stolen) Jeep. After they got all they wanted they decided they'd *helped* enough and said goodbye. When you see pictures of LRPs at barbecues, most likely this is where the food came from.

There are *lots* of stories like that about LRPs, many involving some serious high jinks with women, guns, and liquor. High-spirited, bold, generally horny young men with all the guns and explosives a growing boy could *ever* want, when mixed with alcohol, can make for some rollicking good times. It's tempting to think of it as an *Animal House* with guns, and it did have some aspects of that, but it wasn't really that way at all. Boys *will* be boys but we were still trying to win a war. It was just our little way of working off job stress, but sometimes it could get fairly epic.

Here's an example, and the usual suspects will remain anonymous: LRPs A, B, C, and D were partying with women in a bar one night in An Khe, which everybody considered the best Sin City in Vietnam. The MPs pulled a surprise inspection and LRPs A, B, and C ran out the back door. The MPs caught LRP D in the back in bed with his girl. D reached under the bed, pulled a grenade out of his pants pocket, pulled the pin and went freaking *fugazi*. He jumped out of bed and started screaming, "All right, you straight leg *sonsafucking* bitches! Who wants to die with me? C'mon, motherfuckers! Who wants to die?"

With grenade in hand, he backed the MPs out the door screaming nasty things about their mothers, all the while being stark naked. He then flung the grenade over their heads and across the road, scattering everyone. He ran back into the bar, grabbed his clothes and hauled ass out the back, still naked. There ensued what may have been the greatest manhunt in the 1st

Cavalry Division's history, but the entire 1st Cav's MP Company up against one naked Easy-Company LRP was no contest. He got away after hiding all night in a crawl space underneath another bar.

The only hand-to-hand combat I ever got into was with other American soldiers, and this was usually only reluctantly. (Except for the guy I punched out in the 101st; that's *still* one of my all-time favorite memories.) By this time, I was all for a quiet life and just wanted to spend my off-duty time and money going downtown, drinking beer, smoking some pot, and getting friendly with nice-smelling women. You might say I was winning hearts and minds through direct, grassroots American economic aid. Some LRPs, though, really liked to fistfight, were good at it and would start fights just for fun, especially while drinking. I witnessed quite a few fights, some up real close, too if something impeded me walking backwards.

In November our platoon reassembled in Plei Do Lim in the Central Highlands. We went on patrols and rehearsed working as a platoon. We practiced using the Maguire Rig and also jumped from helicopters. I jumped three times in one day, my highest personal total. I liked jumping. Later, some of our teams made combat jumps, but not mine; that's too bad because a combat jump was the one thing I wanted to do in the Army that I didn't get done.

On one of these patrols, we took along some ARVNs (Army of the Republic of Vietnam soldiers) to train. They were a bunch of bozos, starting fires and talking all night. We made them move away. The next morning, we started off and were moving along a trail when we walked right into two enemy trail watchers. I shot them both and then went into the drill we'd trained to do. I ran to the rear while the others went left and right off the trail, firing their magazines in turn and then retreating to the rally point. (Except the Vietnamese soldiers had already fled down the road! They'd turned and hatted up at the first shot.)

When we caught up to them, we gave them some butt-strokes with our rifles and told them to *didi mau* (get lost). We later worked with Yard scouts; these Montagnards were indigenous peoples of the Central Highlands, who hated the VC/NVA. They were completely different soldiers than the average ARVN.

Most U.S. soldiers had very little respect for the ARVNs. We were fighting harder for their country than they were; we knew it and they knew it. Some of our guys refused to salute the ARVN officers and told them to do something about it or fuck off. Some of our guys could say that bilingually, too.

We went from Plei Do Lim to Qui Nhon, where we stayed at a helicopter base southwest of the city. We ran patrols in the hills to the immediate southwest. We got into a firefight there the day before Christmas, which was cool because then we spent Christmas Day at a helicopter base and enjoyed a turkey dinner with all the trimmings. We thought that was fair because we'd had a Mermite dinner for our Thanksgiving feast.[15]

After that we went to Buon Ma Thuot, (which we called Ban Me Thuot). It was the capital of Dak Lak Province (sometimes spelled Dar Lac) and was a sleepy little farm town though it sat right in the middle of the Truong Son route. This is in the heart of what was called "Indian Country," though truthfully I never saw any Indians there. I did see one hell of a lot of hostile Vietnamese, most of them armed and all of them dangerous.

Indian Country was called that because of the ambience—that and the fact that it was like the American frontier we knew from cowboy stories and TV shows in terms of hostile natives being in residence. It was like the Old West in some ways including the false front stores, the always-open whorehouses and bars, and the fact that everybody carried a gun. Coming into town after a patrol felt a lot like coming into Dodge after a cattle drive. There'd be a certain swagger in our walk. We were paratroopers who'd completed a harrowing patrol and it just felt great to be alive. *It's party time!* (When I was there in 2003, I realized I knew the Vietnamese words for pot and various kinds of sex, but somehow I never learned to say *please* and *thank you*. That about says it all.)

In Ban Me Thuot, we stayed adjacent to a helicopter base and were mortared on our first night. This was the only place where Lt. Stein made

---

[15] Mermite cans were small chest shaped thermos bottles used to transport hot or cold meals to the field in three separate containers: one sleeve was meat, one sleeve was potatoes, and one sleeve was vegetables.

us dig in. We ran patrols out of Ban Me Thuot for a couple of weeks and our teams were running into action everywhere. This was right before the Tet Offensive of '68, and we now know we were watching the Tet buildup. What we observed then was, everywhere we went, there sure were a lot of the little buggers and they were spoiling for a fight, too. They acted like they owned the place and the truth was, they did.

The Truong Son route (what we called the Ho Chi Minh or HCM Trail) was actually a series of trails along the western border of South Vietnam with Laos and Cambodia. The enemy used it for supply and transport. There were eight major land routes and three water routes; all were interconnected. That way if one route was blocked—say by Arc Light, B-52 strikes—they could just reroute the traffic around the blockage. ("Arc Light" was the code name given to the use of American heavy bombers. The B52D model could carry eighty-two 500-pound bombs internally and twenty-four 750-pound bombs on underwing pylons.)

The HCM Trail was actually a huge infrastructure involving tens of thousands of people: camps, roads, hospitals, classrooms, barracks, armories, theaters, and warehouses. It was an enormous human endeavor, a human anthill. The NVA lived on and maintained the Truong Son route (named for the Truong Son Mountains it went through) during the entire war. Everybody in and around it was involved in it; the NVA wouldn't let people live there who weren't, and would wipe out any unfriendly Montagnard village. You could count on everybody you ran into out there as being the enemy. This made it easier for us when determining who to kill, and I mean a *lot* easier.

Along those lines, to keep things accurate I must now say LRPs killed unarmed trail watchers. These were people who were out there to watch trails and report any movement to the NVA. Lots of times they'd be farmers and mostly they'd be unarmed. They were the eyes of the enemy and some real threats to us, so we killed them when we could. Not every time, not even most of the time, just when we were really sure we could get away with it cheap and easy. This would look a lot like cold-blooded murder of unarmed men to many people, but there it was. *Sorry! Don't take this personally; it's good for your country.* Here's another thing I learned in the war that you can take to the bank: when you know your life is cheap, everyone else's life gets cheap also.

Some of this killing was extracurricular; we didn't have to do it. We did some of it just to do it, just because we were soldiers and they were the enemy. *Take THAT, motherfuckers, the U.S. Airborne was here!* It's what they paid us that $65 per month combat pay to do, the same as they paid every cook, clerk, and mechanic in The Nam. (Having low Military Occupation Specialties codes or MOSes, they never even thought of giving us professional pay.)

The Army would give us decks of playing cards with only the ace of spades on them. These were supposed to be left around dead bodies to put the fear of God into the enemy, but only a fool really thought that would happen. I always thought this was so stupid. That was just one of the ways our commanders at the top misunderstood and underestimated the Vietnamese. They weren't afraid of stupid crap like that; it just irritated them, perhaps as you would be if you saw a picture of Jesus that someone had used as toilet paper. It would make you think how low-class the enemy was and how you could do him serious damage, but you wouldn't do anything stupid over it. I tossed the cards in the garbage. You never go wrong thinking your enemy is as human as you are, and at least as smart.

We had a silenced Sten gun that Sam got from some Special Forces guys who probably got it from some Aussies. We could get only two magazines for this gun, so it never was anyone's primary piece. We had to buy our own silenced weapons, just like we had to buy our own uniforms. There is a picture of me wearing Tigers (tiger fatigues) holding this Sten gun with silencer and wearing a really nasty grin on my face. I love this picture because it shows me in an unauthorized uniform, fighting an undeclared war with an unauthorized weapon. How many American teenagers were doing *that* in the '60s?

I can't see why people get upset when they hear farmers beat us. Who says farmers can't be as tough and smart fighters as anyone? They sure as hell know what hard work is, and they know the land and what can be done on it better than anyone. Eisenhower was raised on a farm and so was Grant. The Vietnamese were smart, tough people who'd been fighting wars a lot longer than we had; they were as tough and sophisticated an enemy as

America ever faced, but we thought of them as dumbass little gooks. America was officially a segregated racist country throughout half of the Vietnam War, denying basic rights to our own minorities. That attitude had an effect on how we fought the war and related to the Vietnamese, and how the Vietnamese related to us.

The company culture of the American military in the Vietnam War was racist. We thought we were *so* much better than those "stupid slope-headed peasants," as we called them then. But we really weren't, and we paid dearly for that delusion. Racist attitudes, cultural contempt and misunderstanding, arrogance and truly lousy, extremely fanciful estimates of the enemy are just some of the reasons the Vietnam War was such a struggle for the U.S. throughout many years. Veteran military reporter Thomas E. Ricks provides an example in his book, *The Generals: American Military Command from World War II to Today:* "One of the most striking moments in Norman Schwarzkopf's autobiography is his recollection that in 1965, when he was an advisor in Vietnam, he had tried to take his Vietnamese counterpart to an American officer's club, only to be told by the club manager, 'We don't serve Vietnamese.'"[16]

One morning Lt. Stein dropped us off for a patrol out in Indian Country. We assembled in the high elephant grass adjacent to our landing zone and moved quickly off the field. I moved around a large tree, looked around, and caught my breath. I was looking at an enemy base camp, at least a platoon's worth, with bunks made up and equipment lying around. They had hatted up when they heard us come in, but they were still out there; we could hear them shouting out orders to each other.

This did not look good! We backed up onto a little rise and prepared for a last stand, meanwhile calling for extraction. We were there to locate the enemy and we had done so, now it was time to get the flock on out of there. About four or five of them came into view; we threw grenades and shot at them, and they all went down. We pushed back into the eight-to-ten feet high elephant grass by the landing zone.

We could hear them moving in close trying to find us. We were throwing grenades at them, spooning the handles (letting a couple of

---

[16] New York: Penguin Press, 2012.

seconds run off) before flinging. They were lobbing grenades, too, but wildly since they didn't know where we were out there in the tall grass.

Along with my rifle and pistol, I carried an M79 grenade launcher with the sights removed and the stock cut off at the pistol grip. I had taken the sights off and cut it off because that made it easier to carry slung down my back. I only used it for marking smoke for air support, so I didn't need to be all that accurate. We had another M79 with the sights if we needed better accuracy.

I thought I might fling a few high explosive rounds at them just to keep their heads down and teach them not to be Commies. Looking back down the trail of crushed grass we'd made, I brought up the M79 and fired it with one motion, hardly aiming it. Just as I fired, two heads came into view about thirty feet in front of me, just enough distance for the grenade to arm. I must have hit one of them right in the face and then it was brains for lunch. They both went down ... and up ... and sort of every which way. It's hard to describe adequately.

The helicopter door gunners were working out, trying to keep the enemy in the treeline. Of course this only drove them closer to us. Finally, one of the slick pilots announced, "We're coming in!" and over the top of the trees they came and straight down about forty feet, just splat almost on top of me. The chopper bounced a couple of times and wound up about five feet away. Bullets were flying everywhere, but time seemed to slow down almost to a dead stop. I could hear every *wop* of the rotor going by three feet above my head.

I thought the helicopter was *shot* down since I'd seen it happen in the 101st a number of times. I could only stand there in a huge crater, in shock, goggling open-mouthed through the Plexiglas at the pilots. It was one of those times during the Vietnam War when I absolutely, positively, beyond the shadow of a doubt did not know what to do next. It was one of those times when all the choices looked bad— *really* bad. It's not as simple as it looks in the movies. In the worst periods, this seemed to happen all the time, sometimes sequentially. I was trying to think what to do and I was just not coming up with anything at all. I could only stand there thinking, I'm not ready for this.

I never got all that good at life-and-death combat situations; I was just lucky. It was *always* a scramble for me. I was *always* winging it, trying to figure out what to do … shoot and duck, at the same time hoping God woke up on my side that morning. I was scared shitless a lot and no other time more than this, and that's the true story, too. I kept this Ultra Triple Top Secret at the time for prudent reasons. Only now can the truth be told.

It could have been a few seconds, but in memory it seems like I stood there an hour and a half with that damn *wopwopwopping* sound of the rotors above my head, gaping open-mouthed at the pilots before it registered that they were waving frantically and shouting, "Get on! Get on!" Boy did that seem like a good idea and you may rest assured I needed no further convincing. I went from standing still to jet-propelled in a split second. I was moving as fast as I ever did, but I seemed to be in slow motion. I leaped on the slick and a second later five other guys landed on top of me.

Everyone was screaming, "Go! Go! Go!" The moment the slick took off will remain with me forever: bullets flying everywhere, all my team whooping and hollering, shooting and throwing grenades, and the door-gunners were just ripping it up with gunships firing their rockets and mini-guns. I was lying on the floor at the bottom of the pile with my arms over my head, shaking and muttering, "Oh geez, not after all this time." It took me more than a little while to come down from this; I was helped by a lot of beer and weed.

Sometime after this we lost Perry and Spears but gained Gary Stuart, another cherry. Perry became the lieutenant's driver and Spears went to another team. Gary Stuart became my slack man (behind me on point) and best friend. He was a cocky little guy and a real fighter. We got into a fistfight soon after he joined us; after that we were best friends. That was Team 4-6 as I remember it. I made most of my patrols with these guys: Samuelson (team leader), Sedgwick (assistant team leader/rear security), me (point), Stuart (slack), and Besecke (RTO). We were together on about twenty patrols including radio relay patrols.

On another patrol around the same time, we were watching a road and this three-quarter ton truck pulled up. I'd never seen a truck like that before. It was an enemy truck, probably Russian or Chinese, and they'd sent a couple of squads out to look for us. Fifteen or so guys jumped out, formed up on either side of the road and started moving squads on line toward us, a couple of hundred yards away. We hatted up pronto.

We had our best day ever on another patrol in this area. One of the things we were supposed to do when there was artillery support was to fire in Papa Tangos (preplanned targets) at likely places. We scouted out probable areas of use, for example, trail junctions and possible campsites, and then would fire in spotting rounds and record the site. Later the artillery might use these coordinates for Harassment and Interdiction fire in the middle of the night. Sometimes we'd fire them in and come back to them, or a previous team could have fired them in. We would also use these for artillery ambushes; we'd just lie there and wait for a likely target to step on the big red X.

The day before, we'd fired a Papa Tango on a trail junction and then came back to it on the way out. We set up on a little rise a quarter of a mile away and waited. We remained in place for about half the day and into the afternoon, and then watched as a reinforced NVA company or battalion, perhaps 150 men, walked right into the kill zone. What happened next shouldn't happen to a dog. Sam, our team leader, called for antipersonnel rounds, air bursts, and time-on-target, meaning all six rounds from the cannons of the 105mm battery exploded at once over the target.

We heard a huge thunderclap out of nowhere. This was some *real* shock and awe! I was sure shocked and awed, anyway. Trees were flayed into basket stuff, just shredded in seconds. Sam waited about two minutes and fired again. And again. And again. We fired on those poor fuckers until the battery said they couldn't spare any more rounds. There was no one moving when we left, chuckling and slapping five. *Your tax dollars at work!*

We figured we killed nearly a hundred enemy, with the rest ruined for life. This may have been as big an actual body count as my infantry company had while I was in it! *Five guys!* In terms of what I was trained to do, paid to do, equipped to do, told to do, and what I volunteered to do, this was the best day I ever had in the Army. This was the day they got their most money out of me, and I never fired a shot nor stabbed a stab. I didn't do anything but stroll around the countryside dressed as a heavily armed bush. (I was security.) I didn't realize until much later that this was as important in this life as I ever was, that any of us ever was or ever would be.

I liked that kind of patrol, not in the least because it felt great to get *a little of my own* back—I'd been mortared and shelled a whole lot by that time. Payback's a real bitch, ain't it? I still look back on that day with considerable job satisfaction. *Take THAT, motherfuckers, the U.S. Airborne was here!* That's what I came to do; take the war to the enemy and shove it down his throat in his own comfort zone.

After that, we went back to Ban Me Thuot. That was where we were during the Tet Offensive. As I said before, LRPs would occasionally spend the night downtown for unauthorized drinking and carousing. As long as we showed up for formation, we thought Lt. Stein wouldn't mind too much. And that's what Gary Stuart and I were doing the night the NVA took over Ban Me Thuot.

It was the middle of the night and I was in a hotel room, lying in bed with company, when Stuart came streaking in shouting, *"We gotta get outta here!"* and then I could hear the gunfire. There was lots of it—RPG and machine gun fire—and all I had was my snub-nosed .38 with just the six bullets. I was out of bed in a second, shoving my boots on and running out the door, still pulling up my pants.

We ran down the stairs and out the back, hopped a couple of fences, and hauled ass. There's nothing the Airborne teaches you that's handier than how to run long distances wearing combat boots. We ran all the way back to the base, about five miles. When we got there, the gate was guarded by ARVNs. We just shouldered our way on past them and made it back to our camp.

During the weeks we were there, we met Fess Parker. He was coming around visiting troops with Patricia Blair, the actress who played his wife in the television series *Daniel Boone*. We had just come in from patrol that morning, had been debriefed, and then headed for the shower. Coming out of the shower, I almost walked right in to this big guy. I looked up at him and it was Fess Parker, an icon from my boyhood days. I said, "Holy Shit, it's Davy Crockett!" He laughed and said, "No, it's Daniel Boone." We talked for a minute and I got his autograph. This was one of the biggest events for my platoon; everybody remembers it. (A couple of years ago, someone gave me a photo of Fess and me. I really like it because it shows me with really long hair, the longest I had in the Army. This was really a longhaired hippie haircut for the Airborne.)

Shortly after this I went to Hong Kong on R&R. I had a great time and got back to feeling almost human again. My dad ran an importing business in San Francisco and had an office in Hong Kong. His people set me up and showed me a great time.[17]

After that I went back to An Khe to work out at the Mang Yang Pass. This was a scary place because the enemy could see us come in and would have squads out sometimes in minutes. Every team that went out there ran into trouble. We would search that pass for the mortar and rocket sites that would take out our trucks. (I was on this road many years later in 2003 and I had a chance to take a good look at all the terrain without getting shot at. From the heights you can see everything here.) Although we did many evasive tactics during the war, the enemy would have had no trouble seeing the slicks going in to drop us off. They knew where we were every time; consequently every patrol that went out ran into trouble. The NVA were there within minutes and we would wind up having to shoot our way out.

On one patrol we tried going in at last light. I did not like this because it put us on unfamiliar ground in the dark, never a pleasant experience when the enemy knows the terrain like the back of his hand and you don't. We pushed off the LZ and headed for some thick brush to get our bearings, hang low, and see who'd show up. We had gotten ourselves collected in the twilight and then started moving out. We went about one hundred yards and then, just after I put my rifle down to go under a bush, four heavily armed hostile peasants ran across right in front of me.

I was on my hands and knees, my rifle lying on the ground. I slowly sat back on my haunches and silently pulled out my .38. I didn't speak any more Vietnamese than I needed to buy pot or get laid, but I sure didn't need an interpreter to know they were saying, "You, look over there!" Once again I thought I was watching "The Happy Ending." One of them came back down the trail right in front of me, looked around, and then

---

[17] Sadly, some of the people I met were killed a few years later in a car accident.

pulled out his dick and peed into the bush I was hiding behind. I gripped the .38, looked at his wang, figured he'd let go of it if he saw me and thought, see you in hell, Slope. He never saw me, or if he did, he was one of the coolest heads ever. He shook off his wang, put it back in his shorts, and walked away, but I'm *real* sure he felt no more relieved than I did. I don't know what the record is for the backwards low crawl, but if there is one, I believe I broke it right then.

We'd received the order to pull out and we did so, heading back to the landing zone, which was actually a low place in the bushes not bare ground. On cue, Samuelson threw out a trip flare and then the gunships came in firing mini-guns on the other side of the flare. This was truly horrific. It looked like a wall of horizontal red rain. We were less than 100 feet away and the sight, sound, and sensations were truly terrific, like a wall of sound and shock with splinters and dust flying everywhere and all over us. The forest just disintegrated right in front of us and on top of us. Another thing you'll learn in a war: you're *never* far enough away from this stuff.

Our pilots said they were coming in to pick us up, and as the recovery slick was coming in both door gunners started firing all around us. It looked like they were going to fire right into us. I was jumping up and down with a strobe light in my hand and screaming at the top of my lungs while bullets snapped, crackled, and popped around me like a swarm of angry bees. (Afterwards, I was hoarse for days.)

The slick landed right on top of some bushes but was still five feet up. We had to scramble to get on: Besecke had been shot in the leg, so I picked him up like a child and threw him up on the slick. He's a big guy and he carried the heavy radio, but I was desperate. I was the last one to get up on my side, and was still clambering up on the skid when the slick took off. If someone hadn't grabbed me I would have pitched off the side. We dumped all of our grenades on them and fired off a bunch of ammo. *Yeehaw! Eat that!*

My last patrol was in the very same area. This was the one and only time, out of about twenty-four patrols, that I did not go on patrol as point man. I had become assistant team leader, though still a SPC4. Sgt. Regis Murphy was the team leader; Ron Causey, Gary Stuart, and Juergen

Besecke completed the team. As the assistant team leader I would be tail gunner (rear security). We were going into the same area as before. Our helicopter settled down in a couple of places to try and fake out the enemy, but I think we only attracted more attention. As we were settling down in the third location and preparing to exit out the right side, I looked back and saw an enemy soldier run for cover. I yelled, "Stop!" and I pointed out the door. Right then someone opened up firing from the treeline I was pointing to. Our door-gunner fired back, shooting one of them out of a tree about one hundred feet away.

Bullets started flying everywhere from all directions. Our pilot aborted the mission right away and we circled up above them, watching the gunships going in. We could see several muzzle blasts from the area we'd been about to run into. If I hadn't seen a fragmentary image of that guy diving for cover, we would have run right into them. We flew back to An Khe, and then I just lay on my bunk shaking for quite a while.

There's a point you reach when you know you're not going to make it back. You don't care about anything anymore, including your own safety. You're in an exalted state and nothing can hurt you, but you can only do this so long before your nerve starts to run out. I had been in Vietnam for ten plus months by then, had seen more than my share of combat and tough situations, and I was at the end of it. I was having a hard time knowing what was real. Everything I ever believed in was gone and there was just nothing left in me to give up; nothing more they could take away from me. I was just a robot doing what I was told, but no more. I felt completely hollow inside; like they'd finally beaten out whatever humanity I had left.

The stress was taking its toll (and it did for years to come). I can fake being brave better and longer than most people, but I was at the end of it. I was very close to a nervous breakdown. I just couldn't take it anymore. I could barely put one foot in front of another. Then I got the news that I was going to be going on a special detail to an ARVN Recondo School in Ban Me Thuot. This was a surprise, but it meant I was not going on patrol anymore, which was good because I was truly falling apart inside. So I got to go to Ban Me Thuot for the rest of my tour, about six weeks more. I was an instructor in an ARVN Recondo School. I tried to do the best I could, but the Vietnamese were just not as motivated as we were. Good luck to them, I thought.

We stayed downtown in a place they called The Compound, the nicest place I stayed in Vietnam. It was a walled compound with a nice garden, a restaurant, and a bar. I met an interesting variety of people there since this was also the transient barracks for Special Forces and people who many called *spooks*. I got acquainted with people whom I now know were SOG[18], but you never heard the term *SOG* then. These were America's elite warriors, I guess, but they sure didn't get killed any more dead than LRPs or grunts. I met people I know had to be CIA.

I'd sit in the back, a young kid nursing a beer and listening to them talk, and I realized that these were a pack of true bad asses, some *really* hardcore people—and they showed me respect, too, which was wise. I'm glad I got the chance to sit there. It felt good to be with these people, talking with some *real* jungle pros, hearing how the war was truly going, what was really happening out there in Indian Country. They were talking to me like I was one of them. And there I was at nineteen, as bad as I ever wanted to be.

It's important to understand what was happening historically (sideways to this story) from mid '67 to mid '68 to get the proper context. I remember reading about Westmoreland's "Light at the End of the Tunnel" speech (January '68), where he claimed to have completely knocked out the enemy's capacity to resist. That was not the enemy I was seeing out there in Indian Country, and it finally started to dawn on me that the information we were risking our lives to get was being shit-canned because it did not match the company (Department of Defense) view. That realization can make one bitter over the years and cynical, too. Ask me how I know that.

A few weeks later, the Light at the End of the Tunnel for Westmoreland was the Tet Offensive freight train coming through. Sure we beat them back (we had complete air and sea superiority), but the fact that they could mount a huge offensive right under our noses proved what a liar Westmoreland was. He was getting the correct information all right,

---

[18] Military Assistance and Command, Studies and Observations Group: a highly classified Special Ops unit.

but it did not match the desired company viewpoint so he went with magical thinking. *Your tax dollars at work!*

Others have the same assessment. Thomas E. Ricks notes the following opinions of Westmoreland: "He seemed rather stupid," said Air Force Lt. General Robert Beckel, who was an aide to the chairman of the JCS; "He didn't grasp things or follow the proceedings very well." Russell Weigley, one of the foremost historians of the Vietnam War, concluded that Westmoreland's dullness reflected poorly on President Johnson, because "No capable president would allow an officer of such limited capacities as Gen. William Westmoreland to head Military Command Vietnam for so long."[19]

I left the war in April 1968. I didn't volunteer for another tour because I just never wanted to be accused of trying to hog all the patriotism in the U.S.A. I had long since decided the Army was not my future and that the Vietnam War would have to be won without my further input, another decision I never regretted. I returned to eight more months in the Army at Ft. Bragg, North Carolina. I was in C-Company 1st Battalion/ 504th PIR, 3rd Brigade, 82nd Airborne.

While I was there I was bored enough with police call, unloading sides of beef, and putting salt on the roads to volunteer for another special detail. This was working on a riggers' crew, rigging loads for dropping out of airplanes. The loads could be trucks and Jeeps on platforms. We would push the loads out the back of the C-130s and then jump down after them and pack up the equipment. I liked this and it was interesting and exciting. Doing this, I wound up with forty-three jumps in three years from nine different kinds of aircraft.

I was given a ninety-day early out to go to college, and was honorably discharged Jan 22, 1969, the day Nixon was inaugurated for the second time. After thirty-three months in the Army, I was twenty years and two months old. I was still not old enough to vote nor drink alcohol in my home state of California (though they did lower the voting age to eighteen shortly after I turned twenty-one).

---

[19] p. 234

I got no recognition, medals or rank for being in the Long Range Patrol, or in the 101st, and no thanks either until decades later. The Army left me with the same discharge as an REMF and a very distinguished one, too: no Combat Infantryman's Badge (CIB),[20] no medals but the Vietnam Campaign and Service medals and the National Defense Service Medal (NDSM). You could not have walked away with a more undistinguished official record and still claim to have been in the Vietnam War. After a year's faithful service in the Vietnam War as an airborne infantryman and LRP, at great personal risk and discomfort to myself, all of which I had volunteered for, I walked away with nothing but the *I Was There* medals. After all that volunteering my way into dangerous circumstances, I felt very foolish to say the least.

I always thought I had the CIB because everybody else who was with me had one; we thought of it as a freebie. I have never talked to a 101st vet who saw his CIB orders. I wore it unchallenged for the rest of my enlistment, but when I was being discharged they told me there was no order for my CIB and I would have to take it off. That wasn't the most shocking thing that happened to me in the Army, but it was certainly one of the most. I wish I'd told them to shove their fucking CIB up their Olive Drab asses, but I just wanted to get out of there really badly, so I kept my mouth shut and signed whatever they put in front of me. I walked away from the U.S. Army cursing the day I'd ever heard the name and feeling incredibly ripped off and fucked over. It sure made me wish a lot more I'd gone AWOL, and I don't mean maybe.

Later I had to apply three times to get my CIB; the first two times the Army said there was no evidence I'd earned it. (I have the second one of those letters framed and hanging on my wall in case I ever want to do anything patriotic again.) The problem was this: all the time I was walking point on patrols (which is all I ever did in the Long Range Patrol, E-Co.), someone changed my MOS11B to some *commo* MOS (a rear echelon radio operator). That's what job the Army had me doing in my records. I didn't learn this until I got my official records in the late 1990s. That was

---

[20] Combat Infantryman's Badge: award to infantrymen who fought in active ground combat while assigned to an infantry, ranger, or Special Forces unit.

shocking, too; it was a huge lie. Not only did I get no medals or recognition for anything I'd done in the LRP, they also lied about what I did and later denied I did it. This is also probably why I didn't make sergeant, which I deserved.

I am not the only LRP this happened to. I've never gotten a coherent reason for this and I don't think there is one. It was just one more of those senseless, gratuitously mean, Slap-in-the Face things that impacted me negatively, and that I'd come to expect from the U.S. Army in return for my faithful service. I did not fail them, even in the worst and most horrible circumstances, but they sure as hell failed me in every important way including lying about what I did, and then denying I did it.

Having no CIB or medals other than the *I Was There* stuff pretty well put the kibosh on any bragging rights I might have had for my Vietnam service, a very important reason I quit talking about it. Other people, including REMFs, had their many awards all mounted prettily, but my measly two *I Was There* medals with the NDSM would have looked ludicrous, especially if I'd tried to tell people what I'd done. I was very angry and bitter about this for a long time. Forget spitting hippies. No one has ever insulted me like the U.S. Army, treated me worse, nor ripped me off for my time so badly and by some *real* assholes, too, the kind who punish people for smiling. (No, I'm not kidding about that either.)

I had been used and abused like never before or since and then dumped by the side of the road. They truly did not care about me at all, and it affected whatever nasty things they wanted me to do for them. Other than that I was entirely on my own to get anything I deserved, something I learned much too late (but did suspect at the time). I did not look back at this with anything but overwhelming anger for years; this was the main reason I didn't talk about it. Whatever else had happened in the Vietnam War, I knew I'd gotten screwed by my country *big time,* and I was not happy about it. I was ashamed of what they did to me and knew I didn't deserve it, but after many years I finally saw that it was their shame and disgrace, not mine. That's why I'm writing this to set the record straight. I don't care what their corrupt, lying record says, I acquitted myself honorably as LRP point man on about two dozen patrols in Team 4-6, E-

Company 20th Infantry (LRP). My friends know what I did, and now you do, too. That's enough for me.

Later I discovered that I already *had* been awarded the CIB in 1968. I only found out I'd previously been awarded it when someone else showed me his CIB orders and I was on them, with the MOS of 11B, as far as I knew the only MOS I ever had. The Army had made the award after I'd left Vietnam so I never got it; they didn't forward it, didn't tell me about it, lost the records, and then for decades denied I'd earned it. Again, I am not the only one this happened to; I know two other LRPs it happened to.

The U.S. Army denied for decades there was enough evidence to award me an award they'd already awarded me. Yes, you're reading that correctly! The Vietnam War was just chock full of little ironies like that. They told me to take off a medal they had already awarded me, denying they'd ever given it to me or that I'd earned it. They could have just cut me some orders right then, but instead they elected to tell a Vietnam combat veteran, a paratrooper and LRP to take off his CIB because they were that kind of people; truly mean and mean-spirited right to the very end. Oh yeah, they sure appreciated my service and sacrifices all right.

I have now been awarded the CIB at least twice for Vietnam, another great honor and distinction, especially since they told me twice in writing, and once to my face, that there was no evidence I'd earned it. That turned out to be a big fat lie too. When I got the records, I saw there was plenty of evidence I'd earned it. It's entirely possible, even entirely probable that I was awarded it in the 101st, too. They just didn't pass it on or tell me about that either, which would make three times in all. It's not hard to see why we lost with that level of professionalism. All I can say is if everybody had been as good at their jobs as I was, we might have won that war, but they weren't. That was certainly generous of them and it remains to the day you read this as the only official acknowledgement I ever got for services in Vietnam beyond the *I Was There* medals. That's why I never claim to have been brave, just desperate—and very, very lucky. If I ever looked brave, I was only faking it; take my word for it. Don't argue, I have the official records to prove it. I am not kidding about *any* of this; I am as honest as a point man in the Long Range Patrol can be.

I went back to Vietnam in 2003. Let's call it for completion. I hate the word *closure* since I'm not dead yet. I wanted to see how it turned out for the Vietnamese, whom I actually liked and felt sorry for. I was, after all, allegedly risking my life for their freedom though they never seemed all that grateful for it. I went to most of the places I've told you about and stayed in the same hotel we got run out of in Ban Me Thuot during Tet. We drove slowly down through Mang Yang Pass. I could see the last place where we got shot up on the last patrol. We spent time on the beach, something I only got a chance to do once in the entire year I was there during the war. I saw Saigon, something I'd never done before. I got a chance to see how beautiful the country is, something I had never noticed before—war makes a place look *so* ugly.

Now my memories of Vietnam aren't black and white, but in living color. I got to see the Vietnamese as people acting in normal situations, unlike in a war, which distorts everything. The Vietnamese are, in fact, just like the rest of the world now: businessmen, hardhats, shopkeepers, and soccer mommies. They sure taught the world not to refer to them as *peasants* anymore. I think and hope that they will have some form of democracy in my lifetime. And if they don't, you're going to have to get someone else to ensure they do. The Vietnamese and I are at peace now. As far as I'm concerned, they can have whatever government they want. I wish them well and why not? We walked the Truong Son Route together.

During my return visit I kept thinking, how did we ever think we could beat these people in their own backyard? And in a war they'd been fighting for generations before we arrived. It was easier to believe we could win when they all dressed in black pajamas and wore cone-head hats. Back then, they looked so primitive and backwards and we looked so modern and state-of-the-art. We ran our war right over the top of them, not caring at all what they thought of it. Today there's no way could we fight the same war over the top of them disregarding their casualties so much, because now they look just like people you'd see every day at any mall.

We could not have the same war ever again. Vietnam is a different country now and so are the Russians and the Chinese. So are we. We're no longer afraid of Communism; if they wanted to go Commie now, we'd say, "Be our guests and lots of luck!" The same issues that caused the Vietnam

War would all be negotiated out in the twenty-first century. I think national leadership would now be determined in a closely monitored election. And if Ho Chi Minh won, he would be the leader.

I will always be convinced that if the United States had insisted that the unifying elections of 1956 had been held and abided by, the result would have been no Vietnam War for Americans. It was our refusal for years to negotiate with our adversaries that made the war and made it last so long. I don't think the Vietnam War helped beat the U.S.S.R. in the Cold War. I think it made the Cold War last longer. When I was in the war, I thought that the best thing the U.S. could do, for them or for us, was just get out of it and leave. That's what finally happened, and sure enough the Vietnamese have never been a threat to us since.

Sitting up in Indian Country watching the traffic go by and listening to The Heavies (SOG and CIA) talk up there in Ban Me Thuot, I came to understand that we did not have a prayer of winning that war, nor a clue about how to do it. Our commanders never knew the dimensions of it nor the reason for it from the Vietnamese point of view. That's pretty prescient for a teenage grunt with a worm's-eye view, but it seemed plain as day to me. We were *not* going to win that war *ever*, so we might as well get out of it as soon as possible. I went to war thinking we'd win and left knowing we'd lose.

As history confirmed, I was right about that, too. "'It was the strangest thing we have ever gotten mixed up with,' General Bruce Palmer, who at age 31 had been chief of staff of the 6th Infantry Division in WWII, said not long after the end of the Vietnam War in which he was Corps level commander: 'We didn't understand the Vietnamese, or the situation or what kind of war it was. By the time we found out it was too late.'"[21]

In retrospect, I'm really glad I joined the LRPs. All I really wanted was a hot meal, a good night's sleep, some clean clothes and a shower, and it did lead to a better situation so I never felt heroic about volunteering for it. It was the best decision I made in and about the Army. I look back at the Vietnam War with plenty of mixed feelings, but on one thing there can be no doubt: I got to fight with the best soldiers of the Vietnam War, the

---

[21] p. 218

baddest-ass, do-anything guys you could imagine. It's a great honor just to be with them, to be one of them. I served with the best warriors America put out in that war; they were tough, dedicated fighters who were not afraid to take on the enemy's A-Team. The LRPs were hard, cocky guys who really liked to fight and they sure as hell partied hard, too. These were the epitome of paratroopers taking the war to the enemy and shoving it down their throats. *Take that, motherfuckers! The U.S. Airborne was here!*

Being a paratrooper and LRP set the course of my life. So many things have happened when I asked myself: what would an LRP do? Usually it was something sneaky, unexpected, and really *nasty*. That was pretty much our *modus operandi* or at least we tried to make it so: come out of nowhere, do the job and fade back into nowhere, humming a cheerful little tune. That's the way I like to fight a war. Leave the pillbox charging to the Marines. They're good at it and they like doing it.

Later in life my Army experience in Vietnam became something really special. I was proud of myself for doing it (largely because no one else ever was at least until more recently). I'd look back and think, wow, that was really something! That was really living! It really did take some moxie for a teenager or any other 'ager.

I remember the first time (in the mid '90s) I heard someone say, "Thanks for your service." I looked around to see who he was talking to! I didn't start to tell people about Vietnam 'til long afterwards, not least because it seemed so incredible to me, too, and I don't mean just the war/shooting part, either. It was *really* life on the edge like nothing else, like walking right up and banging on the Gates of Hell *every* day. I felt like I'd walked right up to the cliff and stood there looking over the edge for a long, long time. It's taken a lifetime to get over it and it's a work still in progress.

Sometimes I think about the people I killed. It's not like *I see dead people,* but sometimes there's a consciousness of past extremes, an awareness of how bad things can really get, a tendency to think that others don't really know how tough times can *really* get. It doesn't scare me to think about it, some of it I'm very proud of. I don't think I have enough conscience left to feel survivor guilt; I'm sorta happy just to be alive. I'm glad I survived all of it so I look back on it as an up close, *extremely* realistic action adventure movie with me as the anti-hero cynically wisecracking his way through danger and romance. Sometimes I think of it as the Most Unappreciated Performance Act Ever. I don't think I have enough conscience left to feel guilt. I'm happy just to be alive.

I have to admit there's still a certain amount of job satisfaction about this, and sometimes in the darkest nights of my soul way down deep where I'm still *really* shallow, I take the enemy out and kill them again. I sometimes wrestle with the few remaining tattered shreds of my conscience about how perverted this might be, but not very often. *See you all in hell!*

I look back at the Vietnam War with plenty of mixed feelings, but on one thing there can be no doubt: I fought with the best soldiers of the Vietnam War, the baddest-ass, do-anything guys you could imagine. It's a great honor to be one of them and just to be with them. I think that this was one of the most exciting experiences anyone in my generation could have had. I have been an excitement junkie ever since and have certainly lived an occasionally exciting and far-flung life since then. I am a big believer in the saying, *"To live well is the best revenge."* I have traveled many places in the world. I have been a skier, a professional diver, and I've parachuted again. I've worked construction at heights, oil fields at depths, been a volunteer fireman, and a professional fisherman. I have been in dangerous places doing dangerous things since then. But there was nothing like this, nothing like skulking down the Ho Chi Minh Trail dressed like a bush, trying to look over both shoulders at once and straight ahead, too. Thank God the rest of my life has been an anticlimax compared to that. Soldiering in Vietnam was the supreme experience of my life, the most exciting experience of anyone in my generation. I volunteered for it, I trained for it … and I did it.

The shift from being Long Range Patrol to Rangers happened after I was gone so I wasn't aware of it until the '90s. I'd canceled my subscription to the U.S. Army by then, so I must have missed that issue. It's the same job and the same pay, but with a new hat. Becoming a Ranger was a complete surprise to me, sort of a really nice freebie at the end. It's satisfying to have that connection to a famous unit, but I still think of myself as an LRP. It's what I volunteered to do and it's what I did. I'll always be proud of being one. You're welcome, America.

James Worth's Mother's Story

In 1967, James Worth was living in Berkeley, California with his mother, Jean Reyes, and three younger siblings. He wanted to go to war, but was only seventeen and needed his mother's signature to join the Army. She said she "didn't believe in war of any kind ... except World War II." The two argued for weeks until James finally said, "Mother, if you don't sign this paper, you'll never see me again ... and I mean it!" Jean reluctantly signed and off James went to the U.S. Army.

One week before Christmas, Jean was protesting the Vietnam War in front of the Oakland Armed Forces Recruiting Center. All the protesters were arrested and taken to the Oakland County Jail where they remained for three weeks. Jean's cellmates were the famous singer/songwriter Joan Baez and Baez's mother. When Dr. Martin Luther King arrived to protest the group's imprisonment, it made national news. Reyes said she would never forget listening to Joan's beautiful voice singing in the evenings.

In 2014 *Ghost Warriors* author Bob Stein attended a Joan Baez concert in Chicago. He went backstage to ask if she remembered Jean Reyes. "Of course I do," she replied, "we were cellmates." Baez went on to say, "The jailers took my guitar away for the first two days, but then they returned it."

CHAPTER 7

Fight on and fly on to the last drop of blood and the last drop of fuel, to the last beat of the heart.

Manfred von Richthofen - The Red Baron

PTERODACTYL 22, DOUBLE DEUCE

Capt. Don Williams was the O-1 Bird Dog pilot who provided remarkable support to the 4th Platoon's far-ranging patrols in the field, and frequently was the only link to any American backup. Don's call sign was Pterodactyl 22 (better known as Double Deuce). A typical mission included Don flying into our operational firebase picking up me (Lt. Stein) or the LRP team leader and flying to the AO we were assigned to patrol. Much of the country was covered with heavy vegetation, and identifying a landing zone with an opening for at least a single Huey was critical to each patrol's successful insertion.

The L-19 Bird Dog (which preceded the O-1) was the first all-metal fixed wing aircraft ordered for the U.S. Army since the Army Air Forces separated from the Army in 1947. The L-19 came into service just in time for the Korean War. (The most famous Bird Dog pilot of the Korean War was Ed McMahon, who flew more than eighty combat missions.) Basically a Cessna 172 on steroids, the Bird Dog had a 240 HP Continental 0-470 engine and tandem seats with the pilot in front. In 1962, the Army L-19 was redesignated the 0-1 Bird Dog and it entered its second war in Vietnam.

In 1964 the Department of Defense issued a memorandum directing the Army to transfer its Fixed Wing 0-1 Bird Dogs to the Air Force while the Army began its transition to a "rotor wing" force (helicopters). The Bird Dog name was chosen for its role in flying low, slow and close to the battlefield to identify targets in the manner of a bird dog used by game hunters.

Fortunately for our Long Range Patrols, the Army was allowed to retain some Bird Dogs, and thus appeared Capt. Don Williams, Pterodactyl 22 (Double Deuce). Many considered the Bird Dog to be the most dangerous airplane in the sky. During the course of the Vietnam War, four hundred sixty-nine Bird Dogs were lost to a variety of causes, chief among them enemy ground fire. The Bird Dog flew both low and slow trying to identify targets and were within easy range of thousands of AK-47's.

Don Williams went to Oklahoma State University, joined the Army ROTC program, and was commissioned a second lieutenant. He graduated with a degree in mathematics and went on to earn his Jump Wings at Ft. Benning, Georgia. Since he was on Oklahoma State's free-fall parachute team and was a long-distance runner, Jump School was tame for him— he'd run five miles after the paratrooper trainees were released for the day. Ranger School was another story. It was a three-month grueling test of a man's will and ability to endure all types of pain. Lt. Phil Mayer, an honor graduate of Ranger School and a platoon leader of the 2nd LRP Platoon, recalls *his* ordeal to earn the coveted Ranger Tab. He comments, "I had too much pride to quit, but considered ways to break my leg just to get away from the torture."

After leaving Ranger School with the coveted tab, Don went to Ft. Rucker, Alabama for seven months of pilot training. (His destiny was to be a fixed wing pilot for the next thirty-seven years. Don flew everything from an Army 0-1 Bird Dog to a commercial Boeing 777.) Following the stint at Ft. Rucker, Don's next rather unusual assignment was with the 5th Infantry Recon Pathfinders. He served as Executive Officer overseeing soldiers learning how to use air assets to infiltrate and extract five- or six man patrols as they would in Vietnam. Occasionally Don would ride in the right seat of a helicopter and practice flying approaches to LZ's, but he never liked flying choppers. He said, "I never got comfortable flying those eggbeaters."

New orders took Don to Ft. Knox, Kentucky, where his company of 0-1 Bird Dogs was being organized as the Pterodactyls in the 185th Reconnaissance Airplane Company. Aviators would maintain currency flying short cross-country courses doing touch-and-go landings and formation flying. At Ft. Knox, there weren't any programs for arming the aircraft or flying live-fire missions.

Shortly thereafter, Don's unit was ordered to Vietnam. All the Bird Dogs were flown from Ft. Knox to Oakland, California. Flying into strong headwinds, they travelled at only 110 miles per hour and Don remembers wondering if they would *ever* get there. Sometimes his ground speed was just 55 miles per hour with cars on the highway below passing him. The civilian auto drivers must have been astonished to see twenty-four Bird Dogs with Army decals flying west in formation.

On the way, the pilots landed at an Air Force base north of Little Rock, Arkansas to refuel. Don and the other 0-1 pilots went into the Officers' Club. The Air Force jet pilots were amazed that the Bird Dogs could land "on a dime" and then still need to roll to the first off-ramp. Upon arrival in Oakland, the Bird Dog aircraft wings were detached and loaded onto a Navy transport ship along with the planes.

Don's unit departed Oakland in early June 1967 aboard the *U.S.S. Nelson M. Walker*. A total of 1,700 troops from various Army units were on the *Walker*, a WWII troop ship with no air conditioning. A fuel stop was made in Manila and then on they sailed to Saigon. After sailing for three weeks, the Pterodactyl pilots arrived in Cam Ranh Bay where the port was too shallow for the ship to dock and allow troops to disembark. Large Landing Ship Tanks (LSTs) were brought alongside and rope ladders were deployed. Don was given a small combat pack, an M-16 with a few rounds of ammo, and over the side he went just like the Marines in WWII. Don's unit stepped onto a beautiful sandy beach, boarded buses with wire-covered windows, and headed for Dong Ba Tin. This would be the 185th's staging area until they convoyed to Ban Me Thuot in the Central Highlands, their permanent home in Vietnam.

The pilots married up with their Bird Dogs at Dong Ba Tin where airplane company maintenance technicians reattached the wings and made the Bird Dogs ready for flight, but there was a problem. At Ft. Knox there had been no training for arming the aircraft or flying live-fire missions; it was assumed pilots would drop smoke grenades near the targets and direct fighter-bombers from the colored smoke.

Once in the combat theater, it was obvious the Bird Dogs needed wing pods to fire a variety of rockets. Don was tasked to procure the necessary parts to assemble the 2.75-inch wing-mounted rocket pods. Trips to Cam Ranh Bay and Da Nang were made to acquire the pod parts. Soon all the

Bird Dogs had rocket pods hanging from each wing. Everything that was required for a new aviation company in a combat zone was completed.

The 185th aviators had never practiced firing rockets at targets with the newly mounted ordnance. Experience would be their only instructor. During the next three days, techniques were established for accurate delivery of rocket fire. With a 55-gallon drum target in sight, the pilots learned how to fly an attack approach from one thousand feet above ground level (AGL), arm the four rockets and dive with no aircraft pitch or roll to 500 feet above ground expending the rockets. Usually Don could hit a 55-gallon drum with reasonable consistency. Those on-target results were only successful after gerrymandering an aiming device by cutting a four-inch square piece of Plexiglas with crosshairs scratched across the surface. A small bendable but ridged strap of metal was attached to the top rim of the sight. An extension of that metal strap was secured to the aircraft's windscreen brace. The pilot would bend the sight according to his seat position and, after shooting a couple of dozen rockets, he was ready for war.

Don and his company of twenty-four Birds were ordered to fly into Ban Me Thuot for their first combat flight. The Bird Dogs alternated providing air cover for the 185th's supply convoy all the way to Ban Me Thuot. The road trip was completed without incident.

Although Ban Me Thuot was always home base for Don and used for maintenance and repairs, he normally flew from bases near the patrol's area of operation. Some included Chea Rea, Chu Lai, Oasis, Pleiku, and Tuy Hoa North, where the runway was pierced steel planking (PSP) versus the normal dirt airfields. Tuy Hoa South was a major U.S. airbase with lighted mile-long cement runways.

Don was assigned to the 4th Platoon and E-Company LRP because he was Airborne-Ranger Pathfinder qualified. It was the perfect marriage since Don knew what the small patrols were experiencing on the ground. He would save the lives of many LRPs. Some LRPs gave Don tiger fatigues, which had been made exclusively for the LRPs in Japan. He always wore them. His company commander, a major, was really pissed that Don was out of uniform and called him on it. Needless to say, the major also refused several of Don's requests to accompany a LRP patrol; this remained an unfulfilled desire.

Capt. Williams and I (Lt. Stein) would identify the Long Range Patrol team's potential landing zones, being careful not to fly exactly over the LZ or circle the LZ, which could alert the enemy that a patrol was being inserted in the next two to forty-eight hours. That would have given the enemy plenty of time to organize an ambush. Typically, a primary LZ was selected plus one or two alternate LZs. Alternates were used if the primary was not able to offer a chopper the opportunity to get at least six feet above the ground. When a Huey was on a very short final approach, the slick pilot would determine if the LZ was viable. Frequently, high stumps made insertion impossible. Many times the enemy was on or near the LZ and NVA soldiers, who were looking for the patrol insertions, were spotted in trees.

On one mission, after the LZs were marked, Capt. Williams and I proceeded to look for enemy locations around the river separating Vietnam from Cambodia. The entire area was a free-fire zone; anyone in that zone was assumed to be the enemy. We spotted sampans and an occasional hooch. I pulled the pin from one of the six hand grenades on my lap, held it out the window and threw it at small boats on the river. Don fired his M-79 grenade launcher at targets with an occasional bull's-eye. Perhaps Don and I didn't pass all the required Army safety procedures, but being twenty-three and twenty-five years old, we didn't stop to consider if what we were doing was unusual or even dangerous. The grand finale to our "air bombardment" was Don firing his four amazingly accurate high explosive rockets at the largest hooch in view. With all ordnance expended and fuel low, we returned to base to brief the team on their selected LZs.

Capt. William's had three choices in armament: high explosive (HE), smoke rockets, or white phosphorus (Willie-Pete) rockets. Normally, he selected the HE rockets to provide more firepower to cover the teams he was supporting on the ground. Besides his .45 and M-79, Don also carried a case of twelve multi-colored smoke grenades to mark targets for the supporting helicopters or fighter-bombers. Bird Dogs had four radios—VHF for Air Force and Navy fighter-bombers, UHF for Army Hueys and helicopter gunships, one HF for the 105 and 155 artillery batteries and a second HF to talk directly with the Long Range Patrol team on the ground.

Capt. Williams remembers a mission that took place in late August 1967. On a clear day west of An Khe, a LRRP team came in contact with the enemy (visual reconnaissance had never shown large enemy unit activity in that particular area). South of the contact, squad-size NVA or Viet Cong units would cross the Song Ba River in the evening to attack a Special Forces outpost on the west bank of the river just after dark. Don knew the enemy carried AK-47s because every time he spotted them, those were their weapons. Flying fifty to a hundred feet above the river, he saw stakes made from tree branches and footprints in a sandbar. The stakes were the enemy's way of marking safe passage in the sand and water.

It was too late! Eight NVA, who were standing on the west bank of the river only two hundred yards away, opened fire on Don. He was attempting to gain altitude fast. The endangered LRRP team was nearby, just north of the bend in the river. Rounds were passing through Don's cockpit windshield, wing strut and the empty observer's seat. As far as he could determine, nothing went through the wing fuel tanks or the engine. He executed a climb to one thousand feet, banked hard left, armed the four HEs, dived to five hundred feet above ground and fired all four rockets. The NVA's AK-47s were still rattling off rounds with all four rockets coming straight at them. Now at 250 to 300 feet from the target, there was no time to take a second look. If the engine took a round on that dive, Don's aviation career (not to mention his life) would be shortened. Out of rockets, very low on fuel, and with seventeen bullet holes in his Bird, it was time to go "home" and grab a new aircraft. The distraction caused by Don's Bird Dog gave the incoming gunships and slicks a window of opportunity to successfully extract the Long Range Reconnaissance Patrol team. Don received no medals or recognition for his bravery.

On February 19, 1968, Don was flying a communication relay mission when Chippergate 4-4 called for extraction. He coordinated with the Long Range Patrol team, the Rat Pack and the Bandit slicks, plus four Wolf Pack gunships. The helicopters were from two platoons with the Intruder Battalion and part of the 281st Helicopter Assault Company. In a fairy-tale ending, all five LRPs were saved. The patrol was in Cambodia, forty miles from the nearest friendly forces, under thick triple canopy forest with steep hills and mountains, and no LZs within two miles of the team's desperate battle.

Don's calm demeanor and accurate assessment of the situation, plus coordination of sometimes eight helicopters above the battle scene, resulted in the team being successfully pulled from the jungle. Two soldiers came through the trees on a jungle penetrator carried by a slick from the Rat Pack; the final three were hoisted on a McGuire Rig dropped from a second Rat Pack chopper. In August 2011, forty-three years after their rescue, members of the Chippergate 4-4 LRP team met Don. In a tearful reunion, the men told him, "You absolutely saved our lives."

Don left the military thinking he would teach math in a high school, but Delta Airlines called him soon after he returned to the States. He was hired during a phone conversation on a Friday and told that a class of thirty was starting the next Monday in Atlanta. The Delta employee told Don he could be in the class if he could get there. Don hopped into his Pontiac GTO and drove 85-90 mph from Oklahoma to Georgia to begin training.

Don completed a thirty-four year career with Delta, flying Boeing 777s on the European route. He was flying from Paris, France to Atlanta, Georgia on September 11, 2001when he was told U.S. airspace was closed to all flights due to the attacks in New York City, Washington, D.C., and near Shanksville, Pennsylvania. Don was directed to secure permission to land outside the United States. The passengers, crew and Don spent four days in Halifax, Nova Scotia before receiving clearance to re-enter U.S. airspace.

Today, you'll find Don in Dunwoody, Georgia running an energy management company or at his ranch in Oklahoma, where he was kicked in the knee by a bull, causing him to walk with a limp. Asked why the bull was so angry, Don replied, "I was trying to castrate him but he had an attitude."

CHAPTER 8

Out of every one hundred men, ten shouldn't even be there, eighty are just targets, nine are the real fighters, and we are lucky to have them, for they make the battle. Ah, but the one, one is a warrior, and he will bring the others back.

Heraclitus 535 BC – 476 BC

THE SELECTION PROCESS

Their founder and commander, Maj. Dandridge M. Malone, interviewed virtually all of the officers and enlisted men selected for E-Company Long Range Patrol. He'd assumed responsibility for selecting his troops after the battle death two weeks earlier of his executive officer, Capt. David Tucker. To help select men for E-Company, the major used a number of interesting criteria including: combat experience, medic training, civilian tracking and hunting experience, physical fitness, formal Army jungle training, and Ranger/Special Forces training.

One of the first men Maj. Malone interviewed was **S. Sgt. Tom Workman**, who reported to the major's tent in Phan Rang, the headquarters of the 1st Brigade, 101st Airborne Division. After pleasantries were exchanged, the major asked Sgt. Workman, "Can you run to the top of that mountain (Nui Dat) and back?"

"Yes, Sir, I can," said Tom.

"Can you run to the top of that mountain carrying a weapon, ammo, and LBE (load bearing equipment)?"

"Yes, Sir, I can," replied Sgt. Workman.

Then the major asked, "If I put a fifty-pound sandbag in your rucksack, can you do it?"

Sgt. Workman paused a moment and said, "Sir, I cannot promise you that, but I can promise you that if anyone else can do it, I will do it."

Maj. Malone grinned and said, "I like your attitude; you're in." Sgt. Workman was now assistant team leader of Team 4-3 and a member of the 4th Platoon, E-Company LRP.

S. Sgt. Bob Johnston's initial interview for E-Company began in Chu Lai when Maj. Malone drove his Jeep past Sgt. Johnston and noticed on his shoulder a red diamond patch signifying he was a member of the 1st Brigade's elite LRRP Platoon (Long Range Reconnaissance Patrol).

Sgt. Johnston served with the 101st LRRPs on his first tour in Vietnam and rejoined them on his second tour when fate brought him and Maj. Malone together. The major asked, "How'd you like to be interviewed for a new unit being organized from elite soldiers with combat experience?" Johnston nodded and the major ordered, "Get in the Jeep. I'll look at your records and, if they check out, you can join E-Company as a team leader. If you can get through Special Forces Recondo School in Nha Trang, plus lead a couple of missions without killing anyone, I'll promote you to E-6." Sgt. Johnston asked several of his friends, "What's going on with the LRP Company?" They told him, "It's kinda secret but this new unit has carte blanche on personnel and the latest and best equipment, so it's probably a good deal." Sgt. Bob Johnston signed that day.

Steve Woodson, today a locksmith in Lake Havasu, Arizona, distinctly remembers how he became a member of the 4th Platoon, E-Company LRP. Arriving in Vietnam at age nineteen, he was assigned to the 101st Airborne Division, 1st Battalion 327th Infantry, Charlie Company, 4th Platoon in July 1967. Just a couple of weeks later his entire company was in contact with a strong NVA force exchanging rifle and machine gun fire. U.S. Air Force fighter-bombers were called to drop napalm bombs on the enemy forces.[22] Steve and his squad were occupying the top of a ridgeline and firing at a number of camouflaged NVA in a treeline about ninety meters to their front. He looked to his left and saw an F-100 jet release a napalm bomb that was heading right toward the enemy.

---

[22] In 1942, a team of chemists led by Louis Feiser at Harvard University were the first to develop synthetic napalm for the U.S. Armed Forces. From 1965 to 1969, the Dow Chemical company manufactured Napalm B for the American military. After news reports of Napalm B's deadly and disfiguring effects were published, Dow experienced a boycott of its products. However, the management of Dow Chemical decided that its first obligation was to the American government. Napalm B is the more modern version of napalm and is usually a mixture of the plastic polystyrene and the hydrocarbon benzene. The original napalm usually burned for fifteen to thirty seconds, while Napalm B can burn for up to ten minutes. "Napalm is the most terrible pain you can imagine," says Kim Phuc, napalm bombing survivor from the widely publicized Vietnam War photograph. To put the heat produced into perspective, water boils at 212 degrees. Napalm generates temperatures of up to 2,200 degrees.

It appeared to be spinning in slow motion and then impacted branches on the tallest tree near the squad. One soldier was severely burned and later died in the Medevac chopper. Steve's hair and back were singed with napalm splatter and he tore a ligament in his ankle trying to avoid the flaming napalm. A second responding Medevac chopper was shot down, so Steve was not transported to a field hospital until the next morning. His ankle was placed in a cast and his burns were treated. In time the leg healed, the cast was removed, and Steve was sent back to his unit. However, two days later he reinjured the ankle and went back to the hospital for another cast. When it was removed, and while he was recuperating in the rear doing guard duty and KP, Steve heard that a Capt. Tucker was interviewing volunteers for a Long Range Patrol Company being formed in-country. Steve asked for an interview and met with Capt. Tucker the next day. The captain went through a standard list of question and then asked, "What are you doing in the rear and why do you want to join my Long Range Patrol Company?"

"I've always wanted to become the best airborne soldier in the Army, Sir. My ankle is healed just fine." (Actually it was *not* yet healed.)

Capt. Tucker ordered, "Get on the next aircraft to Phan Rang where the company is being formed and trained."

Steve arrived at Phan Rang and was told, "Capt. Tucker was killed two days ago when he was flying to Chu Lai for additional interviews with volunteer Screaming Eagles." Steve met with Lt. Calvin Greene, the acting executive officer who was filling in for the deceased captain. Greene told Steve to report to the 4th Platoon and said, "You're assigned to LRP team 4-1."

Milt Hendrickson was the only Long Range Patrol Airborne trooper to sail to Viet Nam. He deployed from Oakland, California on a troop transport carrying the 1st Brigade of the 101st Airborne Screaming Eagles Division, arriving in Saigon in 1965. Milt served with the 2nd of the 327th, Charlie Company, 4th Platoon. When Milt joined the Army in 1964 at age seventeen, he had a goal of serving in the best battle-ready airborne unit possible.

He was trained as a rifleman and given an MOS 11BP[23] classification. Milt's company was on stand-down (after having fought in Operation Wheeler) when he interviewed with Maj. Malone in Chu Lai and was immediately impressed by Malone's charisma. When the major asked him if he wanted in, Milt thought, it doesn't take an Einstein to know a team of six makes less noise in the bush than a platoon or a company; my platoon was just shot to pieces and I figure it's just a matter of time. Milt said, "I'm in!"

It was unusual for a U.S. soldier to specifically aim, shoot, and kill an enemy … and then retrieve his weapon. That happened twice to **Ron Causey**. The first time Causey was on a recon patrol with the 101st, they spotted five resting NVA soldiers; one aimed his AK-47 at Ron just as he fired a long burst, killing the North Vietnamese soldier instantly. All five NVA were soon dead without any U.S. casualties. (Causey still has his adversary's necklace of black, white, and red beads with an attached French coin held by a drilled hole.) Later in the same operation, Ron fell down a steep hillside during a mortar attack requiring a visit to the aid station in Chu Lai. The doctor put him on crutches and said, "Stay off that leg." While at the Chu Lai fire base, Causey heard about the Long Range Patrol Company being formed from 101st volunteers and asked to meet Maj. Malone; they met in the major's small tent. When the interview concluded, Malone said, "We're going to go through a lot of tough training

---

[23] MOS (or military occupation specialty) is a nine-character code used by the U.S. Army and other services to identify a specific job. The first three characters are always a two-digit number followed by a letter; thus *11B* is a light weapons infantryman who uses small arms such as rifles, hand grenades, hand held rocket launchers, and similar weapons in close combat. The next number designates an NCO or non-NCO enlisted level, e.g. an *11B4* would designate an NCO and an *11B2* would designate a Specialist. The next letter is a special designation e.g. an *11B4P*, would designate a Paratrooper. Some other designations would be *11C*, which designates heavy weapons such as a mortar or an *11H*, which designates a heavy weapons anti-tank warfare specialist (which in the Vietnam War would be a crew served 106 Recoilless Rifle on a Jeep, a 90mm Recoilless Rifle or shape charge explosive). Most clerical MOS designations began with 71, such as a *71H* which was a personnel specialist. Other characters were not recognized by field troops and infrequently used. Sixth and seventh characters were an additional skill identifier (ASI) and could designate skills such as "master fitness trainer." Eighth and ninth MOS characters are a language identification code (LIC).

and PT and I can't take somebody who's unable to keep up." Ron dropped his crutches and said, "I can do anything you need done."

The major replied, "If you can walk out of this tent you get the job."

Ron replied, "I'll run out if I have to!"[24]

Malone said, "Okay, you're in."

The next day, twelve more soldiers who'd interviewed with Maj. Malone stood in formation at attention as he told them only one, **S. Sgt. Ray Bohrer**, had been selected for the new company. The major told Ray it was his Special Forces training that got him into the unit.

After the men were dismissed, one man, **Bob Shaffer**, stopped Malone.

"I want to be a part of this unit, Sir," he said. "I can fight, kill anyone anytime, and shoot straighter than most soldiers in Vietnam."

The major answered, "Your MOS is 11C, which is mortars. I don't need mortar men."

Shaffer reminded Maj. Malone, "Sir, you said you were looking for soldiers with balls of steel," and added, "I have bigger steel balls than anyone in the 101st."

Malone looked Shaffer in the eyes, smiled, and said, "You're in! Get to the airfield. Go to Phan Rang."

Jerry Shankle's jungle warfare training, his perfect score on the 82nd Airborne's pop up target range plus qualifying as Expert for pistols and rifles caught Malone's attention. When he interviewed Jerry, Malone asked where he lived. Jerry replied, "Cottage Grove, Tennessee, Sir."

Malone said, "I know right where that is … near Paris, right?"

"Yes, Sir."

The major asked if Jerry hunted game.

"All the time; I'll be a great soldier for you," Jerry replied.

"All right. Get to Phan Rang."

Juergen Besecke arrived in Vietnam in early September 1967. Unlike most of the men who were being selected for the new LRP Company, Besecke had no combat experience. He arrived at Cam Ranh Bay via

---

[24] In high school, Ron placed second behind Richmond Flowers, the state high school 100-yard dash champion who went on to play football for the Dallas Cowboys.

World Air Lines, a United States charter airline. The soldiers aboard, about two hundred of them, disembarked and were placed on buses. Behind an adjacent high barbed wire fence, Juergen noticed two hundred more soldiers waiting to board his plane for their return to the States. The veterans, of course, made wise-ass comments including how many days remained before the new arrivals could return home. Most soldiers kept a short-timers calendar that ticked off the days a man had to remain in-country. A common expression was, "Thirty-two (or the number of remaining days) and a wake-up."

The bus took Besecke to the Repo Depot at the north end of the air base where those with infantry MOSes were separated from the rest of the replacements. There were the typical Army lines of men and most of the arriving soldiers were very nervous, not realizing that this day probably would be their safest in Vietnam. Juergen was assigned to the 5th Special Forces Group even though he didn't finish the last ten days of training due to broken ribs suffered in a Jeep accident at Ft. Bragg, North Carolina.[25]

Capt. Tucker approached Besecke, calling out his name but, as usual, butchering it. The captain said that a Maj. Malone wanted to talk to him due to his stateside Special Forces training. Tucker and Besecke met Maj. Malone in a small office, where the brass told him about a new unit being formed. Malone explained the concept of a six-man Long Range Patrol team and gave him an overview of the LRP Company. Maj. Malone said these teams would receive a great deal of support and promotions would come more quickly with his unit. He then asked Besecke, "Do you want to sign up?"

Juergen remembered some training at Ft. Bragg when his twelve-man team had broken up into two six-man teams. He always wanted to belong to something creative, something that was outside the box, and after only a short pause, he replied, "Yes, Sir." Within an hour he and Tucker were on a plane to Phan Rang.

---

[25] Besecke was from a unique family. His father was a German soldier in WWII and ended up as a prisoner of war in both German and American prison camps. He was imprisoned by the Germans for failing an order by the SS to load Jewish prisoners on a train. When the Americans overran his sector of Germany, they put him in an American prison camp. Besecke was five years old when his family emigrated from Germany to the United States.

Maj. Malone liked **Del Ayers'** double MOS designations, 11B rifleman and 91A10 Combat Medic. Del, an Eagle Scout, had completed the 101st Recondo School training at Ft. Campbell, Kentucky. He impressed Malone during his one-on-one interview which finished with the major saying, "Get your shit; you're going to Phan Rang."

When **Sgt. Sam Pullara** was interviewing with Maj. Malone, Sam explained that he was volunteering for the Company Admin position. After telling Malone about his administrative experience, Malone looked very skeptical and said, "Sorry, Sam, you have a good background, but I just don't know how a trained personnel specialist would fit in with all the infantry soldiers and Rangers in the company."

Sam replied, "Sir, I'm not a trained personnel specialist; I enlisted as Airborne Infantry. I was in the second class of the new Preparation Airborne Advanced Infantry Training at Ft. Gordon, Georgia, and spent a year in an infantry company at Ft. Campbell. That's where I became the morning report clerk and I got the personnel specialist MOS when I was promoted. Prior to that, I was the acting Public Information Officer (PIO) for the 3rd of the 187th; I'm a trained infantryman, Sir, who always seems to get clerical and administrative jobs."

"What the hell did you do as a battalion PIO?" Malone asked, half grinning at Sam.

He promptly replied, "Sir, I wrote stories and took pictures of battalion events for the post newspaper. The morning report clerk job was the last straw so I volunteered for Vietnam, but truthfully and obviously, I would serve you better as an Admin than anything else. I know my way around."

Malone asked, "What was your Infantry MOS—what were you trained for?"

"Sir, I trained for nine and a half weeks as an 11H (heavy weapons, anti-tank warfare) crewman on a 106 Recoilless Rifle. I trained for a battle against Russian tanks on the plains of Germany and I haven't even seen a 106 since then. I've been in Vietnam for over a year and have contributed little to the war; I'd like a chance to do so."

Malone said, "You know we don't have anything to start with—just a table and a typewriter. You'll have to create it all as we go along. Think you can do it, Sam?"

"Absolutely, Sir!"

"You're hired," said the major.

Sam says of Malone, "He was the best officer I ever knew at any level in the Army. It was an honor to be selected by him."

1st Sgt. Frank Moore was a massive man by any standards, standing 6'3" and weighing 238 pounds. (He played Army division football as a tackle against other division teams in the States.) By comparison, most American soldiers were about 5'9" and 140 to 150 pounds. The North Vietnamese enemy averaged 5'1" and 105 to 115 pounds, according to the anthropometric survey of the Armed Forces of the Republic of Vietnam.

Moore was just seventeen years old when he joined the U.S. Marine First Division and fought in Korea. He left the Marines in 1954, joined the Army and went to Jump School; he remained with airborne units for the remainder of his military career. Moore accumulated the highest administration and physical training scores in the Army as he made his way up the enlisted ranks. He was serving with the 173rd Airborne in Vietnam and transferred to E-Company, Long Range Patrol.

Lt. Calvin Greene,[26] 1st Platoon leader, sought Frank Moore out as Malone's Long Range Patrol Company was forming. (Greene had been an enlisted man for fifteen years and had met Moore while they were in Raider School with the 82nd Airborne.) Lt. Greene introduced Moore to Maj. Malone and they hit it off immediately. Frank Moore later said, "In the thirty years I was in the Marines and Army, Maj. Malone was the finest officer I had the privilege to serve."

The first sergeant of any combat infantry company in war has huge and unending duties. Frank Moore had that times ten. Some of his responsibilities included:

- Organizing equipment coming from multiple countries
- Setting up training for new troopers coming to E-Company Long Range Patrol

---

[26] Lt. Stein attended the six-month Officer Candidate School (OCS) with Greene, who was the toughest soldier out of two hundred candidates. Greene lacked judgment but was always rugged, hard-hitting, and courageous.

- Arranging air and ground transport for each of the four platoon that operated independently throughout all of two Corps
- Ensuring the company had food supplies
- Managing supplies of ammunition, maps, PRC-25 and PRC-77 radios, plus radio frequencies
- Handling wounded and dead soldiers properly
- Completing administration forms required to get his troops paid
- Making sure soldiers got their R&R
- Arranging safe passage back to the States

When asked how he would contrast the war in Vietnam with Korea, Moore said, "If asked which was the easier war to fight, I'd say Vietnam. The key problems in Korea were always resupply, communications, and the unrelenting cold coupled with marginal winter gear. Vietnam had the oppressive heat, but that was manageable. Both wars had ferocious and brutal enemies from cultures we didn't understand." In later years, Moore said he was proud of his service to our country, but left both conflicts (Korea and Vietnam) with regrets and disappointment, especially after the final chapters were written.

The author will be forever thankful to his first sergeant, Frank Moore, for a wonderful three-day trip to Hong Kong. Company commanders in Vietnam had authority to grant two-day in-country passes. Maj. Malone approved a pass and the first sergeant traded captured weapons to some Air Force guys for a ride to Hong Kong on a camouflaged DC-3, a plane used to drop Airborne troops in WWII. (I didn't know Hong Kong was in-country but Frank Moore made it happen.)

1st Lt. Bob Stein: I'd been a front-line infantry platoon leader with the 1st Cavalry Division for six months, and like nearly everyone had seen many U.S. troops killed or wounded. I received a message asking if I wanted to interview for a general's aide job. I replied, "Sure," and was told to report to Nha Trang for a meeting with an officer named Maj. Malone. When we met, he began describing his vision for the formation of Long Range Patrol Company. As he was talking about the timing of the new company, I interrupted him saying, "I'm in the wrong place, Sir. I'm supposed to be interviewing for a general's aide job."

He smiled, "No, you're in the right place, Lt. Stein, there is no general's aide job. That is just a ruse to conceal from the enemy that the Long Range Patrol Company is being formed and will be sent into the field sixty days from now." Malone knew all about my record and the battles I'd been in. I remember how his questions focused on how I led my men, if I respected them, and my leadership skills. He told me communications skills were the foundation for a platoon leader and gave me six bullet points I remember to this day:

- Take time to listen to soldiers.
- Keep soldiers informed.
- Get new information out quickly.
- Communicate openly and honestly.
- Encourage subordinates to be open and straight with soldiers.
- Do not punish soldiers who tell you bad news.

He answered all my questions and told me I'd have the privilege to lead the best troops in the Army. He would assume an extremely high level of excellence from me and expected my decision by morning. I agreed on the spot.

CHAPTER 9

A real friend is one who walks in when the rest of the world walks out.
Walter Winchell

LT. STEIN MEETS LT. MAYER

Phil Mayer was a warrior, adapting to war and combat as easily as Patton did in World War II. Mayer would have been equally comfortable as a centurion serving Caesar, one of the Persian Immortals, or an *oberleutnant* (highest ranking lieutenant) in the Austrian army fighting in nineteenth century Europe. Lt. Mayer led airborne infantry companies in combat from both the 82nd Airborne and the 101st Airborne Divisions.

I first met Phil in Nha Trang. Maj. Malone, our company commander, had selected us to lead his 2nd and 4th Long Range Patrol Platoons. Lts. Calvin Greene and Gerald Koch led the 1st and 3rd Platoons. (Two months later Mayer would help with the difficult identification of Greene, since there was only a cavity where his head should have been and no dog tags. Greene was following a too-obvious blood trail, walking point with his platoon sergeant Patrick Henshaw when the NVA fired up a thirty-pound Chinese Claymore mine, instantly killing both men.)

Phil was my best friend in Vietnam; my first recollection of him is the two of us having breakfast with Maj. Dandridge Malone in Nha Trang at the 5th Special Forces Group mess hall. The major told us, "The best of the best Airborne troopers from the 101st Airborne Division will be arriving to attend Special Forces Recondo School training in two weeks.[27] It's critical

---

[27] On September 15, 1966, Gen. Westmoreland authorized establishment of the Recondo School to train selected troops in long range reconnaissance techniques developed and employed by Project DELTA. Some referred to Recondo School as "the toughest school on earth" or "the deadliest school on earth." During its four-year existence, a total of 5,626 soldiers attended Recondo training. (U.S. soldiers were joined by 296 Koreans, 193 Thais, 130 Vietnamese, 22 Filipinos, and 18 Australians.) More than a third of the candidates failed, but the 3,515 who graduated were authorized to wear the highly coveted Recondo insignia patch. Mayer's and my platoons had no dropouts. Training, which was all practical, included calling for artillery, tactical/air support, prisoner snatch, reconnaissance, rappelling, McGuire Rig, advanced map reading, land navigation and evasion, combat first aid (which included your buddy inserting an IV into your arm to draw blood), runs of 3.5 and 7.0 miles, timed runs, and much more.

we set high caliber examples for whatever we ask of these exceptional soldiers, which I, for the most part, have hand selected." Unsaid by the major was his concern for our *personal* physical fitness; however, he did say he wanted to run with us and would meet us early the next morning at the Recondo School headquarters.

At 0530 the next morning, we met the major at the mess hall. He removed his glasses, folded them neatly, and put them on the porch railing. We began our sixteen-mile round-trip run in combat boots, wearing our holstered pistols. Phil and I were in good shape, having spent six months in the bush, and we also ran up the Nui Dat Mountain twice a day. For us, the run was a breeze and we were thinking about a nice hot breakfast as we came back to the camp entrance, but we didn't stop. The major continued running down the road circling Nha Trang. Phil and I looked at each other, and with slight grimaces continued to run on and on and on. Both of us were thinking that this thirty-seven-year-old major would not outrun us, and we would die before dropping out. Finally, the major said, "God dammit, where is that camp entrance?" We said, "Sir, we passed it miles ago." We all laughed and jogged back to camp.

Several days later the Special Forces cadre said a six-man Special Forces patrol team was being inserted on a beach down the coast. They were looking for volunteers to help row a raft from a boat to the beach and back. Phil volunteered himself and me saying, "We're up for it." We received an explanation of the insertion at a briefing. The Navy would send a patrol boat to Nha Trang the following night to pick up the team plus the four rowers.[28] We would load a raft onto the boat and execute a night insertion. At the briefing (no Navy personnel were present) the Special Forces team leaders especially emphasized securing weapons and any gear to avoid losing equipment in the event of a capsizing wave. No mention was made of the ocean tides.

The boat arrived at a small dock at 2300 hours and a good-sized raft was placed aboard, much of it vertical since there wasn't much room on the boat that was thirty-one feet long with a 10-foot 7-inch beam. The versatile craft had a fiberglass hull and water jet drives that enabled it to

---

[28] Navy Patrol boats were used in Vietnam from March 1966 until the end of 1971.

operate in shallow waters; it drew only two feet of water fully loaded. The drives could be pivoted to reverse direction, turn the boat in its own length, or come to a stop from full speed in a few boat lengths. It usually operated with four enlisted men; it was powered by dual 220 horsepower Detroit diesel engines with Jacuzzi Brothers pump-jet drives and could reach a top speed of 53 mph. The boat was heavily armed for such a small vessel. The forward area had twin .50 caliber machine guns in a rotating tub, as well as a single rear .50 caliber and side-mounted M-60 7.62 machine gun, plus an MK-19 40mm grenade launcher.

There was just a low rumble from the engines as we went about twelve miles south of Nha Trang. The boat stopped and ten of us scrambled into the raft. As we neared the coastline, the raft picked up a great deal of speed and we felt it being pushed quite far onto the beach. The LRP team was gone in an instant and we turned the raft around to go back into the ocean. I was first in and sat in the front. As I began paddling as hard as I could, I looked up and saw what appeared to be a ten-foot wave of water that grabbed our raft, flipping it completely over and depositing everyone back on the beach. This happened two more times until we broke free of the crashing waves. Back aboard the boat, we discovered two rifles and a radio had been lost. Phil and I had followed directions and still had our weapons. At our debriefing, we highly recommended that ocean tides be considered for all future water insertions. (The next morning Phil told me he was a weak swimmer, but hadn't told anyone else fearing he would have been scratched from the mission.)

In January 1968, the 1st Platoon of E-Company LRP was assigned to the 173rd Airborne Brigade Combat Team to run screening missions for the Sky Troopers of the 173rd. The brigade headquarters was in Tuy Hoa. Phil remembers one mission that a team from the 1st Platoon was conducting near the large Tuy Hoa Air Force base. The 1st had lost both its platoon leader and platoon sergeant and now S. Sgt. Tommy Bragg led the platoon with mission support provided by Mayer.

One LRP team observed 230 NVA moving with small branches and bushes on their backs toward the city of Tuy Hoa and the adjacent large U.S. Air Force base. It was rare to observe such a large enemy formation in daylight. Although the LRP team's mission was to Observe and Inform, it made multiple requests for air strikes on this prime target, but the requests were denied. Finally, Sgt. Bragg, who was at headquarters, found Brig. Gen. Switzer, yanked his sleeve, and begged him to order airstrikes on the NVA target. The general refused saying, "Sorry, all my air assets are committed." Air strikes were finally delivered, but by that time the enemy was gone. Mayer told everyone, "Tuy Hoa will be hit tomorrow."

The next day, January 30, 1968, signaled the commencement of the countrywide attack called the *Tet Offensive*, the largest military operation conducted by either side during the war. Although Tet was a military defeat for the communists, it had a profound effect on the U.S. government and shocked the U.S. public. Our military and political leaders had led them both to believe the communists were, due to previous defeats, incapable of launching such a massive effort. With Bragg and Mayer's information coupled with other intelligence, the United States would have had a 24-hour window to prepare for the Tet attack. History might have been altered.

Here's another example of a missed opportunity to change the war. On the eve of Tet, Team 4-1 was patrolling in the Ia Drang Valley on the Cambodian border. Team members included: Jim Brokaw (team leader), Randy Mills (assistant team leader), Jerry Shankle (scout rifleman), John Higgins (radio telephone operator), and Steve Woodson (point). Steve's recollections of the patrol follow:

It was our first day out. Right away we found a hidden boat docking area along the river with a well-worn embarking area. A large, wide and rutted trail came down the hill to the dock. We moved away into the jungle and stopped next to a small artesian pool; the water that fed it came right out of a small rock cluster. Later we moved up the hill through the undergrowth and came upon a bivouac site that was very recently used with fresh fire pits. The trail to the boat site came directly from there.

The wide trail continued west deep into the jungle and looked ominous like a black cave. We were prepared to go that way when we were directed instead to head south along the river. It was obvious that a lot of foot traffic had passed through there recently, and I was glad to leave the area. Later we found out that this day was the eve of Tet. I've often wondered what might have happened if we had gone out a day or two earlier and began our patrol a hundred yards or so from a large NVA force that was waiting to cross the river. We didn't know Tet happened until we finished the patrol. It may have been the same guys that attacked the Oasis and Plei Me bases.

After leaving the Army I went to college and read Tolkien's book, *The Hobbit*. At one point in the story, the character Bilbo Baggins and the dwarves enter the forest of Mirkwood. Baggins describes the forest trail as looking "very dark, like a black shadow on the trees." I was vividly reminded of the cave-like jungle trail I'd seen in Vietnam.

S. Sgt. Bob Johnston, leader of Team 4-4. Johnston was shot five times and received a grenade wound to his face. After recovering in the U.S., Johnston returned to Vietnam to assume all security responsibility for Four-Star Gen. Creighton Abrams, commander of all Allied Forces in Vietnam. When he left the Army, Johnston served as a U.S. Marshal in the witness protection program for twenty years.

Sgt. Oscar Caraway with his favored AK-47 taken from one of the thirty-two enemy he killed while serving with the 101st Airborne and E-Company Long Range Patrol. Graves registration containers were positioned in areas where significant American casualties were anticipated.

Don Kinton (Team 4-3); later on this day Don was shot and subsequently died on the flight to the hospital in Pleiku.

Donald Ray Kinton is honored on the Vietnam Memorial Wall, Panel 46E, Line 19.

Team 4-3 - Gary Stewart (back left) and Herman Dunklebarger, Ray Bohrer (front left) and Team Leader, S. Sgt. Tom Workman pictured prior to a mission in which they encountered an NVA patrol. Eleven enemy were killed including two Chinese officers. Teammate Darrell Presley took the photo.

Sgt. Ray Bohrer, Assistant Team Leader, Team 4-3.

Sgt. Regis Murphy at his defensive position with the 4.2 heavy mortar in Special Forces Headquarters, Nha Trang. In his second tour, Murphy became leader of Team 4-7.

Milt Hendrickson, Charles Haney, and Oscar Caraway loading for the dangerous Starlight Patrol.

James Worth (Team 4-6) wearing an unauthorized uniform and fighting an undeclared war with a pirated, unsanctioned weapon.

James Worth revisits Vietnam in 2003.

Lt. Bob Stein (beside Pterodactyl 22 "Double Deuce" 0-1 Bird Dog) prior to a flight mission to identify suitable patrol landing zones.

Capt. Don Williams, the 0-1 Bird Dog pilot who supported E-Company on reconnaissance and attack missions in Vietnam, wraps up his thirty-four year career with Delta Airlines by piloting a final flight from Paris to Atlanta.

An 0-1 Bird Dog; 469 were lost (mostly to ground fire) in the Vietnam war.

Rick Ogden, 2nd Platoon, team leader (2-2), snapped a picture behind Pterodactyl 22 pilot Capt. Don Williams. They were locating potential insertion LZs near Kontum. On a later patrol, Rick was shot in the chest and evacuated to a crowded U.S. hospital in Yokohama Japan. Teammate Spec 4 Morrow was also wounded and survived.

Two of the four 2.75 high explosive rockets hanging off the wing of Pterodactyl 22. A good pilot (and Don Williams was) could accurately hit a 55-gallon drum starting from a 1000 foot dive.

185th Reconnaissance Airplane Company patch.

Dead NVA soldiers after gunfight with the 1st Batt/327th/101st Airborne Division. The U.S. press was accusing Sgt. Oscar Caraway's battalion commander of inflating enemy body counts, so he ordered his troops to haul in dead, decaying bodies as proof. Oscar remembers that day as one of the most miserable he experienced in Vietnam.

Randy Mills and Ron Causey at the Ban Me Thuot airfield.

A necklace from one of three NVA shot by Ron Causey; in each case he recovered their rifles. The necklace includes a French coin. Causey gave this necklace to his nephew for good luck when he received orders to deploy to Afghanistan.

Lt. Phil Mayer, Commander of the 2nd Platoon, E-Company, Long Range Patrol at An Khe, Vietnam.

Sgts. Oscar Caraway and Charles Samuelson with a Browning Automatic Rifle.

Commander James M. Fisher in his gunship.

Capt. Perkins, E-Company Operations Officer

Compliments of The Prffessionals

LA LEGION DES ESTRANGER.
SAT VIET MINH
WE KILL FOR FUN IN THE
TRUE AIRBORNE TRADITION.

The 4th Platoon's calling card. (Unfortunately spell-checking software was unavailable in 1967.)

CHAPTER 10

The most important thing I learned is that soldiers watch what their leaders do. You can give them classes and lecture them forever, but it is your personal example they will follow.

Gen. Colin Powell

MAJOR MALONE IN THE FIELD

Recruiting and formal training for the 4th Platoon was complete and the 4th was at full strength and primed for action. Almost every man in the platoon had already seen combat with the 101st Airborne Division in I Corps. Seven six-man teams, each with a team leader and an assistant team leader plus a platoon sergeant and platoon leader, had endured a tough two weeks of very physical training running up the Nui Dat Mountain in Phan Rang twice a day. This was followed by the three-week Special Forces Recondo School. It was as if all the men of the 4th Platoon were race horses just looking to run at full gallop. We were psyched and ready to test our newly learned patrol techniques.

Maj. Dandridge M. Malone had selected a Special Forces camp called Plei Me for our forward operating base and our initial teeth-cutting operation. Plei Me was garrisoned with a twelve man Special Forces A-Team and 350 Montagnard mercenaries. It was located thirty-seven miles southwest of Pleiku and seventeen miles east of the Ia Drang Valley. The Drang River runs through a valley northwest of Plei Me. October of 1965 saw the beginning of heavy combat between the 1st Cavalry Division and major units of the North Vietnamese army, principally the 32nd, 33rd, and 66th NVA regiments. Initially Plei Me was attacked and surrounded until a relief column of 175 South Vietnamese Rangers led by Special Forces Maj. Charlie Beckwith broke the siege and saved Plei Me from being overrun. Beckwith was the hero that day and became the founder and first Commander of today's Delta Force. Several weeks later Lt. Col. Hal Moore, commander of the 7th Cavalry Regiment, tangled with those same three enemy regiments in the nearby Ia Drang Valley, a battle depicted in the book, *We Were Soldiers Once ... and Young* by Harold G. Moore and Joseph L. Galloway, and later in the film, *We Were Soldiers.*

In December 1967 main force North Vietnamese soldiers were miles from Plei Me and the enemy consisted almost entirely of Viet Cong soldiers. The Vietnamese Communists, or Viet Cong, were the military branch of the National Liberation Front. There were some mainline Viet Cong units, but most were regional forces that only operated in their own districts. Unlike the mainline troops who saw themselves as professional soldiers, local Viet Cong groups tended to be far less confident. For the most part, recruits were young teenagers, and while some were motivated by idealism, others had been pressured or shamed into joining. They also harbored real doubts about their ability to fight the heavily armed and well-trained American soldiers.

During an initial briefing about Plei Me camp security, which was attended by the Special Forces camp commander (a captain) and a couple of his NCOs, Sgt. Crowe, my platoon sergeant, Maj. Malone, and I (Lt. Stein) discussed local patrolling to enhance security. The captain asked if he could send some of his "Yards"[29] on our patrols and Maj. Malone agreed. The terrain around Plei Me was not jungle, but rather like some African geography with shrubs, trees, and open elephant grass fields.

I chose Bob Johnston's Team 4-4 and assigned a walk-out mission from Plei Me. Bob was a pro and held in high esteem by the five men in his patrol. When told he'd have four Montagnards on his patrol, he had some concerns about the language barrier, their unfamiliarity with our Long Range Patrol tactics, and how missions were conducted. Maj. Malone informed Bob that he'd also be going along as a team member and that Johnston would remain the mission commander. That night Sgt. Johnston conducted a briefing for a first light walk-out in the morning. He recalls thinking, I sure don't want to be the team leader who's remembered for losing our beloved Maj. Malone!

The major told Johnston that he would carry his own weight on the patrol, so Sgt. Johnston had the major walking point the first day, carrying the radio the second day, and responsible for rear security the third day.

---

[29] *Yards* was U.S. military slang for the Montagnard soldiers.

Each night Malone took his shift at radio watch along with the rest of the men. The major had a Ranger Tab, and to no one's surprise he was an outstanding team member. At noon on the third day Malone told Johnston to call a chopper (the platoon had four slicks and two gunships attached to it) to pick him up since it appeared there would be no action for Team 4-4. Malone knew another team was scheduled to be inserted into their AO via a night combat jump and he wanted in on that mission. A slick stopped by and returned Major Malone to Plei Me.

Johnston's team continued their patrol; about six hours later four individuals were spotted about three-quarters of a mile away. Johnston looked through his binoculars and thought they looked like Montagnard soldiers, so he handed his "glass" to the Montagnard sergeant to get his opinion. The sergeant excitedly yelled, "VC, VC, VC!"

Johnston chose a direction to intercept the four enemy soldiers, however, when they were about sixty yards away the Viet Cong (VC) spotted Team 4-4 and opened fire. The VC were screwed—they were pinned between Johnston's team and a steep ravine to their backs—and lucky for the Americans, the enemies' marksmanship skills were lacking and most of their rounds shot high. Team 4-4 plus the four Montagnards opened fire killing three enemy soldiers, their bodies tumbling into the ravine. The fourth VC dropped his rifle and ran parallel to the ditch, with Team 4-4 in a foot race to catch him.

Sgt. Johnston kept shouting, "Prisoner, prisoner!" trying to capture the fleeing VC. When the men got within ten yards of him, the VC soldier stopped, spun around, and put his hands over his head. Team 4-4 quickly taped his arms around his back and returned to the three dead VC in the ravine. The steep embankment proved difficult to traverse so Johnston told his team to retrieve only the three rifles. Meanwhile, he was calling for a chopper to take the prisoner back to Plei Me for interrogation. As they were awaiting the chopper, Johnston had all he could do to keep the Yards from killing the prisoner. They had him against a tree and were beating the shit out of him. The Montagnards were fierce fighters and hated the VC.

When I arrived on a Huey, the soldiers dumped the VC plus the four captured rifles aboard. The VC looked terrified as the chopper took off on the short flight back to Plei Me. Our group was met by Special Forces soldiers and a translator who took charge of the prisoner and later told me that he "gave up all he knew." The prisoner said his unit reported to the NVA and they were supposed to map the movements into and out of Plei Me. He didn't know if the NVA was planning another attack on the camp.

The four captured rifles were a hodgepodge of weapons; there were two French MAS-36 bolt-action rifles with five-clip magazines (first introduced to the French military in 1936), an MAS-49 French semiautomatic with a ten-clip magazine and an M-1 U.S. .30 carbine with a twenty-round magazine. The more respected NVA soldiers would always carry the AK-47, the Soviet RPK light machine gun, and the RPG anti-tank grenade launcher.

Johnston believed his mission was compromised by the gunfight and the helicopter picking up the prisoner, so the team and the Yards headed back to Plei Me. Spirits were high, having killed three VC and taken a prisoner. To show their appreciation and thanks for the mission's success, the Montagnards gave their red scarves with blue piping to the men of Team 4-4. The Americans immediately put on the scarves (and continued wearing them until they left Vietnam); they reciprocated by giving the Montagnard soldiers LRP patches.[30]

From radio reports, Maj. Malone knew about the prisoner and gunfight; he was disappointed that he'd missed it. My final briefing for the scheduled night combat jump was just beginning at 1600 hours when the major joined the group, told me to continue and announced, "Lt. Stein, *you are still in command*."

---

[30] Three months later Sgt. Johnston was in a U.S. military hospital in Pleiku with five gunshot wounds; his fatigues were being cut off prior to surgery. Del Ayers, also wounded, noticed a nurse untie the sergeant's red scarf and asked her to save it for him. Months later, while recovering in a Valley Forge, Pennsylvania hospital, Johnston received a box containing the scarf, his canteen (which had an entry and exit bullet hole in it), plus a knife Johnston's uncle had made in a Pittsburgh Steel Mill, carried during WWII, and then gave to his nephew for good luck in Vietnam. Bob Johnston has all three memorabilia at his home in Pittsburgh.

CHAPTER 11

Just because nobody complains doesn't mean all parachutes are perfect.

Benny Hill

NIGHT COMBAT JUMP

I (Lt. Stein) recall being more nervous than any time in my Vietnam tour as I looked at Maj. Malone, founder of the Long Range Patrol Company and a Ranger, professor of leadership and psychology at West Point and a man with twenty-plus years in the Army. My briefing included the major, a first sergeant, four Huey helicopter pilots, and S. Sgt. Clay, the leader of Team 4-7. After I completed the briefing, there were only a few questions. The major was aware of the big picture, as it was his idea and he had authorized the mission.

The operation was simple and consisted of two jumps. The initial drop was scheduled at 2300 hours and would include the major, 1st Sgt. Frank Moore, our company medic, and me. It would be a static line jump from the normal altitude (1250 feet); it was critical we exit the chopper together (two on each side of the Huey) using T-10 parachutes so that we would land together.

We would be armed with M-16s except Maj. Malone, who would jump with his favorite M3A1 fully automatic .45 caliber Grease Gun with a thirty-round magazine. The gun had been introduced to the Army during WWII, was all metal and 29.8 inches long. With the stock retracted, it was only 22.8 inches long. The major allowed us to shoot his Grease Gun, but no one liked it. It was inaccurate and, when a second magazine was fired, the all-metal M3 was almost too hot to hold.

Upon landing, the four of us verified there was no enemy on the drop zone and marked it with strobe lights so Team 4-7 could jump. Sgt. Clay, the only black team leader in the platoon, would lead them. Clay was cool under fire and highly regarded by his team. Sgt. Hutchison was the assistant team leader and the other four team members were 4th Platoon soldiers who asked or begged me to allow them to go on this jump mission.

(Three of patrol Team 4-7's soldiers were on R&R or sick call, so the rest of them were mixing with soldiers from various 4th Platoon patrols.)

Meanwhile, Team 4-7 was "chuted up" and seated with their backs against a sandbagged revetment adjacent to their chopper. All the men were silent; five of them were smoking. These soldiers had less than twenty-five jumps to 1st Sgt. Moore's one thousand jumps.[31] Ron Causey had made only five jumps at Ft. Benning, the minimum needed to earn Airborne Wings. He asked Sgt. Clay for a cigarette. Clay lit it for Ron and remarked, "I didn't know you smoked." Causey replied, "I don't; this is my first."[32] The chopper pilots were in the cockpit with the crew chief untying the rotor blade and the gunners ensuring the belt ammunition would feed clean. Clay and his men climbed aboard.

At 2400 hours, Team 4-7 lifted off. They were very well trained; every airborne soldier had completed a three-week Airborne Course at Ft. Benning, Georgia. At a minimum, soldiers are required to complete Basic Combat Training and Advanced Individual Training. Airborne school requires excellent physical condition and is broken into three phases: Ground Week, Tower Week, and Jump Week. Ground Week focuses on the parachute landing falls (PLF), and Tower Week features jumps from the 34-foot and 250-foot towers. Jump Week was fun and included five aircraft jumps from planes flying at 130 miles per hour and from 1,250 feet above the ground. Now this training was going to be put to the test.

The Huey pilot looked at his passengers, gestured by chopping his hand, and shouted, "Go, go!" The men plunged into absolute darkness. After a short ride to the ground and a successful PLF, they collapsed their wind-blown chutes and went looking for each other. To identify *friendlies* and help find each other, they were hitting two metal-on-metal strikes with the respondent replying with a single metal strike—somewhat like the airborne soldiers landing with their clickers in Normandy twenty-four years earlier. When everyone was accounted for except Sgt. Hutchison, the men began searching for him.

---

[31] 1st Sgt. Frank Moore finished his thirty-plus year Army career with over 2,000 jumps.
[32] Ron Causey smoked for the next seventeen years.

Hutch had a bad night after landing in one of the few trees in the drop zone and fracturing his ankle in four locations. He was in terrible pain, but unable to get down from the tree and couldn't send the metal-on-metal signal. When he was trying to fire a pin flare to signal his teammates, Hutch accidentally shot off the end of his thumb. He was rescued at first light, picked up by a Huey, and transported to the hospital in Pleiku. The rest of Team 4-7 continued their three-day mission with no enemy contact.

My team also spent the night in the jungle, but didn't make contact with Team 4-7. At first light, I requested a pick-up chopper. As it was preparing to land, one of the pilots reported seeing a wild boar in a nearby field. Maj. Malone heard the transmission and yelled, "Pick me up! I want to catch him." When the chopper arrived, Malone jumped on, grabbed a rope, and quickly fashioned a lasso. While approaching the field, the major got out on a strut and was holding onto the helicopter with one hand, while twirling the lasso and trying to rope the 200-pound boar. When the chopper got close, the wily boar would take quick evasive action, avoiding the lasso.

After twenty minutes, the major gave up the rodeo act and called me to say he was going to herd the boar toward the soldiers so they could shoot him. M-16 automatic rifle rounds quickly killed the boar. We loaded the big animal on the chopper and flew to the nearby Montagnard Special Forces Camp. Later in the day, Major Malone and I enjoyed tasty boar barbecue with the Yards.

CHAPTER 12

The Marines I have seen around the world have the cleanest bodies, the filthiest minds, the highest morale, and the lowest morals of any group of animals I have ever seen. Thank God for the United States Marine Corps!

Eleanor Roosevelt, First Lady of the United States, 1945

MARINE FORCE RECON

Sometime in November 1967 the commander of First Field Force, Lt. Gen. William B. Rosson, was scheduled to brief Gen. Westmoreland in Nha Trang on the status of all operations in his AO. One agenda item Westmoreland requested was the status of the Long Range Patrol Company he'd authorized. Westmoreland wanted specific information regarding the LRP's organization and administration, command policies, training, logistics, personnel and equipment, as well as helicopter support and operations. Rosson told Maj. Malone, E-Company (LRP) Commander, to join him for this briefing. Maj. Malone's notes follow:

Company-E (LRP) was organized on 25 September 1967, and formed within South Vietnam from in-country assets. The original personnel fill was comprised for the most part of combat veterans. It was initially filled to 100 percent by drawdown primarily from LRP volunteers from the 1st Brigade, 101st Airborne Division under Modified Table of Organization (MTOE) 7-157E. This unit is authorized a total strength of two hundred twenty-one enlisted men and nine officers. Since the company was organized it has been kept at close to one hundred percent authorized strength.

The unit was activated in Phan Rang, RVN with all the Table of Organization and Equipment (TOE) provided on requisition by the G-4 supply, IFFV (First Field Force Vietnam). These requisitions were placed through the 1st Logistics Command depots in Cam Rahn Bay and Qui Nhon. E-Company (LRP) was relocated to Camp Enari base camp of the 4th Infantry Division on 22 October 1967 with supplies, pay, and administration now provided by the 4th Infantry. In addition, a number of items have been laterally transferred from other units and directly from

Japan e.g. camouflaged uniforms. The original TOE for Army Navy/Portable Radio Communications (AN/PRC) was twenty-five and a recommendation to forty-eight has been sent to Headquarters, U.S. Army, Vietnam (U.S. ARV) with immediate approval expected.

The original procedures called for two platoon mission support sites but it is anticipated E-Company (LRP) could and would run four mission support sites and such tactics would be beyond the capability of the communication platoon as presently equipped. Other than this there are at present no serious logistic problems that adversely affect the accomplishment of the unit mission. E-Company (Long Range Patrol) 20th Infantry (Airborne) has the following missions:

- To provide long range reconnaissance, surveillance, and target acquisition patrol capabilities to First Field Force Vietnam (IFFV).
- To provide personnel and equipment to train, administer, plan for, and employ patrols as directed.
- E-Company will employ two patrol platoons at a time, with the other two undergoing stand-down, training, and refitting at the company base camp. The two deployed platoons operate from a mission support site where they are further supported by a base radio station from the Communications Platoon and necessary personnel from the operations section. The LRP platoons are normally not capable of providing their own security and therefore must be located in a secure area: i.e. a battalion fire base, Special Forces camp, etc. Based upon discussions with IFFV staff we now anticipate deploying all four patrol platoons simultaneously which triggered our request for an additional twenty-three radios. Each platoon consists of seven six-man patrols led by a Team Leader, usually an E-5 or E-6 plus an Assistant Team leader, normally an E-5. The platoon commanders are lieutenants supported by E-7 platoon sergeants. The company commander is a major rather than a captain because of the complexities of the missions, the platoons' geographic isolation and the need for daily interaction with other U.S. and foreign commands. A captain serves as executive officer with another captain as the S-3 (operations) with a lieutenant

assistant. E-Company (LRP) includes a communications (commo) platoon reporting to a lieutenant to ensure quality communications are available throughout the II Corps area that represented a very large AO (fifty percent of Vietnam's geography). The balance of the company includes the company clerk, supply clerks, generator operators, cooks, and other support personnel.

Each platoon operating from mission support sites will have direct air assets of four Huey helicopters, two gunships, and access to an O-1 fixed wing aircraft. Most of the time patrol teams will operate outside of artillery fans. Every patrol mission briefing includes an identification of the reaction force. Normally this will be a Special Forces-led Montagnard company or an American infantry company held in battalion reserve while securing the battalion fire base. The reality is these forces are not standing by choppers and would not be capable of being on the ground for a minimum of twelve hours, usually the next morning. If patrols are discovered and a firefight begins, the small task force of six helicopters, one Bird Dog, thirty-two soldiers (thirteen pilots, six crew chiefs, six gunners with a Command and Control commander) and the combat skills of the six-man patrol team will determine the patrol's outcome.

These task forces have considerable firepower: 26,000 M-60 machine gun rounds, 4,000 M-16 rounds, twenty-eight high explosive rockets, twelve hand grenades, twelve M-79 grenade launcher rounds, plus marking smoke grenades. The advantage the team on the ground will enjoy is enemy confusion as to the size and strength of the ghost-like American warriors. An immense amount of focused firepower will be unleashed allowing a slick to drop down and extract the patrol.

Each platoon receives three weeks of Special Forces Recondo School training in Nha Trang. The four patrol platoons were filled with personnel in sequence and phased into a special Recondo course at the Military Assistance Command, Vietnam (MACV) at one-week intervals. Prior to attending this course, each platoon had a minimum of ten days hard preparatory training. After completion of the Recondo course, each platoon will complete a one-week field training exercise (FTX) at Plei Do Mi Special Forces Camp in the Central Highlands south of Pleiku, RVN. After this training is completed platoons will be declared combat ready. The last platoon to complete its training will be declared combat ready on 23 December 1967. This will be, in effect, E-Company's Christmas present to IFFV, a combat ready Long Range Patrol Company, organized and trained from the ground up in less than three months.

The generals seemed pleased with the briefing and Westmoreland offered the opportunity to have several patrols work with Marine Force Recon patrols in Da Nang to understand U.S. Marine patrolling tactics. That afternoon Maj. Malone told me (Lt. Stein) to send two teams to Da Nang and report to Marine Maj. Walker. I selected Team 4-1 and Team 4-3 for the assignment based on the fact that these team leaders were my most senior NCOs. The teams arrived at the An Khe airfield in an Army truck. Unlike airports today, there were neither gates nor flight numbers anywhere. Team leaders went to Airfield Operations to locate their plane. An Khe was home of the 1st Cavalry Air Mobile Division and there were hundreds of helicopters and planes on the vast air field.

S. Sgt. Henry Swift was the leader of Team 4-1 and a veteran of the Korean War. I thought Sgt. Swift was one of my best team leaders, and each of Swift's soldiers was honored to be on his team. However, the Army had a somewhat different persuasion. Swift, nearing twenty years of service, normally would be considering retirement and career options, but found himself only a recently promoted E-6. His exceptional field service was countered by many counseling sessions, reprimands, and extra training, plus a few Article 15s (also known as "non-judicial punishment") used for relatively minor "crimes,"[33] a sort of a mini court-martial with the commander acting as judge and jury. Swift's home-based track record didn't trouble me in the slightest; in a war I wanted as many Sgt. Henry Swifts as possible on my side!

---

[33] The primary purpose of the United States justice system is to dispense justice, but that is not the primary reason for the creation of a separate justice system for America's Armed Forces. The paramount purpose of the military's system is to provide the military commander with necessary tools to enforce good order and discipline. That's why, for example, it's not considered a crime to be late for work at your civilian job, but it is a crime to be late for work in the military (violation of Article 86 of the Uniform Code of Military Justice, or UCMJ). Swift's "crimes" in the military caused him delayed promotions or loss of stripes. He never faced the "biggies" of military justice: summary, special, or general court-martials.

The teams found their aircraft, a De Havilland C-7B Caribou, which was originally designed and built by the Canadian government. The United States purchased 307 of these $800,000 airplanes, which carried a crew of three with a load capacity of thirty-two passengers and were capable of landing on the many dirt strips in Vietnam.

The C-7 aircraft commander introduced himself, his copilot, and crew chief to our twelve LRP soldiers. "Please take out your magazines and clear your weapons," he ordered. Soon the men were off to the Da Nang Airfield, about a ninety-minute flight to the coast of Vietnam. Upon arrival, Maj. Walker of Marine Force Recon met the troops, showed the men their billets, and scheduled a briefing for the two LRP teams and his Marine Force Recon men after lunch. These Marines had their paratrooper wings so that made for instant camaraderie and bonding with the LRP teams.

Milt Hendrickson remembers that the teams were split into two- or three-man elements and attached to Marine Recon units for their operational missions. He and John Higgins were assigned to a twelve-man team led by Marine Staff Sgt. Mills; the second in command was another sergeant whose name escapes Milt, but who was nicknamed "Frenchy." Milt's recollections follow:

The mission started with the usual Warning Order and briefing. Our infiltration wasn't executed in helicopters as we'd trained, rather we traveled to our AO in a Deuce-and-a-Half (a medium-weight class truck designed to carry five thousand pounds but known to haul twice as much as rated) north on Highway One to where we were dropped off and walked into our assigned patrol area. The French colonists constructed Highway One in the early twentieth century; this 1,078-mile asphalt road connects Hanoi and Saigon (a 700 mile trip by air) and has 874 bridges.

I remember thinking that everyone (and their brother) knows we're here ... and probably where we're going! Our patrol area began at Hoa Hiep Bac; we dismounted and moved directly west through light-to-heavy vegetation with single-to-double canopies. The first day and night proved uneventful. On the second night we set up on the military crest of a ridge, overlooking the nearby valley. (The military crest of a ridge refers to the shoulder of a hill or ridge rather than its actual or topographic crest, i.e., the highest point.) My watch was 0200 to 0300. As I scanned the valley and the adjoining jungle, I spotted a long line of lights and woke our team leader, Sgt. Mills. He called in pre-plotted artillery from two batteries, a 105mm and a 155mm. As the initial rounds impacted, the lights went out immediately, but the Marines continued to adjust artillery on that area for another hour.

On day three, tensions were high and we moved cautiously now that enemy troops were confirmed in our area of operation. During the briefing we were told if enemy contact was made we were to break contact, make our way to high ground, and repel the NVA using artillery until a Marine infantry company could relieve us. Our luck held and no contact was made. That night we set a Night Defensive Position (NDP) usually designated for a small number of soldiers (i.e. five to fifteen) as opposed to a perimeter defense used by company-sized units. At about 0200 hours, lights were again spotted, but this time they were farther up the valley. Sgt. Mills was calling for a fire mission from destroyers and cruisers positioned just off the coast of South Vietnam. Heavy cruisers like the *U.S.S. Saint Paul* were armed with 8-inch guns able to fire 26,000 yards (about 15 miles), and the shorter range 5-inch guns, which are accurate to 15,000 yard (8.5 miles).

About ten minutes later, I heard different explosion signatures from both the five-inch and eight-inch guns. The sounds of friendly artillery and enemy mortars impacting the ground were significantly different than rounds fired from the Navy. It shouldn't have surprised me that the rounds hit the exact requested coordinates, but considering the ships were bobbing in the South China Sea, their accuracy was remarkable. The teams returned from the four-day patrols without casualties.

The Marines were outstanding warriors, but lacked significant helicopter air support and their tactics differed from the Army's principally because the Marines patrolled with eight to twelve men vs. the Army's five to six-man LRP patrols. Should the Marines engage in a firefight, they would make their way to high ground and fight until relieved by a Marine infantry company, as opposed to LRP tactics calling for movement to the closest LZ aided by airborne fire-power and helicopter extraction. Not surprisingly, the Marines benefited by great fire mission coordination with the Navy vessels off the coast.

The U.S. Navy fleet aided the allied ground command in South Vietnam with gunfire support. The 1200-mile coastline allowed the Navy to take advantage of the mobility and firepower of its surface ships. They used both their brown water (shallow) and blue water (deep) strategies in Vietnam. Because the waters off the northern and central regions of South Vietnam were deep, the guns on many Seventh Fleet cruisers and destroyers could reach targets in large segments of II Corps. Relatively safe from the enemy, the gunfire support ships operated day or night and often in the foul weather that swept the South China Sea. I regret that the U.S. main battleship, *New Jersey*, didn't arrive on-station until September 1968. I wanted to hear and perhaps see the impact of its nine massive sixteen-inch guns.

When all the teams returned to Da Nang, Maj. Walker asked S. Sgt. James Nobles, leader of Team 4-3, "Would your soldiers like to earn their Vietnamese Jump Wings tomorrow morning with a couple of jumps before returning to An Khe at 1600 hours?" The men were told that it only took one jump to earn Vietnamese paratrooper wings.[34] Sgt. Nobles enthusiastically agreed and all the team members were pumped when they heard the news.

At dawn, the LRP patrols and their newfound Force Recon friends were loaded in two trucks and heading for the Da Nang airfield. They were going to jump from two C-7s using the rear cargo door for a static line jump from 1200 feet, which was high enough to pull the reserve chute should the main malfunction. The teams would be jumping "combat light" with no enemy activity expected, and they carried only a single rifle magazine. They parachuted onto the beautiful Da Nang beach, collected their chutes, and returned to the airfield for their second jumps. Back at their billets, Maj. Walker thanked the LRP teams and wished them success in their future missions.

---

[34] This was never confirmed, nor were wings ever given to our teams.

CHAPTER 13

Onward we stagger, and if the tanks come, may God help the tanks.
>Brig. Gen. William O. Darby
>Commander of the First Ranger Battalion in WWII

U.S. ARMY RANGERS

The Army deactivated its Ranger companies in 1959 after heroic battles in WWII and Korea. Effective February 1, 1969, E and F Long Range Patrol Companies, plus other Long Range Reconnaissance Patrol units' successful war records caused the United States Army to flip and reflag these combat organizations, and reactivate Ranger units into today's elite 75th Ranger Regiment. Team member Ken Taylor said he remembers going out on a mission in E-Company, Long Range Patrol and returning as a member of a Ranger Company!

In 1756, a frontiersman, Major Robert Rogers, recruited nine companies of American Colonists to fight for the British during the French and Indian war. Today's modern rangers can trace their roots and heritage back to Major Robert Rogers, who provided the famous Rogers' Rangers Standing Orders, which are included in the front of every edition of the Ranger Handbook and follow:

ROGERS' RANGERS STANDING ORDERS
Maj. Robert Rogers, 1759

Don't forget nothing.

Have your musket clean as a whistle, hatchet scoured, sixty rounds of powder and ball, and be ready to move at a minute's warning.

When you are on the march, act the way you would if you was sneaking up on a deer; see the enemy first.

Tell the truth about what you see and do. There is an Army depending on us for correct information. You can lie all you please when you tell other folks about the Rangers, but never lie to an Officer or Ranger.

Don't ever take a chance you don't have to.

When we're on the march, we march in single file, far enough apart so one shot can't go through two men.

If we strike swamps, or soft ground, we spread out abreast so it's hard to track us. When we march, we keep moving until dark so as to give the enemy the least possible chance at us.

When we camp, half the party stays awake while the other half sleeps.

If we take prisoners, we keep 'em separate till we have had time to examine them so they can't cook up a story between 'em.

Don't ever march home the same way. Take a different route so you won't be ambushed.

No matter whether we travel in big parties or little ones, each party has to keep a scout 20 yards ahead, 20 yards on each flank, and 20 yards in the rear, so the main body can't be surprised and wiped out.

Every night you will be told where to meet if surrounded by a superior force.

Don't sit down to eat without posting sentries.

Don't sleep beyond dawn; dawn's when the French and Indians attack.

Don't cross a river by a regular ford.

If somebody's trailing you, make a circle, come back onto your own trail, and ambush the folks that aim to ambush you.

Don't stand up when the enemy's coming against you. Kneel down, lie down, hide behind a tree.

Let the enemy come till he's close enough to touch. Then let him have it and jump out and finish him up with your hatchet.

The term *Ranger* came into use in 1622 after the Berkeley Plantation Massacre in the English Colony of Virginia. Grim-faced men had gone forth to search out the Indian enemy. The men were militia, citizen soldiers, but they were learning to blend the methods of Indian and European warfare. As they went in search of the enemy, the words *range, ranging,* and *Ranger* were frequently used. The American Ranger had been born.

When the American Revolution began, Gen. Washington ordered Lt. Col. Thomas Knowlton to select an elite group of men for reconnaissance missions. This unit was known as Knowlton's Rangers, and is credited as the first official Ranger unit (by name) for the United States. This unit, however, carried out intelligence functions rather than combat functions in most cases, and as such they are not generally considered the historical parent of the modern day Army Rangers. Instead, Knowlton's Rangers gave rise to the modern military intelligence branch (although it was not a distinct branch until the twentieth century).

The most famous Rangers of the American Civil War fought for the Confederate States Army, but some fought for the North. In January 1863 John S. Mosby was given command of the 43rd Battalion, Partisan Rangers. Mosby's Rangers became infamous among Union soldiers due to their frequent raids on supply trains and couriers. Their reputation was heightened considerably when they performed a raid deep into Union territory and captured three high-ranking officers, including Brig. Gen. Edwin H. Stoughton. Weeks after the surrender of the Confederate Army, Mosby disbanded his unit rather than formally surrender. The most successful attacks against Confederates were carried out by the Union Army's Mean's Rangers. Mean's Rangers became famous when they successfully captured Gen. James Longstreet's ammunition train.

In World War II the 1st Ranger Battalion was sanctioned, recruited, and began training in Carrickfergus, Northern Ireland in May, 1942. Of the five hundred volunteers who formed in Carrickfergus, only eighty-seven were alive by the end of the war. The birth of the Ranger Motto occurred on June 6, 1944 during the assault landing on the Dog White sector of

Omaha Beach as part of the invasion of Normandy. Under fire, Brig. Gen. Norman Cota, Assistant Commanding Officer of the 29th Infantry Division, approached Maj. Max Schneider, Commanding Officer of the 5th Ranger Battalion and asked, "What outfit is this?"

Schneider answered, "5th Rangers, Sir!"

To this, Cota replied, "Well, God dammit, if you're Rangers, lead the way." From this comment, the Ranger motto "Rangers lead the way!" was born.

At the outbreak of the Korean War, a unique Ranger unit was formed. Headed by 2nd Lt. Ralph Puckett, the 8th Army Ranger Company was created in August 1950. It would serve as the role model for the future Ranger units. Instead of forming into self-contained battalions, the Ranger units of the Korean and Vietnam eras would organize into companies and then attach to larger units, to serve as organic Special Operations units.

In total, sixteen additional Ranger companies were formed in the next seven months of the Korean War, many with volunteers from the 505th Airborne Regiment and the 82nd Airborne Division. During the course of the Korean War, Rangers patrolled and probed, scouted and destroyed, attacked and ambushed the Communist Chinese and North Korean enemy. Rangers destroyed the 12th North Korean Division headquarters in a daring night raid and they made a combat airborne assault near Munsan. Crucially, the Rangers plugged the gap made by retreating Allied forces and helped stop the Chinese 5th Phase Offensive. As in World War II, after the Korean War, the Ranger units were disbanded with final deactivation of the Rangers in 1959.

The modern 75th Ranger Regiment represents the culmination of 250 years of American soldiering. As the nation's oldest standing military unit, the regiment traces its origins to Robert Roger's Rangers during the pre-Revolutionary French and Indian Wars, to the five active Ranger battalions of the Second World War, and finally, to the four battalions of the current Ranger regiment engaged in modern combat. Over that period, a standard of professional excellence and the forging of that excellence is distilled in the selection, assessment, and training of today's Rangers.

The 75th Ranger Regiment is a unique and distinct culture among the American military establishment. They stand alone, even among our other

Special Operations forces, as the most active brigade-sized force in the current global war on terrorism. Since September 11, 2001, the regiment is the only continuously engaged unit in the Army, and has had forty percent of its number deployed in harm's way for the last fifteen years. Today their mission is unique. Rangers do not patrol, they don't train allied forces, nor do they engage in routine counterinsurgency duties. They have a single-mission focus. They seek out the enemy and they capture or kill them. This sets Rangers apart as pure, direct-action warriors.

CHAPTER 14

Only those who will risk going too far can possibly find out how far one can go.

T. S. Elliot

THREE UNIQUE PATROLS

Quy Hoa Leper Colony

Subsequent to the Long Range Patrol Company launching in late November 1967, my (Lt. Stein's) 4th Platoon conducted seventy-six patrols in our first six months in the field; thirty-seven of the patrols were completed without an exchange of gunfire. Team 4-1 conducted one such patrol.

The team leader, Sgt. Randy Mills, and his six-man team including Steve Woodson (point), Rich McKenzie (slack), Jerry Shankle (RTO), Milt Hendrickson (scout-rifleman), John Higgins (rear security), and a Montagnard scout flew by chopper to a U.S. Air Force communication site just south of Qui Nhon. This radar/communication compound, located on the crown of a small mountaintop, overlooked the beautiful beaches of the South China Sea. The site was manned by about seventy-five airmen/technicians who provided their own security and thought they had tough duty until they met the men of Team 4-1.

The team's mission was to support the 5th Special Forces Group; the insertion method they used was called "Stay Behind." With this method, a small reconnaissance team or combat team attaches to a larger unit, typically an infantry company. (Stay Behind was used frequently in Vietnam, particularly by LRRPs directly supporting combat battalions or brigades. Airborne/Infantry Divisions frequently used this method, as well, with a platoon staying behind after a company swept an enemy area.) The 5th Special Forces Group would conduct a Search and Destroy operation in an area of suspected enemy and then, at an appropriate location, Team 4-1 would drop off and begin their mission.

The entire Long Range Patrol Company graduated from the three-week Recondo School staffed by Special Forces instructors in Nha Trang. Our patrol teams quickly bonded with these men; Randy and Milt especially relished working with the cool dudes of the Special Forces. Their briefings were excellent and backed with solid intelligence. Team 4-1's Quy Hoa mission was to locate a Viet Cong battalion operating in the Qui Nhon region and, if pinpointed, maintain contact until 5th Group units could move into position to develop the situation.

Team 4-1 married up with a MIKE (Mobile Strike Force) company from 5th Group consisting of Montagnard soldiers led by Special Forces advisors. At dawn the team met the MIKE company about a mile down from the mountain summit. The Montagnards usually traveled single file with a three-man point leading the way and fire teams guarding their flanks. The Americans were always amazed at how little water (usually just a single canteen) or equipment the Yards carried, and how easily they traversed the jungle. These small soldiers always seemed happy and were constantly joking with each other, but they had a sixth sense and knew when danger was close at hand. These marvelous warriors were well respected and liked by the American soldiers. Older Montagnard veteran fighters told us they would rather fight with U.S. soldiers than with the French since we provided as much ammunition as they could carry. The French, on the other hand, would count and document individual bullets for each Montagnard soldier. Randy Mills and the Special Forces advisor, a master sergeant, selected a drop-off point, and then the sergeant motioned his company forward. As each diminutive Yard soldier passed by Team 4-1, they lightly touched hands with Randy's men.

After an uneventful four days, Team 4-1 hiked back to the radar site to regroup and recharge. Tomorrow would be New Year's Eve. The officer-in-charge (OIC), a major, was thrilled having six combat-proven Airborne Rangers defending his post. Wherever they were based, the LRPs found they were viewed as security blankets by the "legs," especially the REMFs. Since there'd been an accidental shooting at the radar site, the major had locked up his soldiers' weapons except for the men on guard duty. He assigned Mills' team a concrete bunker with overhead cover to eliminate danger from mortars. That amenity coupled with hot food and showers made Team 4-1 feel like kings in their own suite. The major also provided Randy's team with two M-60 machine guns on tripods and unlimited ammunition to target shoot during the day. The soldiers enjoyed shooting these guns, but didn't like carrying the weapon that weighed twenty-three pounds and its hundred-round bandoliers of ammunition in the field.

New Year's Eve 1968 found the team with no responsibility for security and invited to a party in a large underground bunker. At the foot of the bunker stairs sat a big cooking pot containing screwdrivers (orange juice and vodka), complete with a ladle and cups. The drinks were free and the nineteen-year-old soldiers took full advantage. Yikes! Steve Woodson, a calm and mild-mannered trooper, got drunk and into fights and shouting matches with the airmen. The next day he awoke in his sleeping bag to hear about his antics. Steve and his team recovered from the party, albeit slowly.

Two days later Team 4-1 learned about their second patrol; it would be a very difficult, one-of-a-kind mission. However, these men would not push back on their assignment. In the Army, orders are given and carried out with few questions asked. These men knew their job was to "get 'er done!" That's why they'd volunteered, so forward they'd go.

The new mission was to investigate the nearby Quy Hoa Leper Colony for signs of the Viet Cong battalion rumored to have their headquarters near Qui Nhon, a coastal city in central Vietnam. The lepers were suspected of providing cover and safety for the Viet Cong. The mission was a "walk out," with the men leaving at 2200 hours and arriving outside the colony before dawn. They would observe the leper colony for three days and, if no enemy was observed, patrol in and throughout the colony. On the fourth morning, they were to report and return to base.

After the briefing by the Special Forces senior NCO, Team 4-1 was checking their equipment, ammo, and cleaning their weapons when John Higgins said, "I heard leprosy is contagious. Dammit, I don't like this!" McKenzie replied, "Come on; they wouldn't send us somewhere to get sick." The men looked at Mac in silence. This would be the only time when LRPs were more fearful of something other than the enemy!

A quarter moon was offering some light for the team's three-mile trek to the leper colony, which was on the seacoast and nestled in a valley encircled by hills. The men found an exceptional observation site offering substantial cover, but also having direct sightlines into the colony and the only road accessing Quy Hoa. The road was actually only a path best traveled on foot and by goats.

Team 4-1 monitored the colony through their one set of binoculars (*aka* their glass) for three days, seeing only a handful of peasant women come and go. On the third night they were wondering what they'd find in the morning; no one quite knew what to expect. Randy said, "We're under the operational control of the 5th Special Forces Group, and they're responsible for thirty square miles of territory including this small leper colony. These guys are smart, and it's interesting they chose us to patrol this small area of their AO. Do they know or suspect something they're not telling us?" Randy's teammates didn't speculate.

The next morning Team 4-1 walked into the 175-acre leprosarium occupied by about nine hundred Vietnamese lepers, most of whom were gathering in the doorways of their thatched roof huts and giving the Americans puzzled looks. None were smiling. Randy's team had their weapons at-the-ready, but after a while felt comfortable they were not in danger. They shouted, "VC? VC?" Some lepers were shaking their heads indicating no, when two French nuns appeared. Since they didn't speak English and the team members knew very little French, the two groups used sign language and some interesting charades to communicate. Finally, the Americans were satisfied there were no Viet Cong in the colony.

Many of the leper colony residents were encrusted with skin sores; their lesions were lighter in color than their normal brown skin. Their toes were bent and misshapen fingers were attached to clawed hands. It looked as if their muscles couldn't control their eyes, so the lepers were staring at the soldiers with an unfocused gaze. It was weird at first, but after a while the team became accustomed to and accepted what they termed the Halloween Show. After inspecting each hooch, Randy's team collected all the food and candy bars they were carrying in their rucks and placed them at the colony's well. With a wave to the residents, Team 4-1 trudged back to the radar site.

The next morning, they said goodbye to the radar operators and awaited the chopper that would lift them to Ban Me Thuot to reunite with the 4th Platoon. It had been nearly two weeks of good duty; now it was time to get back to the war.

Today the Quy Hoa Leper Colony is a tourist attraction. Most of the lepers are quite elderly and their descendants populate the village, some of whom work in a small clothing factory or as crab fishermen. The nearby beautiful Quy Hoa Queen's Beach is named for the wife of Bao Dai, the last emperor of Vietnam, who ruled from 1926 to 1945.

Mystery Fort

Sgt. Bob Johnston was staring through his glass and wondering what he was seeing; he handed the binoculars to Oscar Caraway, who examined what appeared to be an illusion. The two men looked at each other and then shook their heads. This was the fifth day of a jungle patrol along the Cambodian border and the five-man Team 4-4 was coming up empty. A light rain was filtering down accompanied by heavy ground fog; Johnston decided to move his team closer to explore whatever it was they were observing. Patrolling in the rain had advantages, of course, chief among them allowing the men to move silently through the jungle. However, a huge disadvantage was that the tracks they left in the wet soil were like blinking neon signs and easily followed. Oscar, the rear security team member, needed to be especially alert for enemy trailing them. He would pause and wait or double back to see if they had any unwanted "company" behind them.

Since his assigned area was quiet, Johnston had taken his team outside his Area of Operations and ventured three miles south. The men were patrolling somewhat parallel to the Mekong River when they found themselves on a low hill overlooking a clearing about a mile across and a half-mile wide. The double and triple canopy jungle disappeared, and was replaced by shorter trees and undergrowth in a large clearing.

Johnston stopped for another look as the heavy fog began to lift and a fort appeared in his binoculars. It reminded him of forts in the American Old West having a blockhouse on each corner. Then he focused his glass on a Jeep with a machine gun mounted on it that was driving out of the fort. Bob could see the driver, a gunner, and what looked like another American looking back at him through his own binoculars. Since this area was nearly fifty miles from any friendly forces, Johnston wondered what was going on.

Team 4-4 waved and the Jeep's occupants motioned them to come closer. As the patrol walked toward the fort, they could see Chinese Nung mercenary guards. They also spotted a dozen or fifteen Americans dressed in Army fatigues without unit patches or rank designations. There were three large cement block buildings plus some smaller living quarters. In addition, antennas of every size with unique shapes and configurations were everywhere! The team wondered who—or what—these antennas were monitoring.

The Americans in the fort were congenial and obviously quite surprised to see the men of Team 4-4. They said they were an Army supply outfit. Sgt. Johnston thought, yeah, right. The supply outfit guys said, "We've been watching you. A flight of Air Force fighter-bombers is on hold and circling, awaiting additional guidance." How they'd spotted Johnston's team wasn't disclosed and the ensuing conversation between the two groups was like a kabuki dance. Neither side wanted to let the other know their mission or what they were thinking.

One of the so-called supply outfit soldiers asked the men of 4-4, "Who's in charge?" Sgt. Johnston replied, "I'm the team leader." He was escorted into one of the blockhouses for a briefing with seven or eight men who were seated at a long table. Johnston noticed a Special Forces E-8 master sergeant, but his was the only rank insignia visible. Johnston assumed the sergeant led the Nungs and was probably in charge of the fort's security.

The Americans in the fort said they were amazed by the uninvited presence of Team 4-4, and that they figured the patrol team had been sent to check them out. Johnston never admitted his team was out of their AO; he just assured them there were no enemy forces north of their compound. Then the "supply outfit" men welcomed Team 4-4 to take a shower, clean off their camo, enjoy a steak dinner, and stay the night. Johnston radioed this unbelievable story back to Lt. Stein and requested a next-morning pickup. Everyone at the fort was taking pictures of Johnston's team as if they were famous celebrities from the States.

When thinking about this encounter later, Johnston says it was good that both groups held their nerve and checked their fire. If Team 4-4 had received fire, they would have requested air strikes on the fort; Johnston was sure the Special Forces troops (or the *supposed* Special Forces troops) in the compound would have done the same. It would have been interesting to be at the Air Force acquisition targeting headquarters when they received requests from two units requesting air strikes on the same target!

Johnston knew his team was somewhere they weren't supposed to be, and that the Americans they discovered were not a supply outfit in the middle of nowhere. No one asked any follow up questions.

Lt. Stein flew in a single bird to pick up the team and observe the installation, but never got out of the chopper. Team 4-4 scrambled aboard and, after much conversation and conjecture, concluded that none of them could understand what was happening at the "mystery fort." Were they a Special Operations Group or the CIA? Almost five decades later, they still don't have an answer. If you know, contact me, Lt. Stein; the team and I are still curious.

Chinese Officers

Team 4-3's four-day mission was almost over. A small one-ship Landing Zone had been selected and the team's extraction was requested. Helicopters were airborne and on the way. Team 4-3 walked around and across the LZ, detected nothing, and was waiting inside the treeline. A soft rain had stopped about an hour earlier so everyone was feeling good and thinking about some downtime back at An Khe. Herman Dunklebarger was lying on a low horizontal tree branch while the rest of Tom Workman's team (Ray Bohrer, Darrell Presley, and Gary Stewart) were chilling on the ground. Their four-day patrol had been uneventful.

Dunklebarger watched as a single file of NVA entered the LZ with their point man only twenty-five feet away from him. He could barely get out the words, as he excitedly whispered, "Goo ... Goo ... Gooks!" The team instantly brought their rifles to-the-ready, shifting their safeties to full automatic with five soft clicks. The NVA point man came to the team's footprints and was looking in their direction, but with their camouflage paint and the jungle cover, Team 4-3 was almost invisible. Tom motioned Ray to take out the point while he cut down the last soldier. One NVA soldier yelled loudly just as Team 4-3 opened up on the column. The shooting was over in less than thirty seconds. The men counted eleven dead or wounded NVA, and then finished off the wounded with a shot to the head to ensure they couldn't throw grenades. Tom's team wasn't too concerned about a counterattack because their own choppers, slicks, and gunships were less than two minutes away with twenty-eight HE rockets, 26,000 machine gun rounds, and full fuel tanks.

Team 4-3 couldn't believe their good fortune. In addition to the AK-47s, they captured an American-made .30 caliber machine gun with a tripod. Two of the dead soldiers were much larger than the other men and were wearing unusual uniforms (brown with red insignias on the collars). While the team was celebrating the captured machine gun and the mission's success, Sgt. Workman called headquarters to report and was told to bring back the uniforms. The men stripped off the two dead soldiers' clothing, took all the weapons, and hopped aboard their pick-up chopper with high-fives all around. Later, the Special Forces Intelligence group told the team that the uniforms were removed from Chinese army officers.

CHAPTER 15

One more dance along the razor's edge finished. Almost dead yesterday, maybe dead tomorrow, but alive, gloriously alive, today.

Robert Jordan

CHRISTMAS PATROL

Team 4-6 conducted a Christmas patrol beginning on December 21, 1967. This nine-day LRP mission would be one of the longest patrols ordered by First Field Force Vietnam during the war. Team 4-6 was selected for the mission led by S. Sgt. Charles Samuelson. Sgt. Regis Murphy, Assistant Team Leader, SPC4 James Worth, newly-arrived PFC Gary Stewart, and recently-promoted Sgt. Juergen Besecke; a sixth team member completed the patrol. The extended time frame for this particular mission was in response to intelligence (G-2) received indicating large battalion or regimental enemy formations were moving from Cambodia into Vietnam. Headquarters wanted continued "eyes on the ground" to verify this G-2. Hindsight later told us these were NVA soldiers being positioned for the nationwide Tet attack four weeks later.

Juergen Besecke, physically the strongest member of the team, was the RTO; he carried the twenty-five pound PRC-77 radio along with extra batteries and antenna. (The men of Team 4-6 believe Besecke carried the first PRC-77 issued in Vietnam.) His Long Range Patrol communications lieutenant, Jerry Ramsey, gave the radio to him. The PRC-77 was an improved version of the PRC-25; the specifications and accessories for the two radios were nearly identical. The only important differences in design were internal so they were virtually impossible to tell apart externally. The 77 included a solid-state power amplifier that did away with the PRC-25 2DF4 power amplifier tube in the final transmitter section. Its completely solid-state design made it more reliable and reduced its power requirements. Filters had been added to reduce interference.

Besecke also carried the longer (ten feet versus three feet standard antenna) folding six-section whip antenna, but the team hesitated to use it since it was difficult to move in the jungle, and was easily seen when patrolling in high grassy areas. The PRC-77 with short antenna had a range of eleven miles, but with the long whip antenna the range extended to twenty-two miles. Of course, effectiveness varied widely depending on geography and weather conditions. Frequently, successful communication depended on airborne or mountaintop relay stations. Thirty-three thousand PRC-25 and PRC-77 radios were delivered to Vietnam. The PRC-25 was, according to Gen. Creighton Abrams, "the single most important tactical item in Vietnam."

The patrol's first two days, December 21 and 22, were peaceful even though there were fresh NVA east/west trails everywhere. The team moved slowly and carefully, not more than five kilometers (*aka* klicks) each day. They left no evidence of their presence; when they urinated, it was always in high grass so it was not detectible. They stored all garbage in their packs, ensuring they left no trace of their presence in the field. The patrol stayed high in the foothills where it was easy to observe the terrain in multiple directions.

Each night, about an hour before total darkness, Sgt. Samuelson chose a good area to settle, one which would provide his team maximum camouflage yet allow for sightlines to see NVA movements. The team would sit back-to-back and some nights got only a couple of hours sleep. They took "Green Hornets," a green pill that kept them awake. Six Claymore mines were always set up about fifty feet out surrounding the men. Each Claymore consisted of a C-4 block with embedded ball bearings; when the C-4 was detonated, the ball bearings became deadly shrapnel flying outwardly toward the approaching enemy. Claymores were a staple of every LRP team.

Each day Team 4-6 ate LRRP meals: packets of dried food that were, when mixed with water, some hot sauce, and a little salt and pepper, not bad! Of course, they tasted better when made with hot water heated by C-4 (ignited with a flame rather than detonated with a primary explosive). In the field, however, LRRP meals were served cold to avoid the aroma of cooked food alerting the enemy.

On December 23, their third night out, the team spied numerous groups of twenty-five to forty lights and lanterns moving to the east. The men were told to hold in place and continue to report, as the area was far beyond artillery fans. They stayed in that location until December 28, and then began moving down from the high ground to an LZ. They had to be careful and go slowly, with James Worth finding the best route to a dry rice paddy that had an adjacent wood line. That's where they would await a pickup chopper scheduled for 1900 hours. Everyone felt good about their mission and looked forward to some hot meals, mail, and a shower. Juergen grinned at his best friend, Gary Stewart; they'd be at base camp in forty minutes.

Suddenly they heard men shouting and saw NVA soldiers crossing the rice paddy from the north and south heading for their wood line. Stewart gasped and yelled, "Holy shit! Holy shit!" Samuelson told Besecke to contact the Wolf Pack chopper pilots to hold the team's pickup since NVA soldiers were on the LZ. Samuelson and Murphy started looking at their maps, trying to figure a way to backtrack to another LZ, perhaps on the other side of the hills. Escaping to the rear would have been difficult and might have split the team because of trees and undergrowth. The NVA soldiers were closing in on Team 4-6. They were being flanked north and south with the jungle behind them and the dry rice paddy in front of them. Besecke saw an enemy come into view from the left less than twenty feet away; he fired a short burst past Murphy's ear, killing the NVA. Samuelson had to make a lightning-quick decision. The bad guys knew where his team was, but not about the six helicopters just sixty seconds away. He decided to call for maximum firepower with their lift ship to be the first over and on the LZ. Sam told the choppers Team 4-6 would pop red smoke and to pick them up right at the smoke.

The extraction chopper appeared over the LZ followed by two gunships firing twenty-eight high explosive rockets and thousands of M-60 rounds. The three other slicks had their door gunners pepper the entire area with fire, as much as to confuse the enemy as to kill them. As the team ran to the chopper, which was just flaring to land, Besecke was shot in the leg. Due to the weight of the radio and Besecke's wound, Worth grabbed him and pushed him aboard. The American's red tracer rounds along with the green NVA tracers were everywhere. It was an incredible scene with the five choppers circling and continuing to fire upon the surrounding LZ as the team fired down at the enemy. At last Team 4-6 was safe above the fray.

During the after-action briefing with the Headquarters group, an assumption was made that the NVA was at least company-size in strength. After Samuelson treated Besecke's flesh wound, the shaken team enjoyed the best holiday meal their platoon could rustle up.

CHAPTER 16

People fly planes; pilots fly helicopters.

Author unknown

WOLF PACK THREE-NINER: DEATH ON CALL

It was February 19, 1968, and Warrant Officer and gunship Aircraft Commander Jim Fisher was feeling good on his twenty-fourth birthday and relaxing in Pleiku, Vietnam. His operations officer had wished him a happy birthday and said he and his gun crew should "take the day off" to celebrate. Jim was also feeling lucky. Only twenty days earlier, the NVA had launched their Tet Offensive on the first day of the lunar calendar and the most important Vietnamese holiday. Both North and South Vietnam had announced on national radio broadcasts that there would be a two-day cease-fire during the holiday, so the attack was a countrywide surprise. Jim spent that first night of Tet in a trench watching a great "fireworks show" that was set off when enemy mortars hit an ammunition dump filled with enormous quantities of white phosphorus. The good news was, the night before Tet, Jim was told to move his chopper because he'd parked it in the major's sandbagged revetment parking space. Jim moved the gunship farther down the airfield flight line. During the night the major's chopper was completely demolished from a direct hit by an enemy mortar. At that point, Jim was feeling very good ... and very lucky.

While Jim was enjoying extra sack time on his birthday, a company clerk ran into his barracks to tell him and his copilot, Ken Donald, that an LRP team from E-Company was surrounded by NVA; their supporting slicks and gun teams were low on fuel, out of ammunition, and returning to Pleiku. The encircled patrol had not been recovered. Fisher alerted his other gunship team and all eight airmen dashed down the flight line to their gunships.[35]

---

[35] A gun team consisted of two choppers; a heavy gun team had three choppers. Each gunship had an aircraft commander and the pilot, plus the crew chief and a door gunner. The commander sat in the right seat with gun sights that were fixed and the chopper had

Their UH-1C gunships were always fueled and armed, so they merely had to fire up the power switch, untie the rotor blade, pull the starter trigger, do a quick check of instrument gauges, pull pitch, and they were airborne to help the besieged patrol team thirty miles away. They married up with four Rat Pack slicks and then their mini air armada followed a direct azimuth to the beleaguered team, passing six returning Wolf Pack gunships and Bandit slicks. While in-route, Jim's group was given the coordinates of the LRP team, and they established communication with the Command and Control helicopter and a Bird Dog pilot to receive an initial situation briefing and confirm the radio frequency of the LRP team. Arriving on station, Fisher was thinking, "It doesn't look good for these guys."

The LRP team was under triple canopy jungle with the nearest potential LZ nearly two miles away. An estimated battalion-sized force surrounded them and four of the five team members were wounded. With dusk approaching, no reinforcements could or would be sent. If the team were to be rescued, they would be coming up through the trees on a Jungle Penetrator (a bullet-shaped device for extracting wounded) or a McGuire Rig (three leather seats affixed to a slick helicopter, each by a single nylon rope).

The endangered LRP team did not know it, but their odds were improved with the 281st Assault Helicopter Company working to save them.[36] Meanwhile, there were a few good things going for the team. Although wounded, the patrol RTO, Del Ayers, was calm in his communications with Fisher and the slick and Bird Dog pilots. Since there was no wind, the colored smoke from their grenades could ascend vertically through the trees, enabling Fisher to pinpoint their exact location. The five-man patrol emptied all their magazines, sending nearly four

---

to be moved to adjust rocket fire on targets. The pilot could move the quad M-60 machine guns up or down, left or right, while adjusting on the target.

[36] The 281st Helicopter Company (aka The Intruders) had become the first organized Special Operations helicopter unit in the U.S. Army. Our Long Range Patrol company had worked with the 281st at Recondo School in December 1967. The Intruders were the primary helicopter support for B-52 Project Delta, Recondo Training, and 5th Special Forces in Nha Trang. This was the first helicopter unit to train and develop Special Operations techniques and procedures. They were decorated numerous times for valor and meritorious service.

thousand accurately aimed rounds and causing the NVA to reckon they were up against a much larger force. If the enemy had realized they were fighting only five soldiers, a direct frontal attack would quickly have wiped out the team.

Fisher began firing his fourteen 2.75 inch rockets in a circle surrounding the team, about fifty to seventy-five yards away. Practically, they weren't intended to deliver lethal force because the trees caused them to explode before reaching their targets. Fisher's intention was to discourage and intimidate reinforcing NVA troops, and the loudly exploding rocket fire seemed to buy the patrol some additional time. On his next pass, Fisher brought his four coaxially mounted M-73 7.62mm machine guns to bear, but all the guns malfunctioned and jammed. His wingman continued firing in support, but there just wasn't enough firepower.

Fisher ordered his crew chief and door gunner to transfer the bullets from the quad guns to the single M-60 machine guns on each side of the Huey. He nearly laid the chopper on its side while the door gunners pumped bullets almost nonstop within twenty yards of the team. The crew chief continued to draw down on the eight thousand bullets from the unusable weapons and resupplied the door gunner ammunition, stopping only occasionally to exchange gun barrels. Fisher realized his gun team's and lift ships' fuel situation was critical; gunships normally carried eight hundred to one thousand pounds of fuel versus one thousand to fourteen hundred pounds for slicks.

Jim Fisher broadcasted over the radio, "The Rat Pack recovery slicks need to make their move now to pick up the team!" This was the team's last chance with darkness approaching and no help being sent. The gunships increased the fire support for the team. The first chopper brought out two wounded soldiers, but one of its door gunners was wounded during the extraction. The remaining three soldiers came up via a McGuire Rig. Just as they started up, the slick was taking lots of hits, so the pilot applied full throttle, dragging the men through the canopy and knocking the only uninjured soldier unconscious. His two buddies held him in the rig until they arrived at a Special Forces camp thirty minutes later.

Warrant Officer James M. Fisher was awarded the Distinguished Flying Cross for his actions on that day, February 19, 1968. The men of Chippergate Team 4-4 will always be indebted to Jim Fisher and the men of the 281st Aviation Company for saving them. Jim and the men of Team 4-4 reconnected in 2012 and are in contact each February 19th to remember the gunfight and celebrate their rescue.

CHAPTER 17

Lead me, follow me, or get out of my way.

Gen. George Patton

MAYER'S SECOND TOUR

Phil Mayer completed his tour with our Long Range Patrol Company in June 1968, and then served as an assistant professor of military science at Georgia Military College in Milledgeville, Georgia. Phil's recollections of his second tour in Vietnam follow:

After completing my tour of duty with E-20th Infantry (ABN/LRP) in June, 1968, I taught military history, logistics, and leadership and I served as tactical officer for fifty cadets who lived on campus and wore uniforms similar to those of the Confederate Army during the Civil War. For some of the ROTC staff, this duty was considered desirable and especially conducive to family life. Needless to say, the wives were overjoyed; we had predictable duty hours and a relaxing social life centered on bridge parties, family picnics, boating at the lake, and plenty of golf and fishing. It didn't take long for me to get my fill of this routine. I was promoted to captain in October 1968 and I volunteered for a second Vietnam tour shortly thereafter. I knew the ultimate challenge for an infantry captain was to command a rifle company in combat. I wanted to make sure I got a shot at this challenge before the war ended.

In September 1969, I reported to the 3rd Brigade, 82nd Airborne Division for subsequent assignment as Commander of Company-D, 1st Battalion 508th Infantry. Its primary missions were to protect Saigon and Tan Son Nhut Air Force Base from rocket and mortar attack, locate enemy battlefield cache sites, conduct combat operations in the pineapple plantation area southwest of Saigon, and "win the hearts and minds of the people residing in and around Vinh Loc Village in Tan Binh District." By late September our battalion was operating in Phu Hoa District just south of the Iron Triangle District, which was the area of operations (AO) for the main force Viet Cong (VC) Quyet Thang Regiment. During the day, combat operations were characterized by company and platoon-size sweeps throughout the AO. These were called "eagle flights" and consisted of three or more Huey helicopters that would insert a rifle platoon to swiftly and efficiently search out and destroy suspected enemy positions. Aggressive ambushing at night was conducted to prevent VC infiltration into populated hamlets and villages.

The terrain throughout our AO consisted of low-lying hills and small valleys interspersed with tall elephant grass and thick stands of wooded vegetation along with open fields dotted by small rice paddies. Our AO lay in the middle of an enemy transition route, which offered a fast avenue of approach from the mountains allowing NVA and main-force VC units to quickly assemble troops and munitions to attack populated areas. Most often, the goal of these attacks was to disrupt our pacification efforts.

My assignment with the 1/508th Red Devil Infantry Battalion was characterized by numerous riverine, air-mobile, and ground infantry combat operations that demanded maximum effort to overcome a wide variety of hazards including difficult terrain, extreme temperature, and an elusive and determined enemy. Most of our engagements with the enemy would be considered minor to moderate skirmishes triggered by both friendly and enemy ambushes, and brief hit-and-run attacks by local VC platoon- and squad-sized units.

One occasion that stands out in my mind occurred during a sweep of a heavily wooded area in search of a reported enemy weapons cache. We'd already discovered an enemy bunker complex and were moving cautiously along a primitive trail showing signs of recent activity when our attached scout dog (a German Shepherd) alerted. The handler commanded the dog to stand fast and then moved up to confer with the point man. At that time, pre-positioned VC opened up with a barrage of AK-47 automatic weapons fire instantly killing the handler and my point man. Seeing his handler down, the scout dog broke command and ran to comfort or assist his handler; the dog was shot and died by his soldier's side. Returned fire was initiated in the enemy's general direction as our troopers moved forward. The VC ambush had exercised the element of surprise; they quickly dispersed and retreated back to their village or hamlet to fight another day. The scout dog prevented many more soldiers from certain death or serious wounds as a result of a well-executed ambush. On that day, the German Shepherd dog was indeed our best friend.

Weeks before I arrived in-country, the focus of ongoing operations was on Vietnamization and pacification. The defense of Saigon and outlying districts was in the process of being turned over completely to the South Vietnamese Army. Rural and local reaction forces were being trained to defend their respective villages and hamlets. News of the draw-down and possible return of the 82nd Airborne Division to Ft. Bragg, North Carolina quickly reached the troops via the unofficial grapevine. Some of my troops became less than aggressive in their pursuit of the VC via daytime patrols and nighttime ambushing.

In an effort to reinvigorate patrol and ambushing aggressiveness, my first sergeant and I implemented an informal incentive program. After conferring with the platoon leaders and NCOs, we decided to offer overnight passes to Saigon and cash stipends ($100-$150) from our beer/soda fund for individuals who killed or captured a VC. A couple of weeks after implementing this program, I was directed to report to my brigade commander, Brig. Gen. Dickerson, regarding a congressional complaint filed by the mother of one of my troopers. It didn't take me long to figure out what this was all about, since the mother's last name was the same as that of one of my troopers who had killed a VC on a recent ambush and received an overnight pass to Saigon.

The next day my Jeep driver drove me to Phu Loi, where the 3rd Brigade Headquarters was located. With some degree of reluctance, I reported to Gen. Dickerson and rendered a snappy salute. He asked if I was aware that one of my troopers' mothers had contacted her Congressman and told him I was rewarding young soldiers with bounty money for killing or capturing enemy combatants. I replied that I didn't know all the details but I had surmised as much.

Gen. Dickerson asked, "Did you put this informal incentive program in writing?"

I replied, "No, Sir.

He looked at me with a slight smile and replied, "Good. That will be all, Captain." After rendering another salute, I did an about-face and headed for the door. As I walked out he said, "And Captain, I suggest you come up with a different incentive program."

The beginning of November, 1969 saw our battalion, The Red Devils, being sent to Phu Loi base camp where we began stand-down and making preparations for the long journey home. Those with more than ten months in-country were processed for early departure from Vietnam. Those with less than ten months became replacements for other units within country.

Situated close to the Laotian border in the northern portion of the A Shau Valley was a mountain known as Ap Bia, identified on U.S. maps as Hill 937. It would later become known as Hamburger Hill. In residence since 1964, the NVA had fortified the area, building log-covered bunkers and camouflaged spider holes to protect all avenues of approach. By May, 1969, the A Shau Valley had become a staging area for three regiments of the crack NVA 29th Division. Lt. Col. Weldon Honeycutt, the 101st Battalion commander, set up a permanent landing zone and a battalion command post near Hill 937 and began to conduct reconnaissance in force (RIF) operations with no reaction from the NVA. At 1640 hours on May 10, 1969, paratroopers from B-Company, 3/187, were ordered to seize the summit of Ap Bia/Hill 937.

What started out as a frontal infantry assault became one of most horrific battles of the war. It was a nightmare of close-quarter fighting that was to continue with little respite for eight days. Day after day, Company-B moved forward, closing with the NVA regulars and attacking fortified bunkers with grenades, recoilless rifles and machine guns, only to be forced to pull back, dragging their wounded to safety. The determination of the NVA was evidenced by what the paratroopers discovered in a clump of trees near the center of Hill 937; there were eight dead NVA soldiers, four of them tied or chained to trees to keep them from fleeing the battlefield, and all of them wearing shirt patches with the words "Kill Americans."

Although the heavily fortified Hill 937 was of little strategic value, it had been captured by a frontal infantry assault only to be abandoned soon thereafter. This action resulted in an outrage, both in the American military and in public opinion. In any other war, the battle of Hamburger Hill would have been hailed as a great victory despite heavy casualties: 70 killed and 372 wounded, including two of four company commanders and eight of twelve platoon leaders. Over 630 enemy bodies were found and a heavily defended stronghold had been taken.

On June 5, 1969, the 101st quit Hamburger Hill, allowing the NVA to return. President Nixon ordered Gen. Abrams to cease offensive operations in NVA controlled territory, accelerating the process of Vietnamization to allow U.S. troops to withdraw. The United States involvement in Vietnam was coming to a close. The 3rd Brigade of the 82nd Airborne Division was going home to Ft. Bragg, North Carolina accompanied by those with ten or more months in-country.

I was among those with less than ten months in-country, so I was reassigned to the 101st Airborne Division, 3rd Brigade, 3/187th Infantry Battalion. Five months earlier this battered battalion had been pulled off Hamburger Hill and relocated to the Phong Dien District, which lay along Highway One. This enabled the battalion to get much needed rest and recover from wounds sustained on Hamburger Hill.

To provide historical context, it's important to note that in the mid-'60s, NVA regulars and the main force Viet Cong began making their presence felt in the Phong Dien District by demands for increased taxes. Residents had to pay two taxes, one to the government and one to the VC. When our battalion (3/187) arrived, civilian resettlement was made even more difficult by the presence of hundreds of mines and booby traps that had been planted during the Tet Offensive. Upon assuming command of Company-B, the specific missions assigned to the battalion were threefold: 1) Pacification of the area by rooting out local Viet Cong infrastructure, 2) Upgrade local territorial forces so they could assume their own defense, and 3) Clear mines and booby traps from the resettlement area (the primary mission).

Upon assuming command of B-3/187 in late November 1969, it didn't take me long to realize that morale had plummeted to an all-time low following the debacle of Hamburger Hill. There were still several survivors of the battle remaining in the company who felt they and their deceased buddies had been needlessly sacrificed by the battalion commander, Lt. Col. Weldon Honeycutt, whose repeated demands to take Hill 937 became the focus of the men's discontent. The soldiers bitterly complained, "If that son-of-a-bitch wanted to take that mountain so bad, why didn't he do it himself?" Although B-3/187 survivors of Hamburger Hill were thankful to be far removed from Hill 937, they were not overjoyed with the task of clearing mines and booby traps from the resettlement area near the Street Without Joy.[37] They thought the South Vietnamese Army (ARVN) and local defense forces should be tasked with this mission. With this as a backdrop, B-3/187, augmented with platoon/company size ARVN and local defense force units, would begin the dangerous and arduous task of clearing mines and booby traps from the resettlement area.

On February 19, 1970, B-3/187 along with another rifle company was assigned the mission of conducting a Cordon and Search of one of the larger villages in the Phong Dien district. Ordinarily, this was considered a routine mission; however, B-Company would be required to move during darkness through an area that had not been cleared and swept for IEDs.[38] During the operations briefing, I voiced my concern regarding this and was advised that visibility would be good due to a full moon and that the route of march would be in an easterly direction for about four kilometers through mostly open terrain to our sector of the village cordon in the coastal lowlands.

I issued an OPORD (Operations Order) to the platoon leaders, who in turn briefed their men. Needless to say, they were not overly anxious to take on this mission, especially since all our troopers had witnessed buddies killed and several maimed for life from IEDs. Shortly after midnight we moved out in one single file advancing toward the village/hamlet objective. I figured one single file would minimize our chances of simultaneous detonation of more than one IED. We moved slowly toward the objective while being ever vigilant and cautious. Although the moon was bright, it didn't afford the same visibility as natural sunlight.

I'd allocated six hours to arrive at the objective and position the troops in their sector of the cordon perimeter. We were about halfway to the

---

[37] Street Without Joy (in French, La Rue Sans Joie), was what French troops in the First Indochina War called the stretch of Route 1 from Hue to Quang Tri. During the Vietnam War, it became an NVA stronghold.

[38] An IED or improvised explosive device is a bomb constructed and deployed in ways other than in conventional warfare.

objective when a loud explosion interrupted the early morning stillness. We all knew that someone had detonated an IED and that it wasn't a toe-popper or fragmentation grenade. Word was passed up the column that Sgt. Larry Harrison had stepped on a pressure device that probably detonated a 105mm or 155mm artillery round. We immediately requested a Dust-Off chopper while our medics initiated emergency life-saving measures as well as pain medications. When the evacuation helicopter arrived, Sgt. Larry Harrison was placed gently aboard the aircraft; he'd died minutes before its arrival. Three weeks earlier, Larry had celebrated his twenty-first birthday and shortly thereafter learned he'd become a first-time father. His death was not unlike the deaths of thousands of others who would become IED casualties, but it was especially heartbreaking to each of us in B-3/187. Larry was well-respected by all and was among the best squad leaders in the company.

I was summoned to report to the battalion commander, Lt. Col. Herbert Y. Schandler. He informed me that we'd been ten minutes late in securing our portion of the cordon, which may have enabled some of the enemy to escape and avoid apprehension. I replied that we were lucky to have avoided more casualties considering that we were moving during hours of reduced visibility through unfamiliar terrain that had not been previously swept for mines and booby traps. The colonel was not happy with me and I was not happy with him.

CHAPTER 18

God created war so that Americans would learn geography.

Mark Twain

GRINS AND GUFFAWS

1st Cavalry Patch

There was always friendly banter about the various units in Vietnam. I (Lt. Stein) remember Phil Mayer asking if I knew what the 1st Cavalry Patch[39] represented. I said, "No, I don't." Phil replied, "It's for the line you wouldn't cross, the horse you couldn't ride, and the color speaks for itself."

101st Airborne Division Motto

The motto of the 101st Airborne Division is *Rendezvous with Destiny*, although some say it's *Homeless People with Guns*, and others claim it's *Screaming Chickens* (versus the 101st's official nickname *Screaming Eagles*). And, of course, we can't forget the 82nd All-American Airborne Division, which is affectionately called "Alcoholics Anonymous" by all who know them.

Target Practice

I remember Herman Dunklebarger, whose Army recognition included being the top pistol marksman in the 82nd Airborne Division, challenging me to a marksman competition in which a beer can was placed on top of a 55-gallon drum about thirty-five yards away. Troopers from the 4th Platoon gathered to see the tournament. As they prepared to fire, Herman said, "Listen, lieutenant, you can shoot at the large drum. My target will be the beer can."

The M1911 .45 caliber pistol held seven cartridges in its magazine and was liked by the Army for its killing power. (Incidentally, Bob Johnston

---

[39] The patch is yellow, has a diagonal line across it, and includes an image of a horse's head on the top section.

was the only member of our platoon to actually kill an enemy with his .45.) I remember seeing Herman holding out his arm with the pistol on its side parallel to the ground, and watching in amazement as he slowly turned the pistol vertically to aim at the target. Herman hit seven different beer cans; I hit the large drum just six times, causing riotous laughter from the assembled men.

Murphy's Briefing

The brigadier general of the First Air Cavalry Division called a leadership briefing to review the An Khe base's defensive plan in response to G-2 (intelligence) indicating an attack sometime in the next week by several NVA regiments operating in the Central Highlands. As usual, all of the division's fighting battalions were far afield on combat missions. A single division battalion was always stationed at An Khe and tasked with the base defense. Every battalion of the division would be rotated into this cushy defense mission for a month. While there, in addition to defending the immense 1st Cavalry's base and airfields, the battalion would also receive new replacements, conduct additional training, and approve as many soldier's R&Rs as possible.

The five thousand to six thousand soldiers garrisoned at An Khe represented G1-Personnel, G2-Intelligence and Security, G3-Operations, G4-Logistics, and G5-Civil and Military Cooperation. There were also cooks, water support teams, mechanics, aviation crews, plumbers, radar and electronic technicians, signal (communications) operators, vehicle mechanics, supply parts teams, ammunition, rocket and bomb handlers, hospital/medical staff, Psy Ops specialists, military police, chaplains, and many other support groups. Senior officers represented each of these groups at the 1400 hours leadership briefing.

Our Long Range Patrol Company had forty-five Rangers scheduled to be on stand-down in An Khe for another three days. Maj. Malone would have represented our company at the leadership briefing, but he was flying to Ban Me Thuot to coordinate our next thirty-day mission. Interestingly enough, he selected Sgt. E5 Regis Murphy to take his place at the briefing. I am only guessing, but perhaps Malone chose Sgt. Murphy over his operations captain, a platoon leader, or senior NCOs to put a humorous stick into senior leadership.

Having just returned to camp from a patrol, Murphy strode past the two M.P.s who were guarding the door to the general's briefing room. The guards looked at the dusty sergeant (who needed a haircut and a shave), but said nothing. "Murph" selected a chair at the back table and then watched the room fill with colonels, lieutenant colonels, a couple of majors, and three sergeant majors.

A large map of An Khe was displayed on a raised platform in the front of the room. It showed unit designations indicating what sector of the perimeter the soldiers were to defend. After the general finished outlining responsibilities for the entire perimeter, he began to outline a plan should the defensive line be breached.

Murphy raised his hand, said he was from the Long Range Patrol Company along with forty-five Rangers, and asked, "Where do you want *us*, Sir?" The general turned and looked at Sgt. Murphy, who was sitting with all the colonels and senior officers. He paused and then said, "If the enemy's pouring through our lines, you tell your forty-five Rangers to surround me!" The room erupted in laughter. Obviously, the general had a great sense of humor. He told Murphy the Rangers would be An Khe's Quick Reaction Force and would be sent to close any breach in the lines.

Lt. Stein Remembers Recondo School

My 4th Platoon had just been organized and we were going through the Special Forces Recondo School in Nha Trang. The school cadre announced a walk scheduled to take place at first light. At 0500 we assembled and the Special Forces major gave us a brief orientation. He said we'd be going on a ninety-minute walk and that the rules were quite simple. "You need to keep within twenty meters of the pace leader, but cannot pass him." We looked at each other and tried not to snicker. Within our total platoon you'd be hard pressed to find more than six ounces of fat. A walk? A walk? We were in superb condition and incredibly fit. Certainly for us this would be just a walk in the park.

A Special Forces sergeant from Australia was introduced as the walk leader He looked cool with the brim of his hat flipped up on its side; he was wearing shorts and walking shoes. Our platoon was dressed in camouflage fatigues and combat boots. A major who was commanding Recondo training asked me, "Are your men ready?" I replied, "Yes, Sir."

The Aussie was out the front gate in a flash. (We later found out he was on their Olympic race-walking team.) We went a little over ten kilometers and it was torture the entire way. We had to jog and speed walk to keep up, but we couldn't run to pass the sergeant. When our group finished the walk, not a snicker was heard from our platoon.

Team 4-3 and the Monkey Attack

It was a typical night halt for Team 4-3; they were in thick brush with limited line-of-sight, but with enough trees to tape their Claymores on for 360-degree security. Team leader Ray Bohrer, Tom Workman (alternate team leader), Darryl Presley (RTO), Gary Stewart (rear security), and Richard Gosnell (point) settled in for the night. Ray recalls the team's experience:

That night seemed a little darker than usual. A light misty rain fell, but all was quiet and we were back-to-back in a 360-degree defensive circle, or "rucksack to rucksack." We would pass the PRC-25 radio handset around at the end of each watch (usually every hour) although some team members stayed up longer. I was more tired than usual, as we had humped some good-sized hills that day. Sometime around 0200 hours Tom (Workman) woke me by nudging me with his elbow and whispering, "Bo." (Tom usually called me Bo because he didn't remember my last name.). I lowered my poncho liner and looked at him. He said, "I hear a snake." We both listened carefully—then I heard rustling in the near brush that sounded like individual footsteps and whispered, "Tom, snakes don't walk." I was about to alert the rest of the team when a monkey appeared, screeched at Tom, and ran up a nearby tree. After muffled laughs, we settled down.

Tom, however, wasn't amused. He handed me the handset and said, "You've got watch." Tom had his M-16 on full auto while covering himself with his poncho liner and leaning back against his ruck. Not much more than fifteen minutes later, the monkey, who had a "thing" for Tom, came screaming down from the tree above and landed square on his stomach. Tom had his weapon against his chest and came out firing on full auto, catching his poncho liner on fire, and waking the rest of the team. The guys instinctively punched their Claymores, thinking we were under attack, and began firing their weapons in a defensive manner.

At that point I was laughing so hard! Tom was cussing and stomping out his poncho liner fire. The rest of the team were trying to figure out what had just happened. The explosions of Claymores and automatic fire echoed throughout the dark valley, causing the radio relay (X-ray) to call area teams to find out what was happening. I called in this message: "4-3 monkey attack."

An Up-Close Encounter

Steve Woodson recalls a patrol launched in April 1968 from our base camp in Ban Me Thuot. The team included Jim Brokaw (team leader), Oscar Caraway (assistant team leader), Richard McKenzie (slack), Jim Higgins (RTO), Jerry Shankle (rifleman), and me, Steve Woodson (point).

We flew northwest to a Special Forces Camp and I remember it seemed like a long flight. Upon arrival, a Special Forces officer gave us our patrol orders. Along the border of Vietnam and Cambodia, there were hills believed to be used as enemy bivouac areas. We were there to search them out. As we flew west from the Special Forces Camp, the vegetation was grass for as far as we could see. Occasionally a wavy treeline would appear, and we knew that it was a near a stream flowing west to east.

We heard the pilot say our objective was ahead. To the west forested hilltops came into view, but most of them weren't very big and they gave me the impression of islands in a sea of grass. When I found out this was where we were going, I became a little concerned about getting out of the chopper without being seen. The only place we could jump out was into the grass where anyone could see us go in. When we did jump on the south end of a long hill, we disappeared into elephant grass over our heads. Even

Jim Brokaw, who's about six feet tall, was hidden. Down came our sleeves and on went our gloves to protect us from the sharp grasses.

We started going west and then turned north, so we eventually came to the north end of the hill where we left the grass and went into the trees. They were tall and the canopy was thick, blocking out the sun. I had an eerie feeling as we left the grass. It wasn't fear—it was a feeling of going into a different world. The canopy was so thick that very little grew beneath it. Some vines climbed the trees and a few saplings were scattered around. To our left (east) was a cut in the top of the hill running north to south with some brush in it, but for the most part the hilltop was fairly open under the trees. A faint path ran the length of the hill, but the ground was covered with leaves, inches thick in places. If this area had been used as an enemy camp, apparently it hadn't been used recently. It was late in the day when we arrived and we needed to find a good place for our night halt; we couldn't.

There just wasn't any cover where we were; night was approaching and the tall, thick canopy made it get dark fast. We found two large trees, just off the trail, with three smaller trees between and behind them. This was going to be our night position. We lined up five across with Higgins at our feet. We had the three small trees behind us, but there was nothing covering Higgins.

Brokaw, on my left, took the first watch. When he woke me for my watch, it was so dark I could only see the two guys next to me. The only break in the darkness was a faint bit of light some distance out to our front, so I suppose the moon was out. I remember all this detail because of what happened later.

I woke McKenzie for his watch and then lay down to sleep. Very soon, Mac was waking me up. He told me he'd heard something walking around to our front. We sat and listened, but heard nothing. After a while, I decided to lie down again and told Mac to wake me if he heard anything else. I had just lain down when he was poking me. Something had just walked up to Higgins and then walked away.

I whispered, "What did you see?"

Higgins replied, "I can't see much, but I heard something in the leaves."

I figured it was only some small animal, so I was lying back and watching out to the front when Higgins said, "Something's behind you standing beside Brokaw."

I turned my head to look up and saw a dark form. As dark as the night was, the form was even darker and it seemed to be right next to me. Although it was very big, I knew it wasn't a man. Being left-handed, I had to turn completely around to bring my CAR-15 on target, but by that time it was gone. Brokaw was already awake and we awoke the other guys.

Suddenly from behind us came a deep, deep roar and we knew it was a tiger. Hearing another roar and then another, we watched as he began to circle around us. His circling got bigger and bigger until he passed through the faint bit of light to our front. All we could see was a big, dark form but that was enough. We were almost to the point of not knowing what to do—we didn't want to fire if we didn't have to. Giving away our precarious position and killing this beautiful animal weren't good options. Then we heard, off in the distance, some wild cattle lowing. As suddenly as the roaring started, it stopped and we heard the tiger take off in the direction of the cattle. We didn't sleep anymore that night—too much adrenalin, I'm sure.

The next morning, we learned the rest of the story. At one point, Oscar awoke and was looking directly into the tiger's face, but he checked his fire hoping the tiger would go on its way. Brokaw said he woke up and the tiger was so close to him it was standing over his M-16. Jim wore a shoulder holster with a .38 revolver. He took the pistol out and pointed it straight up at the tiger's neck, but the tiger quickly walked away. Higgins was very lucky. The tiger could have easily grabbed him without even being seen.

Since we were so far out in the jungle, we were using a radio relay via a small plane so we had to wait until dawn to call in the incident. When we did, we got a message back that if we encountered the tiger again to shoot it because Westmoreland wanted a tiger skin (true or not). We radioed back the following, "If he wants a tiger skin he can shoot his own fucking tiger." None of us wanted to kill him. We were guests in his home.

Nevertheless, all the next day, as we continued to patrol the other half of the hill, I kept in the back of my mind, the tiger lunging out of the bushes at me. After another day my thoughts were back where they should have been and we continued our patrol. One of the best things about being in a Long Range Patrol team was that, since there were so few of us men, the animals would come out and "do their thing" while we sat quietly observing. This was so different from being in a rifle platoon in the 101st and it was, in comparison, very cool.

An Early Transfer

John Wisheart was on a patrol pulling point, followed by Lou Hansen at slack (no one seems to know where the term slack originated, only that it means the second soldier in line behind point); the group was rounded out by team leader Bob Johnston and RTO Del Ayers with rear security covered by assistant team leader Oscar Caraway. This mission was a reconnaissance of the western border of Vietnam that was marked by a river. Their insertion was unopposed and it was hot and humid at dawn on the second day; they were finding only well-used human trails, probably NVA. They came to a substantial river, a tributary of the Mekong,[40] delineating the border between Vietnam and Cambodia.

As the team walked along the low river bank, they spotted five dugout canoes sunk upside down beneath crystal clear water and attached to the shoreline by yellow ropes. Nearby were several paddles with "U.S. Navy" etched on the handles. Team 4-4 wondered where the small paddles could have originated. Team leader Bob Johnston wanted to check out what was going on in Cambodia (even though it was outside his AO) with the team using one of the canoes as their transport. His men weren't as enthusiastic about the plan, but the decision was made. They cut the lines and then pushed and sank all but one canoe into the deeper waters of the Mekong. They taped rocks to the extra paddles and threw them into the river, as well. Then Team 4-4 lifted the last canoe off the bottom of the river and turned it over; its buoyancy carried it to the surface.

---

[40] The Mekong begins in the mountains of Tibet and is the world's twelfth-longest river. The English name, Mekong River, comes from the Thai and Lao languages and means "the mother of waters." The river flows through China, Burma, Laos, Thailand, and Cambodia, exiting Vietnam via the Mekong Delta and into the South China Sea.

The dugout canoe was made from a large log with space for occupants obviously chopped and dug out with hand tools. The canoe probably could accommodate eight Vietnamese, but was a tight fit for the five heavily-laden American soldiers. Lou Hansen was the only team member not able to swim, and of course, there were no life preservers.

The canoe began sinking in the middle of the river frightening the entire team. As it slowly sank into the Mekong, Lou was thrashing wildly and thinking his end was near when Bob yelled, "Lou, just stand up!" The entire team was laughing so hard Johnston had to remind them to cut their noise. Fortunately for Lou (and perhaps the entire team) it was January, and since Vietnam has only one rainy season from May through September, the river was only about four feet deep!

The men continued their recon patrolling south along the river bank. John Wisheart remembers seeing an immense bolder in the middle of the river with two snakes sunning on it. One looked like an extremely long, large boa constrictor and the second snake was small and multicolored. No one wanted to find out if it was poisonous!

In Cambodia the team found nothing of note. Lt. Stein, riding behind Capt. Don Williams (Pterodactyl 22), flew overhead and requested a location check. Johnston signaled with a mirror (mirror flashes have the advantage of pinpointing the team's exact position without the enemy seeing any smoke signals) to the O-1 Bird Dog and Stein asked, "Do you know where you are?"

Johnston replied, "Affirmative."

The lieutenant ordered, "Get back to your AO now!"

Johnston answered, "Roger that."

The United States government and military had issued orders that Cambodia was neutral territory and no American Forces were authorized to be there.

Six weeks later, Wisheart was recovering from several enemy gunshot wounds that shattered his tibia and fibula, and since the human leg has only four bones, he was in bad shape. The hospital staff asked who they should notify and John replied, "My brother Carl, who's with the 3rd Battalion, D Battery, 319th Artillery near Bien Hoa supporting the 173rd Airborne Brigade Combat Team."

Carl Wisheart received a three-day pass to visit his wounded brother, John, at Cam Ranh Bay, but when he arrived he was told John was sent to Camp Zama in Japan. The Army gave Carl a seven-day pass to go to Japan, but when he arrived he discovered John had been sent to the U.S. Army Hospital at Ft. Devens, Massachusetts (where he would spend the next eight-and-a-half months convalescing). The Army gave Carl a thirty-day pass to visit John in Ft. Devens, where they finally connected. At the end of thirty days, Carl reported to Oakland, California for transport back to Vietnam and was told he was "too short" to return. He spent most of his brief remaining tour driving ladies from the Women's Army Corps around Oakland. Carl never thanked John for his early transfer from duty in Vietnam.

Frank's Night At The Club

According to Lt. Phil Mayer, Frank was quite a guy. Shortly after E-20th's activation, one of the patrol platoons acquired an adult male baboon from a Montagnard. The baboon soon became our unofficial mascot and was named Frank after the company's first sergeant, Frank Moore. Frank the Baboon had apparently been mistreated in his formative years and would frequently resort to aggressive and vicious behavior (e.g. unprovoked biting). The meaner Frank became, the more the troops liked him. They would encourage him to be more aggressive by pitting him against stray dogs. Frank never lost a fight and would be rewarded treats for his aggressive behavior.

One day Maj. Malone suggested to Lt. Jerry Ramsey, Communications Officer, and me (Lt. Phil Mayer) that we join him after dinner at the Officers' Club, which was adjacent to the 4th Division Commanding General's Mess (dining facility). Jerry and I took that invitation as an order. Maj. Malone didn't socialize all that much and, at the time, we were the only two officers at Camp Enari, our company's rear area.

Upon arriving at the Officers' Club, we immediately noticed that the major was in a jovial and relaxed mood. (In retrospect, I realize it was because he would be getting an infantry battalion upon his promotion to lieutenant colonel in the near future.) As the evening progressed, we ordered more rounds of drinks, ate popcorn, and shelled peanuts. Later in the evening Frank became the topic of discussion. I jokingly said, "I wonder how the division staff would react if we brought Frank to the club." Maj. Malone laughed and said, "Let's find out."

One of us called the charge of quarters (CQ) and had him arrange to have Frank driven to the club. The baboon arrived riding on the front hood of the Jeep and holding onto the windshield! The driver brought Frank into the club. He was sporting a collar and leash and someone had dressed him in a small jungle fatigue blouse with first sergeant insignia. After securing Frank's leash, he jumped on a chair and dove into the popcorn and peanuts. He began devouring the peanuts, shells and all.

By that time the club was filling up with staff officers in starched jungle fatigues and shined boots; they appeared to be only mildly amused by Frank. They were more interested in looking at and flirting with the female nurses and the Red Cross Donut Dollies.[41] Someone came over to our table and offered Frank a drink, which he immediately grabbed and gulped down in one swig. More drinks arrived and Frank obliged all who offered them. It wasn't long before we noticed he was becoming intoxicated. When anyone with a tray of drinks came near, Frank would lunge and try to snatch one.

We decided it was time to get Frank back to the company area. While waiting for the Jeep and driver to pick up Frank, he jerked his leash loose from the table and started jumping from one table to another, grabbing peanuts and knocking over drinks. The division staff along with the nurses and Red Cross Dollies vacated their chairs and began hugging the walls. Some chose to leave and those who stayed had a look of disbelief and horror on their faces. The women appeared to be in a state of shock.

We couldn't believe what was happening and hoped Frank wouldn't go on a biting rampage. At that moment, he emitted the most god-awful gaseous smell, which rapidly turned into diarrhea. He jumped onto the bar and began guzzling down leftover drinks while continuing to squirt diarrhea.

---

[41] Young women, recent college graduates, hired by the Red Cross to provide audience-participation recreation and games for servicemen stationed in isolated parts of Vietnam.

Someone summoned the club officer, a panic-stricken lieutenant, who announced the club would be closing. Thankfully, the driver arrived and he and the Vietnamese club staff were able to corral Frank, drag him out to the Jeep, and return him to our company area. I don't think any of us ever went back to that Officers' Club.

A week later, Capt. Perkins, our operations officer, and some troops were giving Frank treats and enjoying his company. Without any warning or provocation, Frank suddenly bit the captain's hand. One of Frank's giant incisors was sticking out the other side of Perkins' hand! Frank would *not* let go of him. Everyone (except the captain) was laughing hysterically. Someone began hitting Frank to make him let go, but he would not. His jaw was firm! At last, someone dazed Frank with a rifle butt and Capt. Perkins was rushed to the aid station.

CHAPTER 19

No duty is more urgent than that of returning thanks.

Author unknown

WHY THIS BOOK?

I began keeping a Vietnam diary forty-nine years ago, but never read any of my lengthy notes until I responded to a call for an E-Company Long Range Patrol reunion. In eager anticipation of renewing distant but strangely close relationships, I finally read the diary that recorded my platoon's combat experiences.

I knew when the 4th Platoon was being organized in late 1967 that these forty-four men possessed an inner confidence in their abilities and in their new mission. In addition, they were developing a bond and commitment to their five patrol teammates. Almost all the enlisted men were paratroopers from the 101st Airborne Division, most with three to six months of combat experience, and some with years of fighting mainline NVA troops in I Corps.

These airborne soldiers were given the opportunity to volunteer once again for what was expected to be very dangerous assignments. The company commander and visionary for the Long Range Patrol concept, Maj. Dandridge Malone (it's unusual for a field grade officer to be a company commander), or Capt. David B. Tucker, the executive officer, interviewed each "re-volunteer." Sadly, Capt. Tucker was our company's first casualty; he was killed while flying to a 101st Division fire base near Chu Lai on October 1, 1967. Rumors suggested Tucker was on a fast track by the Army for a general's star. Tucker came to our LRP/Rangers from Alpha Company, 2nd Battalion, 7th Cavalry, 1st Airmobile Division.

Capt. Tucker's father was Col. Reuben Tucker, Commander of the 504th Parachute Regiment in WWII. He was awarded two Distinguished Service Crosses, the Army's second highest award for wartime heroism. President Franklin Roosevelt presented one of the awards to him in honor of what happened on September 13, 1943. Col. Tucker led the 504th Parachute Infantry Regiment as they parachuted into Sicily, near Salerno,

Italy, and attacked the Germans who had launched a counterattack against the American amphibious forces that had earlier landed on the beaches. As the Germans attacked, the 504th was short one full battalion. The American commander of the Sixth Corps suggested that the unit withdraw. In response to that, one of the most notable rally cries of WWII was uttered by an undeniably heroic Col. Tucker, "Retreat, hell, send me my other battalion."

His son, Capt. Bruce Tucker, was in a Huey helicopter in Vietnam when he was shot by a 12.7 x 108mm round fired from a Russian heavy machine gun (the equivalent of the U.S. .50 caliber machine gun and slightly more powerful). The captain was the only passenger injured in the chopper. He was completing interviews and troop selection for E-Company LRP. Tucker was serving as company commander of the First Cavalry Division's Long Range Reconnaissance Patrol Company when he joined E-Company Long Range Patrol as executive officer.

Capt. Tucker was wounded through his neck and the helicopter was shot from the sky with engine failure. Only a masterly autorotation by the pilots enabled the helicopter to avoid a crash. The pilots and crew placed a bandage on the captain's neck and formed a perimeter around the chopper awaiting the Dust-Off chopper and an infantry platoon to rescue them. Unfortunately, Capt. Tucker, a very good soldier and by all accounts a great man, bled to death before medical help arrived.

As you would imagine, reuniting with my platoon at our reunion in October 2008 brought back many memories, some as crisp as that morning's. Several platoon members asked if I would write a book about their year-long life-changing experience. I had always felt a great sense of guilt about not recognizing my platoon members with adequate Army commendations for their extraordinary, and indeed, daily valor in the most desperate circumstances. Recognition is very important. Napoleon said, "A soldier will fight long and hard for a bit of colored ribbon." Partially to document and establish the historical record, and selfishly to come clean with my conscience, I have tried to tell their stories and honor these brave men.

One mission illustrates my point. Team 4-7 (our platoon had seven six-man patrols which were designated 4-1 through 4-7) was discovered by the

NVA so the team called for extraction by our helicopters and gunships, the only method of returning to base camp safely. This patrol's area of operations was twenty miles from any friendly forces. Helicopters arrived on-station, and with colored smoke grenades and a compass azimuth reading from the team, I vectored the patrol to a suitable landing zone. At the same time, our gunships noted the enemy's last known position and began strafing runs. The six-man patrol ran to the landing zone, hopped aboard the chopper and, with the exception of their after-action report, their mission was complete.

During the exchange of rifle fire with the NVA, Sgt. Regis Murphy was shot in the chest, but was still conscious during the helicopter ride back to base. My diary for April 12, 1968 reads, "We put 4-7 in and they quickly made contact. Sgt. Murphy was wounded. We got them out and the gunships expended their rockets and machine gun rounds; we dropped Sgt. Murphy off at the Pleiku hospital." Murphy went into the hospital by himself, was admitted and treated for two days. He had been shot, but the 7.62 x 39mm AK-47 Soviet cartridge impacted initially on his binoculars and then directly on his compass. Sgt. Murphy had fragments of the compass and the tip of the bullet lodged in his body. After release from the hospital, Murphy found his own transportation back to our base camp via a South Vietnamese commercial bus, and one day later rejoined Team 4-7 for another mission.[42]

These five- or six-man patrols would be on missions ten to forty-five miles from any friendly forces normally outside of artillery fans; they were sometimes not even in Vietnam. The patrols were always outnumbered and operating in a territory familiar and comfortable to the NVA/Viet Cong, but not to them. At times, because of the low mountains or weather, they were without any communications with U.S. forces. Fixed wing O-1 airplanes, helicopters, and mountaintop stations sometimes were available for relay transmissions, but not always. Long Range Patrol reconnaissance soldiers (plus Special Forces and helicopter pilots) had bounties on their heads, formally put there by the North Vietnamese army. When a mission

---

[42] Regrettably, no one thanked Murphy or visited him at the hospital, and no one ever prepared the paperwork for an unquestionably deserved Purple Heart.

was completed, three to nine days later, these teams were reinserted and new missions were ordered.

Perhaps now it's clear how I would answer the question, "Why did I write this book?" The least I owe these American heroes is recognition of their talent and courage. During the war, I was busy with ongoing operations: inserting teams, coordinating patrol extractions, flying O-1 VRs (visual reconnaissance) that identified landing zones for future patrols, and performing many other critical tasks Thinking back, I realize that I could have—and definitely should have—made the time to recognize the men, but I didn't.

Major units had a formal Awards and Decorations department within their Adjutant General's staff to recognize valor and gallantry in action. However, our Long Range Patrol Company was unique since our orders and missions came directly from the II Corps Commander, 3-Star Lt. Gen. Rossen (and sometimes even 4-Star Gen. Westmoreland). Our platoon was assigned to the 4th Infantry Division for pay, rations, and quarters, but did not have access to their Awards and Decorations department. We were at a real disadvantage since actions for commendations needed to be witnessed by an officer and, of course, most of the time no officers accompanied the teams. Later in the war, this restriction was lifted, but that didn't help the 4th Platoon.

Even when I wrote commendations for valor, I received no guidance as to what award was appropriate. The process, as I remember, was this: an OIC (officer in command) submitted an initiation of award to the company battalion, brigade, and commanding general for final approval depending on the level of award. Silver Stars, Bronze Stars, and ARCOM (Army Commendation) service awards were usually approved as recommended. The Medal of Honor always went to the Department of Defense for final approval or downgrade. If I could have a do-over, I'd recommend a Bronze Star with "V" device (a letter on the award that designates combat valor) for every man who went on patrol, and I would recommend higher awards for many others.

Captured NVA prisoner Corp. Quang (2nd Company, 7th Battalion, 18th NVA Regiment) assisted American troops in the battle of Vien Thien (3).

One of 101 confirmed dead NVA soldiers after the battle of Vien Thien (3); perhaps he was one of the enemy shouting, "Americans you die tonight."

Lt. Stein on the morning after the battle of Vien Thien (3), June 21st, 1967. Stein served in the 1st Cavalry Division, Bravo Company - 1/5.

An AK47 recovered from the battle of Vien Thien (3).

Edgar L. McWethy, Jr. - Battle of Vien Thien (3), June 21st, 1967
Congressional Medal of Honor awarded posthumously.

Carmel Bernon Harvey, Jr. - Battle of Vien Thien (3), June 21st, 1967
Congressional Medal of Honor awarded posthumously.

The Medal of Honor is the highest military decoration presented by the United States government to a member of its armed forces. The recipient must have distinguished himself at the risk of his own life above and beyond the call of duty in action against an enemy of the United States. Harvey and McWethy served in the 1st Cavalry Division, Bravo Company - 1/5.

One of our battalion's six 105mm artillery guns which supported Bravo Company - 1/5 during the battle of Vien Thien (3).

Sgt. Ray Clark, 2nd Platoon on patrol.

The word was out, "Don't make our 1st Sgt. Frank Moore unhappy." Moore is in the Ranger Hall of Fame.

A WWII Air Force C-47. 1st Sgt. Frank Moore requested two 3-day passes from Maj. Malone and traded captured AK-47s for seats on this plane. He and Lt. Stein headed to Hong Kong.

LRP soldiers, camoed up and motionless, are practically invisible in the jungle.

Battle-weary soldiers, Larry Clark and George Carter, exhibit the "thousand-yard stare."

Larry Clark of Team 4-5 at a 4th Infantry Division fire base.

3rd Platoon Leader Lt. Gerald Koch transports soldiers to the flight line for a patrol mission.

Ron Causey and Team Leader James Clay. Both participated in the 4th Platoon's night combat jump.

An Khe: A helicopter which had been shot down was used to practice rapid loading and unloading.

An Khe: Training to rappel while carrying a wounded buddy.

Ron Causey and Bob "Balls of Steel" Shaffer

Team 4-1: Steve Woodson (front left), John Higgins and Paul Kuebler, Jerry Shankle (back left), Jim Brokaw and Henry Swift

A 4th Platoon training jump.

A 4th Platoon soldier practices rappelling from a helicopter at Recondo School.

Major Malone (carrying his British Sten gun) prepares to join one of his twenty-eight patrol teams.

Sam Pullara, E-Company's admin, prepared the paperwork authorizing the formation of the Long Range Patrol Company.

SFC Albright, 2nd Platoon Sergeant, E/20 LRP Airborne

S. Sgt. Charles Samuelson, leader of Team 4-6

A Chinese mine, which had been aimed at soldiers of the 4th Platoon, but failed to explode. A second mine exploded causing minor casualties. Four months prior, the same type of mine killed Sgt. Henshaw and Lt. Greene, both from the 1st Platoon.

Sgts. Charles Samuelson and Regis Murphy with weapons they traded for captured AK-47s.

Lt. Stein with the proverbial "monkey on his back" at Plei do Lim Special Forces camp.

Frank, E-Company's pet baboon, chases a stray dog at camp Enari in the Central Highlands.

Field gear taken from one of two enemy trail-watchers killed by Sgts. Jim Brokaw and Oscar Caraway.

When Oscar Caraway was in the field, he wrote letters to family and friends and kept his correspondence in a cloth bag taken from a dead NVA soldier. Upon returning to a fire base, he'd send the letters. Postage was unnecessary when a soldier wrote "Free" on the envelope.

S. Sgt. Ray Bohrer with an American .30 caliber machine gun, a Chinese AK-47, and a French rifle taken from eleven NVA soldiers killed in an ambush by Team 4-3.

James Worth and Juergen Besecke of Team 4-6 train at the Plei Do Mi Special Forces Camp.

Lt. Jack Daniels replaced Lt. Bob Stein as leader of the 4th Platoon in May, 1968.

Phil Mayer, Honor Graduate of the Army Ranger School, commanded the following units in combat:
Rifle Platoon Leader: 2nd Platoon, 3/8 Infantry, 4th Infantry Division.
Platoon Leader: 2nd Platoon, E-Company (Airborne) Long Range Patrol
Company Commander: Delta Company, 1/508, 3rd Brigade, 82nd Airborne Division
Company Commander: Bravo Company, 3/187th, 3rd Brigade, 101st Airborne Division

Four-Star General Creighton Abrams, left, thanks Bob Johnston for his year of service. Bob Johnston (team leader of Chippergate 4-4) recovered from five gunshot wounds in U.S. hospitals and then returned to Vietnam for a third tour. He was selected to lead General Abrams sixteen-man security team.

General Creighton Abrams, commanding general for all Allied Forces in Vietnam, served under General George Patton in WWII. Abrams led the armored columns that relieved the 101st Airborne Division when they were surrounded by Germans at the Siege of Bastogne in Belgium. Today, America's main battle tank, the M1A1 Abrams, is named for the general.

CHAPTER 20

WHY AMERICA LOST THE WAR

You will kill ten of our men and we will kill one of yours, in the end it will be you who tire of it.

Ho Chi Minh

Television brought the brutality of war into the comfort of the living room. Vietnam was lost in the living rooms of America—not on the battlefields of Vietnam.

Marshall McLuhan

Within the soul of each Vietnam veteran there is probably something that says bad war, good soldier.

Max Cleland

The conventional army loses if it does not win.
The guerilla wins if he does not lose.

Henry Kissinger

I see light at the end of the tunnel.

Walt W. Rostow
United States National Security Advisor
Rostow's comment was made in December 1967;
the Tet Offensive began in January 1968.

Ghost Warriors Weigh In

The 4th Platoon did not realize the Vietnam War could not ... or would not be won. In 1967 our commanding officer, Gen. Westmoreland, had just informed President Lyndon Johnston that the end of the war was in sight, but it would continue for eight more years ending in an embarrassing withdrawal by the United States. It struck most of the men of the 4th Platoon as quite unimaginable that the United States lost the Vietnam War, and over the years each of us wondered how it happened. The U.S. Army won every company-size battle and virtually all platoon-size fights. We could control and hold any terrain of our choosing for as long as we were so inclined. Our nation provided us the best weapons and equipment, excellent ongoing supply support, quality troops and until the end, a belief that the cause for which we fought was just. The contrast between the North Vietnamese soldiers and their counterparts to the South always amazed us. When a skirmish developed between the NVA and American/ARVN (Army of the Republic of Vietnam) troops, the South Vietnamese soldiers frequently would melt away only to reappear back in base camp. Why?

Unlike their southern cousins, the NVA would always press their attack or defense until their drubbing by American forces required a tactical retreat. Why?

The South Vietnamese enjoyed excellent weapons and far more ammunition and supplies than their counterparts to the North. Without American support, the South Vietnamese would lose most of their battles to the warriors from the North. Why?

The South Vietnamese were fighting in their own country. Their families were nearby. The North Vietnamese could be almost a thousand miles from their homes, and would not see their families until the war's end. The NVA still clobbered the ARVN every time Why? Why? Why?

An Attempt at Answering the "Whys"

Sam Pullara, our LRP company admin, has endeavored to answer many questions about the Vietnam War. Sam's thoughts follow:

Interestingly enough the officers of the North Vietnam Army had a question of their own that may help to explain the answer to our *whys* about the war. Their question was: Why did Americans fight with such dedication in a war that would have not personally, or as a country, gained anything even if they had prevailed, and cost them so much in lives and treasure? I will try to answer the former by first answering the latter.

Texas Tech University in Lubbock, Texas, has an entire building and staff dedicated to the study of the Vietnam War. The reason for historians to study this conflict is the obvious fact of its impact on American society, politics, and culture decades ago and the influence it has to this day. Many foreign and domestic issues we are still fighting over stem from that conflict. In an effort to understand that war, Texas Tech has in the past invited combatants from both sides of the Vietnam War to the university to talk about the war from their perspectives. NVA Officers and U.S. soldiers have met and discussed their roles and thoughts during the conflict. The question of why Americans fought so well came up time and again from the Vietnamese.

When I joined the Army in March 1965, Lyndon Johnson was the president and the congressmen were overwhelmingly Democrats. The government had embarked on the Great Society experiment and the Vietnam War was just warming up. My family was, and had been, Republicans since before the Civil War. We opposed the Great Society and thought that control of the Congress by Democrats was a disaster that would lead to certain ruin. My family, myself included, was very political and we discussed such issues all the time. Yet, I enlisted to be a paratrooper and was quite prepared to go to war wherever the country needed me. Would I go to war for the government? No, I would go to war for the country.

For most Americans those are two different things. Governments come and go but the country, its values, its culture, and its basic law remains much the same regardless of who controls the government. The same goes for our military. When Americans take the military oath, we don't swear to support and defend the government; rather, we swear to support and defend the Constitution, which is the basic law and without which the country can't exist. We honor the flag, which is the symbol of that law and the nation created out of it. As a soldier my loyalty was to my country, the flag, and the military and by extension to the men with whom I served. I did not fight for Lyndon Johnson, the Congress, the Supreme Court, or any other part of government. Our government is not the nation, just the temporary keeper of the keys that we can replace, change, or even restructure.

My country was at war; I was a U.S. paratrooper, proud of my Screaming Eagle patch and my fellow paratroopers fighting in Vietnam, and therefore I would fight, too. I couldn't care less, in that context, who were the temporary leaders of our government. The North Vietnamese were fighting for their country, too. They saw the conflict's purpose to unify the north and south again as one nation. In contrast, the South Vietnamese were content with the French government's administration of their country. The North Vietnamese had bristled under that administration and sought total freedom from all colonial powers. In 1956, the United States government canceled a promised election in Vietnam because its leaders knew that Ho Chi Minh would win the election; he had rid the entire country of the French colonialists and was a hero, regardless of government, of both the north and the south. The army of the Republic of South Vietnam in contrast would fight for the government of South Vietnam, which changed all the time and was corrupt. The NVA fought for the ideal of a united Vietnam nation, also supported by many South Vietnamese, just as Americans fight for America and not for the government.

The United States refused to allow the election because it felt the North Vietnamese government would operate under the thumb of Communist China, and all of Southeast Asia would fall under the so-called domino theory. The United States Departments of State and Defense sent President Kennedy a memo stating, "The loss of South Vietnam would make pointless any further discussion about the importance of Southeast Asia to the free world; we would have to face the near certainty that the remainder of Southeast Asia and Indonesia would move to a complete accommodation with Chinese Communism."

The entire U.S. government, including Presidents Kennedy, Johnson, and Nixon, bought into this thinking and launched the tragic Vietnam War that ended with more than 58,000 American names on the Vietnam Veterans Memorial Wall. A history of Vietnam reveals that over centuries Vietnam fought Chinese domination, sometimes successfully, sometimes not, but always they resisted the Chinese. There never was or would be a domino effect. In fact, as recently as 1979 China launched a limited invasion of Vietnam, but the Chinese foray was quickly rebuffed by the very skilled Vietnamese soldiers. Territorial disagreements along the China/Vietnam border and in the East Vietnam Sea, that had remained dormant during the Vietnam War, were revived at the war's end. In addition, a postwar campaign engineered by Hanoi to limit the role of Vietnam's ethnic Chinese community in domestic commerce, elicited a strong protest from Beijing. China also was displeased with Vietnam because of its improving relationship with the Soviet Union.

North Vietnam won the war because their strategy was superior to that of the United States and its Saigon ally. North Vietnamese strategy operated at several levels simultaneously to address both total and limited war objectives. Against the Saigon government, Hanoi's war aims were total. They never relented in their objective of disestablishing South Vietnam as an independent country and unifying the country under a single communist system.

Hanoi's war aims against the United States were comparatively limited. All that was necessary was to compel Washington to withdraw its forces and abandon the Saigon government. Major battlefield victories were not needed to achieve these goals. Hanoi opted for a war of attrition, betting their determination and willingness to sacrifice would endure longer than American patience. They were right. For our soldiers, this is a difficult lesson to understand, and even today just a few cannot accept the Vietnam War outcome. The 4th Platoon didn't understand the strategic aims of the North Vietnamese government. They were focused on staying alive and defeating the enemy they saw in front of them. Most of the men only understood what was happening years after their unappreciated service in Vietnam.

Military Strategy: Search and Destroy

The United States military strategy for victory in the Vietnam War was fairly straightforward; force the Viet Cong and the North Vietnam army into large unit battles and use American superior firepower to destroy them. The tactic used to engage the enemy was termed Search and Destroy. Infantry units would move into our adversary's suspected strongholds, be attacked by NVA forces, and then call in superior firepower to kill as many of the enemy as possible. Victory was determined by body counts. By killing large numbers of the enemy we would force our foes to quit the struggle. Body counts were our measure of victory and progress in the Vietnam War.

Search and Destroy was a very successful tactic in that we were able to engage the enemy and, using our superior firepower, win every large engagement. We never lost a single large unit battle nor most small engagements. There is simply no question that the tactic worked. Unfortunately, the strategy was flawed because the enemy was never going to give up regardless of their losses. Yes, body count was very successful; it was successful for the North Vietnamese, not us. Returning home, Westmoreland was criticized as the general who "won every battle until he lost the war."

There was a cost for Search and Destroy. In order to find the enemy, we exposed our troops to attack. U.S. troops engaging in Search and Destroy missions were essentially bait, so once attacked we would know where the enemy was and could then bring to bear other units, gunships, aircraft, artillery, naval gunfire, and even B-52 bomber strikes on them. The grim reality about being bait is that you end up being hit first with the resultant loss of life. In Vietnam, where ordinary citizens supported both sides, American troops were at a disadvantage when hunting the enemy. We became the hunted and endured unacceptable losses.

Vien Thien (3): Search and Destroy

The following is the author's description of the Battle of Vien Thien (3) in the Binh Dinh Province. It details a typical Search and Destroy mission in which every man of E-Company Long Range Patrol participated multiple times:

This battle in June 1967 took place while I was a platoon leader in the 1st Cavalry Division. Battle deaths were almost exactly as forecasted by U.S. Gen. Westmoreland and North Vietnamese Gen. Vo Nguyen Giap: ten North Vietnamese dead for each American. At the time, this battle was pronounced a victory for the United States. Tactically it was a victory; strategically it continued as an unrecognized losing hand for the United States military and foreshadowed our eventual defeat in 1975.

On June 21 and 22, 1967, B-Company engaged in the battle of Vien Thien (3) in which two troopers of Bravo Company, Carmel Bernon Harvey, Jr. and Edgar Lee McWethy, Jr. were posthumously awarded the Medal of Honor. The battle began on June 19, 1967 when the 41st Army Republic of Vietnam (ARVN) captured an NVA prisoner, Cpl. Quang, in a night ambush. He was a member of the 2nd Company, 7th Battalion, 18th NVA Regiment. During interrogation, Quang seemed bright and willing to talk; he said his battalion was on the ridgeline just west of a small village, Vien Thien (3). The battalion commander, Lt. Col. Daniel S. Rickard from the 1st of the 5th Cavalry ordered his B-Company to air assault from LZ Uplift the next morning to conduct a Search and Destroy mission. The NVA corporal was flown to fire base Uplift the night before and was attached to Lt. Tom Cox's 1st Platoon. The prisoner was told he would be the first to die should our troops be ambushed.

We were at LZ Uplift awaiting our fourteen slicks to arrive and lift us to Vien Thien (3). Half of the company, my 2nd Platoon and Cox's 1st Platoon, were on the initial air assault into a dry rice paddy about one klick (one thousand meters or one kilometer) southwest of the village. My platoon was assigned to use seven Yellow Flight choppers. Fourteen choppers landed simultaneously as the division's 105mm artillery battery (six guns) began firing on the target LZ. I found the Yellow Flight leader who told me only two birds were identified as Yellow Flight. He shouted above the din of the choppers and artillery saying the others "were down for maintenance." I yelled, "What should I do?" The flight leader put the palms of his hands to the sky and shrugged his shoulders. I thought, welcome to war, and told my NCOs to get my platoon on any empty birds.

I was seated between the pilots and could see HE (high explosive) rounds blowing up on the LZ. The last artillery round was white phosphorus signifying the barrage was finished. This was immediately followed by aerial rocket artillery fire delivered by multiple helicopter gunships on the LZ. Door gunners chambered rounds and, as the helicopters flared to briefly touch down, they began firing on any brush or trees that could conceal enemy. The infantry troopers were firing their rifles and machine guns as they were jumping from choppers. Almost instantly there was silence with only the faint crackling of burning brush and undergrowth from fires started by rockets and artillery.

Our initial air assault with half the company was unopposed; thirty minutes later the entire company of 135 men was on the ground. Capt. Edgar J. Findeisen, newly arrived in Vietnam, called his four lieutenants to join him to plan our route into the ridgeline.[43] Bravo Company was preparing to move toward the west ridgeline with an order of march of the 1st, 2nd, and 3rd Platoons followed by the Weapons Platoon, when an OH-13 Sioux Silver team helicopter (a crew of two pilots), observed an armed man in a brown uniform moving from a house in Vien Thien (3) into a bunker. Capt. Findeisen dispatched one squad from the company's Weapons Platoon to apprehend this individual. The NVA prisoner, Cpl. Quang, told us that his battalion of more than two hundred men was in the low hills just west of the village. Since we believed the enemy troops were west of the village, Findeisen sent his 1st Platoon, along with the well-fed NVA corporal plus an attached German Shepherd scout dog and handler, toward the western hills to locate the enemy force. The rest of our company waited for a report on the armed man.

Six U.S. soldiers approached the village over a dry flat rice paddy, not realizing over two hundred NVA troops awaited them. SPC4 Ronald B. Zachery, a surviving member of the doomed squad, later described the scene: "We were all spread out, well-organized, three in front, three in the

---

[43] Shortly thereafter, one of the four lieutenants, Robert Neilan, would be in a field hospital with an AK-47 round through his shoulder, another, Lt. Bob Wagner, would be shot dead, and a third, Lt. Tom Cox, would be shot three times. Half of his platoon would be dead or wounded and two of his soldiers would receive the Medal of Honor. (Neilan, Wagner and Cox had graduated from the same Officer Candidate School class at Fort Benning, Georgia.)

back. Our squad leader, Sgt. Thomas Johnson was in the front line; he received a burst across the chest killing him instantly. Zachery, the next man in charge, was wounded in the back while on his belly trying to avoid the murderous fire. Everyone in the squad was dead or wounded." (The NVA didn't kill them all to prevent air strikes from being called on their positions.)

Capt. Findeisen ordered the 3rd Platoon Leader, Lt. William P. Wagner, to assault from the south and aid the wounded from the Weapons Platoon. Wagner's Platoon got to the southern edge of the village where they reported many fortified enemy positions.[44] Wagner's platoon sergeant, Billy J. Watkins, was shot in the neck by an AK-47 round and later died at the field aid station.

My 2nd Platoon was firing at obvious NVA weapons positions that were mainly directing fire at the 3rd Platoon in the southern tip of Vien Thien (3). I called Lt. Wagner and suggested I swing my thirty-five man platoon north of the village and drive south to squeeze and kill the remaining NVA. Fortunes of war probably saved my life and many others when Wagner said it would be best for me to move south, hook up with his platoon, and assault the village with combined platoons. It prevented masking each other's fire and eliminated crossfire. We didn't realize the enemy's strength, only that both sides wanted to fight on that day and in that place.

After moving my platoon to the south, we started to cross the dry rice paddy without cover to marry up with the 3rd Platoon. I heard on the radio that American armor was on the way to support us, so I called Wagner and asked if he could hold out until the armor, one M-48 tank and two dusters (tracked vehicles armed with twin 40mm cannons and medium machine guns) arrived. Wagner agreed since much of the firing had died down. My platoon waited for the armor.

2nd Lt. Robert J. Neilan, standing a few feet from me and in his first day in the field, was shot through the shoulder with a single round; the Medevac helicopter took rounds, but flew him to the safety of a field

---

[44] Later we learned Quang's entire battalion had moved into the village and were holed-up in pre-prepared rebar (steel mesh reinforced) cement bunkers that were disguised as hooches.

hospital at LZ Uplift.[45] Ironically, I remember thinking (in an oddly detached way), that the NVA soldier who nailed Neilan from nearly a quarter of a mile away, had fired a great shot.

The NVA attacked Lt. Bob Wagner's platoon again and he was shot in the chest.[46] The armor arrived (the tank and two dusters) and acted as a shuttle service moving the dead and wounded to a perimeter one hundred meters south of the village. All Americans were now out of the village and a response by the division was coming. Two additional companies were air assaulted into probable avenues of NVA escape; (Alpha Company, 1st Battalion, 5th Cavalry went to the west and Bravo Company, 2nd Battalion, 5th Cavalry blocked escape routes to the north).

The enemy was fixed in the village of Vien Thien (3). A battalion record was set, as more than 1,240 rockets were fired in a single day into the village from the helicopters of the 20th Artillery, Battery-A. There were as many as six Aerial Rocket Artillery gunships firing at one time. Thirteen tactical air strikes (fifty-two "fast mover" fighter-bombers) rained 500-, 750- and 1000-pound bombs into Vien Thien (3) just ninety-five yards from Bravo Company (three platoons). B-Company's 1st Platoon was still up in the hills to the west. I remember bitching to someone about the 1st Platoon seeing a great air show while we got all of the fight. The skies were deep blue with fluffy white clouds as U.S. fighter-bombers circled overhead waiting their turn to drop ordnance on the village.

The NVA prisoner, Cpl. Quang, was still with the 1st Platoon. Through our interpreter, he said since there was heavy fire coming from the village, his battalion must have moved there. Sometime during the afternoon, Capt. Findeisen ordered me to prepare to assault the village after he received word that the air strikes were over. I would lead with my 2nd Platoon followed by the 3rd; I didn't see the men of the 3rd Platoon having much fight left in them since so many were dead or wounded.

---

[45] Neilan was to be the leader of the 2nd Platoon and I was to be promoted to platoon leader of the Weapons Platoon. Neilan was in the field less than forty minutes having just completed the 1st Cavalry's three-day Vietnam orientation. He completed an excellent Army career and retired as a colonel.

[46] Lt. Wagner died on the operating table.

I was peering into the village to find the best route to minimize casualties during the assault when a guy approached me and asked, "What's your plan?" I turned and saw my 2nd Brigade Commander, Col. Fred E. Karhos, (a full bird colonel). I outlined my plan and the colonel said, "Sounds good, son." Col. Karhos told me he had authorized a CNB gas attack to blanket the village followed immediately by my platoon's assault into the village. Soon two choppers flew by and pushed out gas masks in dusty cardboard boxes. I was told the CS gas to be used was much more powerful than the tear gas used in basic training. This type of gas agent (CNC or CNB) would cause immediate vomiting and prostration and could be lethal. Col. Rickard, the battalion commander, told me to ensure all my men's gas masks fit tightly. At that moment I wished I'd paid more attention to the chemical instruction during my gas basic training at Ft. Leonard Wood, Missouri. Immediately after helicopters finished dispensing the gas, my 2nd Platoon, led by the tank and two dusters and followed by the 3rd Platoon, carefully entered the village with the Weapons Platoon remaining south of Vien Thien (3) to guard our equipment.

Because of the light breeze, the gas soon evaporated and the soldiers were able to remove their masks just as they entered the southwest corner of the village. S. Sgt. Jerry Cook and SPC4 Robert Johnson were walking dual point when Cook heard someone holler, "VC!" He looked to his left and saw an NVA soldier coming out of a hole ten feet away. Cook fired twice at the enemy's head and then his M-16 jammed; he screamed and dived behind a palm tree when the enemy soldier opened up with about ten rounds from his AK-47. SPC4 Johnson saw the enemy fire his rifle at Cook and he opened up. It was Johnson's first time killing a man; hesitating only for an instant, he quickly fired four or five bursts. The enemy fell and the platoon continued through the village.

I picked up the NVA's AK-47 and gave it to Lt. Reilly, the platoon leader of the attached dusters, and asked him to keep it for me, saying, "I'll retrieve it at LZ Uplift."[47] I was behind Cook and Johnson when the AK-47

---

[47] Later, I disassembled the AK-47 as my "illegal" war souvenir. One of my soldiers famously said, "What can they do, send you to jail? You could use the vacation!"

rounds kicked up around me and I hit the ground next to a well. Before we assaulted the village, I told our two platoons to kill or destroy everything we passed so we weren't ambushed from behind. I then popped a grenade and tossed it into the well causing a huge geyser to soak me on a day when temperatures were over 100 degrees.

The two platoons continued through the southern part of the village, killing three more NVA and taking no casualties. We thought the NVA 7th Battalion's back was broken. We were wrong! Gunships from the 1st Squadron, 9th Cavalry noticed a lot of activity down in a stream bed that ran east to west from the village. The NVA soldiers were using the creek for cover and concealment; the enemy was fleeing the bombs, CS gas, and the troops of Bravo Company. Brigade commander Col. Karhos' chopper was on the west side and he saw two gunships make a run along the creek. He heard one gunship pilot, Lt. Campbell, exclaim, "I've got two! ... I've got three! ... I've shot eight! ... Hell, there's twenty or thirty in here. We're killing them all!" At that moment, Campbell's gunship was shot down, crashing just to the west of the village. The Battalion Commander, Lt. Col. Rickard, ordered the 1st Platoon back from the hills to the downed gunship to find survivors. The first platoon found the chopper blown apart and all the crew dead just as the NVA cut loose chopping down everything in sight with machine guns, automatic weapons, hand grenades and sniper fire. PFC Frank Constintino, the platoon leader's RTO, fell with one bullet in him, shot dead in the head. 2nd Lt. Thomas Cox was also shot, but ran to his fallen RTO. Cox was shot again and again. SPC5 Edgar Lee McWethy, Jr., the platoon's medic, rushed across the fire-swept area to his comrades' assistance. Although he could not help Constintino, the mortally wounded radio operator, McWethy's timely first aid enabled Lt. Cox to remain in command during this critical period.

Hearing a call for aid, McWethy started across the open area toward more injured men, was wounded in the head, and knocked to the ground. He courageously got up and continued toward the injured, but was hit again in the leg. Struggling onward despite his wounds, he reached his comrades and treated their injuries. Observing another fallen rifleman lying in an exposed position raked by enemy fire, the brave medic moved toward him without hesitation. Although the enemy fire wounded him a third time, he reached his fallen companion. McWethy was weakened and in extreme pain, but gave the wounded soldier artificial respiration. SPC5 Edgar Lee McWethy, Jr. suffered a fourth and fatal head wound and died on his last patient's chest.[48]

Carmel Bernon Harvey, Jr., SPC4, was a fire team leader. He and two members of his squad were in a position directly in the path of the enemy onslaught and received the brunt of the fire from an enemy machine gun. In short order both of his companions were wounded, but Harvey covered this loss by increasing his deliberate rifle fire at the foe. The enemy machine gun seemed to concentrate on him and the bullets struck the ground all around his position. One round hit and armed a grenade attached to his belt. He quickly tried to remove the grenade but was unsuccessful. Realizing the danger to his wounded comrades if he stayed there, and despite the hail of enemy fire, Harvey jumped to his feet shouting "Fuck you!" and raced toward the deadly machine gun. He nearly reached the enemy position when the grenade on his belt exploded, mortally wounding him and stunning the enemy machine gun crew.[49] Lt. Cox of the 1st Platoon called for a Medevac ship for his wounded men, but as it came down about fifteen feet from the ground, machine gun fire raked it, wounding a door gunner and forcing the pilot to abort and return to LZ Uplift. Help would *have* to come from the rest of Bravo Company. Cpl. Quang, the NVA prisoner still with the platoon, helped bandage the wounded and carried water from one position to another in their small perimeter.

At this time, I received the order from Col. Rickard to discontinue our attack into the village and go to rescue the 1st Platoon. I reassembled Bravo Company (minus the Weapons Platoon) south of the village and had the tank lead my column of two dusters followed by the 2nd Platoon and 3rd Platoon. The Weapons Platoon was left behind to secure resupply equipment such as gas bladders, water cans, C-rations and ammunitions.

---

[48] McWethy was posthumously awarded the Medal of Honor for his heroism and fearlessness.

[49] A Chicago city community college, Olive-Harvey College, honors Carmel Bernon Harvey, Jr. for his valor on that day. President Richard Nixon posthumously awarded him the Medal of Honor.

Capt. Findeisen stayed with the Weapons Platoon so the rest of Bravo Company were on their own since all the officers except me and almost all the senior NCO's were dead or seriously wounded. Our column got about half way to the 1st Platoon when the tank's transmission broke down and it couldn't move forward or backward. I decided to continue with the two platoons and two dusters and leave the tank. (I never heard how the tank and its crew were recovered.)

It was almost dark, but we could see our objective by the light of the still burning chopper from the 1st Squadron of the 9th Cavalry. My column was still taking automatic weapons fire, but so far it was ineffective. I remember thinking that the two lines of soldiers had great discipline; everyone was keeping up with five to seven yards between them. The column was only seventy-five yards from the 1st Platoon when one duster fell off an unseen twelve-foot embankment. The driver broke his leg and was screaming in pain. The duster's twin 40mm guns were facing the ground so it couldn't move or be effective. Meanwhile, the NVA were shouting repeatedly, "Americans, you die!"

I sent the 3rd Platoon to reach Lt. Cox's 1st Platoon, but they were turned back because of enemy fire and returned. (I sent the 3rd Platoon forward since I knew that, with their loss of leadership, they probably could not come to our aid should we be pinned down). Lt. Cox was on the radio saying we must come to their rescue, or they would all be wiped out. I'd read a bit of American military history and outside of Custer's 7th Cavalry, could not think of another American unit fighting to the last man. I absolutely could not let this happen!

I got on the radio to give our Battalion Commanding Officer, Col. Rickard, a status update. He was flying over us in his command helicopter. I rapidly shouted, "We're out of water, short of ammunition, the tank is disabled, one duster is down, and the 1st Platoon is decimated, surrounded, and calling for help." I gave him a quick report on everything else we were facing. Col. Rickard said something that's stayed with me throughout my life. He calmly stated, "You sound excited." His remark helped me to focus on the task at hand. I decided to hold our position and bring back the 1st Platoon. We then transferred the ammunition from the stuck duster to the remaining duster positioned in the center of the perimeter. I called Lt.

Cox to ask if he could possibly move his 1st Platoon to our location, but he could not since they required help to bring out his wounded and dead soldiers. I was assessing the situation that seemed without a viable solution when SSG Jerry L. Cook, my first squad leader, said he'd try to reach the 1st Platoon with his squad of eight men.

Cook and his men made it to Cox's position; I asked if any of the wounded required immediate medical attention (thinking perhaps we could wait until dawn). I was told if they didn't get medical aid, two of the twelve would be dead by morning because of the seriousness of their wounds, plus their medic had been killed earlier in the fight.

I called for another Medevac to attempt a very dangerous night landing to pull out the two most seriously wounded, and ordered all three platoons and the duster to shoot suppressive fire when the chopper was inbound. Squad leader Cook popped a white flare to allow the chopper to land, but again enemy fire drove it off, wounding a pilot. Cook told me he couldn't bring back the five dead or all the weapons, but would try to bring the twelve wounded soldiers to my perimeter. Cook's squad was loudly shouting our company name "Mongoose Bravo" to help distinguish friend from foe. Soon they were inside my perimeter. SPC4 William Getz, an artillery observer with the 1st Platoon who was now working for me, called fire around our position. Spooky gunships also arrived on-station and fired on potential NVA escape routes.[50] The Spookies fired with a very loud roar and made a continuous red stream of tracer bullets. The last sniper round came in around two o'clock in the morning. An hour later, four ARVN armored personal carriers arrived with American advisors. They took out all the wounded and left us water and ammunition.

Dawn broke and SPC4 Getz was calling for artillery on possible NVA escape routes when SPC4 Judy was seriously wounded in the neck. We didn't know if an errant artillery round or an enemy sniper caused his wound. I called for another Medevac helicopter and was not surprised that they were very reluctant to send one; three Medevac choppers had been

---

[50] The Douglas AC-47 Spooky (also nicknamed "Puff the Magic Dragon") was the first in a series of gunships developed by the U.S. Air Force during the Vietnam War.

shot out of the various LZs with their crews wounded in each case. My request was finally granted and a Medevac arrived.[51]

That ended the Search and Destroy, Battle of Vien Thien (3). The scout dog and handler were okay. NVA Cpl. Quang was sent to train as a scout to work with other American units, and Bravo Company requested that he be returned to them upon completion of the training.[52] In the morning all of B-Company units took part in policing the battle area. Thirty-two NVA bodies were found where the gunship was shot down. In the gunship cockpit, outlines of the pilots' bodies were distinguishable and they were still wearing their helmets. I was so grateful we didn't have to remove their bodies since they had burned all night. Their unit, the 1st of the 9th, flew in a blue team (an Infantry Platoon) to take them out.[53] Another fifty-eight enemy bodies were found in the village. The large bombs completely destroyed several large bunkers; it was never determined who or what still lay buried beneath the rubble.

The First Cavalry Division flew in two bulldozers and Vien Thien (3) was leveled. Our sister company, Alpha Company 1/5, had a tracking team follow enemy blood trails; they found a grave with eleven bodies and abandoned equipment including packs and weapons. The Republic of Korea army area of operations was to the south of this battle area. The ROK commander pressed his two battalions into the search, but they could find no trace of the NVA battalion. Friendly losses counted fifteen men killed and twenty-seven wounded. NVA losses were 101 confirmed dead and an undetermined number of wounded or unconfirmed dead.

When debriefing my men, it was very concerning to hear them say their weapons had jammed; in fact, as many as one third of them reported the problem. Immediately new M-16 rifles arrived and were available without paperwork or questions to anyone who wanted a new weapon. I thought, what a great country, giving out weapons like so much candy. I also felt I was responsible for not insisting on better weapons field care and rifle cleaning. I was somewhat of an expert on the M-16 since I served for

---

[51] SPC4 Judy came out of the battle alive, but with a jagged wound on his neck caused by a U.S. artillery round; he returned to the States.
[52] I don't know what happened to Quang after this incident.
[53] The 1st of the 9th Cavalry was the unit featured in the war movie *Apocalypse Now*.

a year as the safety officer on a range comparing the M-16 and AK-47 at Ft. Ord, California in 1966 and 1967. I recall that the AK-47 would malfunction once for every 50,000 rounds fired; the M-16 malfunction rate was eight times higher.

Only weeks before our Vien Thien (3) battle, *Time* magazine reported that Marines fighting on Hills 881 and 861 had many casualties due to M-16 rifle malfunctions. "We left with seventy-two men in our platoon and came back with nineteen," wrote a Marine Corps rifleman to his family after the battle. "Believe it or not, you know what killed most of us? Our own rifles! Practically every one of our dead was found with his M-16 broken down next to him where he'd been trying to clear it." Television newsmen, in particular, took up the cry, *"U.S. troops were being betrayed by their own weapons."* As we were fighting the battle of Vien Thien (3), two congressional subcommittees were studying the M-16 controversy. The committee's and other ordnance research findings resulted in the M-16 being quickly changed and improved in three ways:

- Making the barrel bore and chamber from hard chrome. Hard chrome seals the pores in the metal of the barrel and chamber, making it much more difficult for residues and particles to adhere to the surfaces.
- Reintroducing stick powder. Stick powder has granules that are shaped like small extruded cylinders and they minimize residue issues, as opposed to ball powder that left a very sticky residue in the barrel and gas tube of the M-16. This would swell the cartridge casing and cause jamming. The 5.56mm cartridge was designed to use IMR 4198 powder, but in a cost-cutting move the Army had substituted surplus WCC-846 powder, which burned dirtier. Originally, the M-16 was falsely billed as self-cleaning (no weapon has ever been), and cleaning kits were not issued.
- Adding the forward assist to all M-16s in Vietnam. The forward assist is a button found on the M-16 located near the bolt closure that when hit will push the bolt carrier forward, ensuring that the bolt is locked. It will close the bolt even when the weapon is excessively dirty. It can be used to close a bolt that was gently let

down, rather than released under full spring compression, to keep the noise of closing the bolt to a minimum.

As every Vietnam soldier with the CIB (Combat Infantryman Badge) realizes, for almost all battles fought so much is unknown. However, the battle of Vien Thien (3) can be accurately portrayed since I wrote my Search and Destroy battle report the day after the battle. The fifty-page document contained my honest recollections. In addition to my record, all the key players in this battle were interviewed in the field within two days by 1st Lt. Steven M. Schopp, Staff Historian, and by Maj. William S. Witters, Information Officer. They also had the input of the NVA Cpl. Quang. The body count for this Search and Destroy battle was about ten-to-one favoring the Americans, almost exactly the ratio experienced during the entire Vietnam War. The *victory* was ours that day.

Long Range Patrol Strategy

Our company admin, Sam Pullara, and others have envisioned a different strategy for Vietnam, one that would not have changed the ultimate outcome of the war (since the enemy would never have given up its effort to unite the north and south), but it would substitute the ubiquitous Search and Destroy campaigns with an unconventional tactical approach using lessons acquired by the Long Range Patrol companies formed in-country and subsequently becoming today's 75th Ranger Regiment. The strategy change would have resulted in saving tens of thousands of American lives.

The Long Range Patrol strategy, for lack of a better term, envisions thousands of small teams doing trail watching, infiltrating, and withdrawing from the enemy's area of operation countrywide, and would have inhibited the movement of even the smallest enemy units. This strategy would have broken up any serious infiltration of the south by army units from North Vietnam. The NVA could never attempt a nationwide attack like Tet, or even a less serious attack anywhere in the country.

Why didn't we use this somewhat obvious strategy? Politically it would have rendered the large unit structure of the United States Army quite irrelevant; it would have been composed of small teams led by NCOs with officers in support roles. The thinking about how to conduct a war came from war foundations established during WWII and Korea. The training and experiences of virtually all the American Officer Corps was to "fight the Soviets on the plains of Germany." Our military leaders simply were not trained to fight the war we faced in Vietnam.

Sam Pullara's experience is a case in point. In 1965, his Army training was for infantry anti-tank warfare as a crew member of a 106mm Recoilless Rifle team; the Recoilless Rifle would typically be transported by Jeep into a major tank battle. In Vietnam, Sam never saw a 106mm Recoilless Rifle during the entire seventeen months and nineteen days he was in-country. Our military leaders simply were not trained to fight the war we faced in Vietnam.

We learned lessons, but much too slowly for many of the soldiers whose names are engraved on the Vietnam Veterans Memorial Wall. Today's Special Forces, Delta Force, Rangers, Seals, and similar elite groups all have competencies and histories learned in and from the Vietnam War. Their success in recent wars, minimizing casualties with battle victories, is a testimonial to the ability of the American military's flexibility in adjusting to today's warfare. Total casualties in Vietnam were more than 58,000 versus a combined 7,000 in the Middle East (Iraq and Afghanistan), with both wars lasting ten years.

Oddly, our LRP teams' accomplishments, as compared to those of the average infantry company, are due to the belief at the time that soldiers of combat infantry companies thought they were more safe being in a large unit (135 or more soldiers versus five or six). The truth was just the opposite, but this seemed counterintuitive. The issue was training, which didn't catch up to the war being fought until well into the Vietnam conflict.

Today, it's hard to realize that the Army was not organized to fight this kind of war. Officers were not trained to think in terms of teams of infiltrators spying on enemy locations and calling down superior firepower to take them out. The tactic was only used as an aside to the big picture. Ordinary infantrymen could have been trained to do this job if that was the central point of their training, which it was not. It was not the training of virtually all officers and enlisted men, with the exception of the LRP/Rangers and Special Forces.

The enemy always knew where the U.S. Army was located. Whether it was in fixed unit headquarters, fire bases, or company-sized units on Search and Destroy missions, they had the option of attacking or not. The LRP/Ranger tactic of small teams inside their area of operation shifted the initiative to us, because the enemy did *not* know where we were and as they tried to move, we discovered where they were without absorbing casualties to find out. Once located, the proper level of firepower could be launched to destroy the adversary.

Having thousands of teams in the field raises a number of questions about this different countrywide strategy, primarily, would it work? The security of major population centers would be the responsibility of the ARVN (Army of the Republic of Vietnam). Granted, the South Vietnamese soldiers were unassertive and feeble in combat missions, but would prove adequate in a policing and protection capacity.

Reaction forces would be organized on a template provided by the 1st Cavalry's Airmobile Division. Helicopter forces, particularly gunships, would be tripled. Battalions and brigades would be located at air bases with half their forces on alert each week. They would be sent forth on a moment's notice, but only after the enemy received a continuous pounding from every available weapon in the U.S. arsenal.

Five- and six-man teams work because they can normally be silent and stationary for days at a time once they establish their trail-watching positions. There would not be large numbers of American troops banging and crashing in the bush. Other "Hamburger Hills" attacked by a frontal assault by U.S. Infantry forces would not happen along with the concomitant tragic loss of life that type of warfare entails. Men would be used as a last resort, not as the first point of contact. The entire goal of the tactic was to *not* be seen, whereby the Search and Destroy tactic was to *be* seen and, indeed, to be attacked so we would know the enemy's location. The NVA would be unable to foil the LRP/Ranger tactic as they did the Search and Destroy scheme.

Yes, we would lose men and teams, but in vastly smaller numbers because they would be the hunters and not deliberately used as bait to invite attack—and the evidence of this claim is that during the war very few American teams were completely wiped out. Of course, some teams would be killed or captured and attempted to be used to create tiny Dien Bien Phus,[54] and that would be tragic. Sam Pullara recalls seeing an issue of *Life* magazine that listed the names and included pictures of one week's KIAs in the Vietnam War. It was one of the most effective antiwar propaganda documents he ever saw. Young face after young face of the men killed in action were staring out at the reader. It was heartbreaking. Over two hundred soldiers died in just one week—and the war continued for ten years. This was the kind of thing that destroyed the American public's will to support the war. The LRP/Ranger strategy would have minimized the casualties and refocused our military so that we were the hunters and the enemy was the hunted instead of the reverse.

---

[54] The Battle of Dien Bien Phu was the decisive engagement in the first Indochina War (1946-54). After French forces occupied the Dien Bien Phu valley in late 1953, Vien Minh commander Vo Nguyen Giap amassed troops and placed heavy artillery in caves of the mountains overlooking the French camp. The French were defeated on May 7, 1954. The battle signaled the end of French influence in Indochina.

CHAPTER 21

Tomb of the Unknowns - Sentinel's Creed
You are guarding the world's most precious gifts; you, you alone are the symbol of 300 million people who wish to show their gratitude and you will march through the rain, the snow, and the heat to prove it.

Ken Carrolan

3RD US. INFANTRY: THE OLD GUARD

Prologue

Team 4-6 had been successfully inserted by choppers two days prior; this was a relief since the area of operations was very difficult for teams to arrive unseen by the enemy. The team had identified multiple trails and reported movement of squad-size VC or NVA units (they were too far away to specifically identify the enemy type). Team 4-6 (Perry, Worth, Spears, Besecke and Sedgwick) had just settled in to their night defensive position when they heard enemy shouts and saw flashlights and lanterns coming closer. The team watched and listened; they were being hunted. Team Leader Sgt. Charles "Sam" Samuelson moved the men west. He observed about fifty lights following them, but Team 4-6 wasn't using lights so their movement was slow with the aggravating wait-a-minute vines also impeding their progress. The enemy, aided by lights, kept closing on them. (Samuelson's team had flashlights, but it would have been foolish to resort to using them.)

Occasionally their pursuers would take a different bearing and Team 4-6 would enjoy more distance between them and the enemy, but the lights would always reappear. (The men assumed their stalkers were tracking them. Two nights before it had rained so the team's footprints were relatively easy for the enemy to follow.) They'd never been followed with such zeal; it was obvious the enemy wanted to find and kill them. It was around 2200 hours and totally dark when Sgt. Samuelson called An Khe to request extraction.

The base camp radio watch soldier quickly found me (Lt. Stein) and said 4-6 had requested extraction since they were in danger of being overrun. I took the radio, received the Sit Rep (situation report) from a calm Samuelson and realized he was in an extremely precarious situation. Sam was one of the most effective team leaders in the platoon and knew just how dangerous a night extraction would be; it was nearly impossible for the pickup chopper pilot to accurately access the landing zone. Three major problems loomed: 1) unseen trees and branches could tear the pick-up chopper's rotor blades apart; 2) the unarmored pick-up chopper presented an easy target with no way to deflect AK-47 rounds, and 3) it would be extremely difficult to safely coordinate rocket and machine gun fire from the gunships. Rounds and rockets would need to be "danger close" to be effective, but avoiding friendly-fire deaths was an equally important consideration.

I called the Wolf Pack air commander and told him we needed his air team to immediately evacuate Team 4-6. Wolf Pack gunships and Rat Pack slicks had put the team in two days earlier and knew their approximate coordinates. I thought this conversation was going to be difficult with the pilot wanting assurances about the exact nature of the emergency and telling me how dangerous the mission would be. It was a pleasant surprise when he said, "Roger that; meet you on the flight line in five minutes." (I loved those guys!)

The air team had the usual complement of four slicks and two gunships. I grabbed my LBE, .45, and rifle, and was running to my Jeep with men from other 4th Platoon LRP teams wanting to go aboard to help Team 4-6. I was so proud for everyone to be pulling together with the single purpose of getting 4-6 back safely.

I jumped on the Command and Control chopper, coordinated maps with the flight commander, verified radio call signs and frequencies, and then we were off. As we were flying, I talked with Sgt. Samuelson and learned things had stabilized a bit on the ground. The team had left the lights behind (they were still visible in the distance) and found deep jungle cover, but here's the mystery. The team reported a loud buzzing sound associated with the lights coming closer, so Samuelson moved them another quarter of a mile, again finding deep jungle cover but with the same result. The buzzing became louder and the lights closer. It seemed the sound was homing in on their location and must be picking up a signal from the team's PRC-25 radio. We agreed to shut down the radio for ten minutes. When Sam came back on line, he reported the buzzing had stopped and the lights were holding in place.

Chopper fuel was not critical, but was becoming a concern. If we were to pick up the team, we would need to make our move in the next twenty minutes. I told Samuelson it was his call and highlighted the dangers of an extraction. (Sam's other option was to shut down the radio, keep a tight NDP, and wait until dawn.) He told me to stand by while he ran it by his men. He came back and said they would stay in place. With a "Roger that," their radio was silenced and the six helicopters rolled east, returning to An Khe. Flying back, I wondered what would happen to 4-6 in the next eight hours and what we would discover the next morning.

Dawn came and the team reported all was quiet with no additional signs of the enemy. Later, I asked whomever I could find if the NVA was using homing equipment. No one had any knowledge of that tactic being used. To this day, I wonder what happened that night; it's one of many unsolved mysteries of the Vietnam War.

The Rest of the Story

Sgt. Charles Samuelson was a great soldier. After completing his second tour in Vietnam, he applied for the Army's six-month Officer Candidate School. He graduated number one in his class, was promoted to lieutenant, and was given the option to select his first post. He chose the 3rd United States Infantry Regiment (known as The Old Guard) based near Washington, D.C. The regiment is comprised of three active battalions, with two of them residing at Ft. Myer, Virginia and the third at Ft. Lewis, Washington.

Arriving in Washington, D.C., Lt. Samuelson enjoyed a luncheon with the Old Guard commander, a full bird colonel. It was decided Lt. Samuelson would spend three days with each unit in the Old Guard before being assigned to the Tomb Guard Platoon.

The 1,900-member 3rd U.S. Infantry Regiment is the oldest active duty infantry unit in the Army, serving our nation since 1784. The Old Guard serves as the official U.S. Honor Guard and Escort to the President; in addition, it provides security for Washington, D.C. in time of national emergency or civil disturbance. A further distinction of The Old Guard is the time-honored custom of passing in-review with fixed bayonets at all parades. This practice was officially sanctioned by the War Department in 1922 and dates to the Mexican War in 1847 when the 3rd Infantry led a successful bayonet charge against the enemy at Cerro Gordo. Today this distinction is still reserved for The Old Guard alone. The following describes units in the Old Guard.

Tomb of the Unknowns and the Tomb Guard Platoon

On March 4, 1921, Congress approved a resolution providing for the burial of an unidentified American soldier from World War I at Arlington National Cemetery. On Memorial Day, 1921, an unknown was exhumed from each of four cemeteries in France. The remains were placed in identical caskets and assembled at Chalon-sur-Marne, France. On October 24, 1921, Army Sgt. Edward F. Younger, wounded in World War I combat and highly decorated for valor, selected the unknown soldier by placing a spray of white roses on one of the caskets. Those remaining were interred in what is now known as the Meuse-Argonne American Cemetery in France. The Unknown Soldier was returned home to lie in state in the U.S. Capitol Rotunda until Armistice Day. On November 11, 1921, President Warren G. Harding officiated at the interment ceremonies at Arlington National Cemetery.

President Dwight D. Eisenhower signed a bill to select and pay tribute to the Unknown Soldiers of World War II and Korea on Memorial Day, 1958; they were also interred in the Tomb of the Unknowns. Better battlefield medical care, speedier evaluation of the wounded, and a more thorough accounting of the dead meant that by the early 1980s, there were only four sets of unknown Vietnam War-era remains. Two were subsequently identified; a third was considered to be non-American and a fourth set was selected for burial on Memorial Day, May 28, 1984. President Ronald Reagan presided over the interment ceremony for the Vietnam Unknown service member who was laid to rest in the Tomb of the Unknowns.

Fourteen years later the Pentagon removed the remains after a lengthy investigation ordered by Secretary of Defense William S. Cohen concluded that the remains very likely belonged to one of nine Americans killed in Vietnam, including 1st Lt. Michael J. Blassie. The lieutenant's family had urged the Pentagon to conduct the DNA tests after news reports raised questions about the identity of the Unknown Soldier. The remains were exhumed and identified through genetic testing that was not available in 1984. The serviceman was identified as 1st Lt. Michael J. Blassie, an Air Force pilot whose attack jet crashed on May 11, 1972 near An Loc in South Vietnam. Blassie's family took his remains back to Missouri for burial at Jefferson Barracks National Cemetery, near the grave of his father, George, a World War II veteran who died in 1991.

Originally, a civilian watchman was responsible for the security of the Tomb of the Unknown Soldier. In 1926 a military guard was established and assumed protection of the Tomb. In 1948 the 3rd U.S. Infantry "The Old Guard" assumed the post following the unit's reactivation in the nation's capital. Members of the 3rd Infantry Honor Guard continue to serve in this distinguished duty today. The Changing of the Guard takes place in an elaborate ritual every hour on the hour 24 hours per day, every day of the year, and has taken place without interruption since 1937. Neither weather nor acts of terrorism have prevented the guard changing from taking place.

Lt. Charles Samuelson (formerly the leader of E-Company Team 4-6) served as a platoon leader of the guards at the Tomb of the Unknowns. The following describes the duties he performed during a Changing of the Guard ceremony at Arlington National Cemetery. Nearly fifty years later, the ceremony remains the same.

A trim six-feet-six-inch, impeccably uniformed Lt. Samuelson walks out to the Tomb and salutes. He faces the spectators, asks them to stand and to stay silent during the ceremony. He conducts a detailed white-glove inspection of the incoming guard's M-14 rifle, checking each part of the weapon once. Samuelson and the relieving sentinel meet the retiring sentinel at the center of the matted path in front of the Tomb. All three salute the Unknowns and the lieutenant orders the relieved sentinel, "Pass on your orders." The sentinel commands, "Post and orders, remain as directed." The newly posted sentinel replies, "Orders acknowledged," and steps into position on the black mat. When Lt. Samuelson passes by, the new sentinel begins walking at a cadence of ninety steps per minute.

The Tomb guard marches twenty-one steps down the black mat behind the Tomb. He turns, faces east for twenty-one seconds, turns and faces north for twenty-one seconds, then takes twenty-one steps down the mat and repeats the process. After the turn, the sentinel executes a sharp "shoulder-arms" movement to place the weapon on the shoulder closest to the visitors to signify that the sentinel stands between the Tomb and any possible threat. Twenty-one steps were chosen because they symbolize the highest military honor that can be bestowed—the 21-gun salute.

Only under exceptional circumstances may the guard speak or alter his silent, measured tour of duty. He will issue a warning if anyone attempts to enter the restricted area around the Tomb, but first will halt and bring his rifle to port arms. The Guards of Honor spend time when they're not on duty in the Tomb Guard Quarters below the Memorial Display Room of the Memorial Amphitheater.

The Guards of Honor at the Tomb of the Unknowns are highly motivated and are proud to honor all American service members with the words "Here Rests in Honored Glory an American Soldier Known but to God." The men of the Long Range Patrol's 4th Platoon are very proud of their friend and brother, Charles "Sam" Samuelson, and of his time serving in the Old Guard.

Presidential Salute Battery Platoon

The Presidential Salute Battery, founded in 1953, fires cannon salutes in honor of the president of the United States, visiting foreign dignitaries, and official guests of the United States. The battery also fires in support of memorial affairs for all military services in Arlington National Cemetery. In addition, the battery fires for ceremonies and special events throughout the National Capital Region. The Presidential Salute Battery is the only unit of its kind in the Army, and its busy schedule includes more than three hundred ceremonies each year.

The Salute Battery Platoon is equipped with ten M5, 75mm anti-tank cannons mounted on the M6 howitzer carriage. Each gun weighs 5,775 pounds. The M5 cannon saw service in North Africa, Italy, and Northwest Europe from 1943 until the end of World War II. Today, the Presidential Salute Battery fires the 75mm blank ceremonial shell with 1.5 pounds of powder.

Ceremonies require a five-man staff and a two-man team for each gun. The staff consists of the battery commander, who initiates fire commands and ensures the proper number of rounds are fired; the sergeant of the watch, who marches the battery into position, controls the firing of the backup gun, and monitors the watchman and his assistant; the watchman, who controls the timing between rounds and gives the command to fire; the more experienced assistant watchman who ensures the watchman stays in time; and the counter, who counts the rounds and signals the last round to the battery.

Each two-man team consists of a gunner who fires the cannon and a loader. The loader has the most difficult job. He must fit a 75mm shell into the block at a particular angle and he does not have time to place the shell by sight. He has to learn to do it by feel and do it quickly. This skill can take up to six weeks to master before the soldier is proficient enough to participate in an actual ceremony.

Caisson Platoon

The Old Guard has sixty-one horses stabled at Ft. Myer and Ft. Belvoir, Virginia; the horses rotate between the two forts working one week and off the next. Their duties include pulling flag-draped caskets on black artillery caissons to a veteran's final resting place in Arlington National Cemetery. The caissons are pulled by six horses matched gray or black. The horses that pull the caisson through the quiet lanes of Arlington National Cemetery are paired into three teams: the lead team is in front, the swing team follows, and nearest the caisson is the wheel team. Although all six animals are saddled, only those on the left have mounted riders. This is a tradition which began in the early horse-drawn artillery days when one horse of each team was mounted while the other carried provisions and feed.

The caissons were built in 1918 and used for 75mm cannons. They were originally equipped with ammunition chests, spare wheels, and tools used for the cannons. Today these have been removed and replaced with the flat deck on which the casket rests.

One of the oldest and most evocative of military traditions in a full honor funeral is that of a riderless or caparisoned[55] horse. A handler behind the caisson leads the horse, which wears an empty saddle with the rider's boots reversed in the stirrups indicating the warrior will never ride again. Tradition allows a caparisoned horse to follow the casket of any Army or Marine Corps commissioned officer in the rank of colonel or above. Presidents of our nation, as Commanders-in-Chief, are accorded the same honor. Over the years, millions have witnessed caissons bearing the flag draped caskets of Franklin D. Roosevelt, Douglas MacArthur, John F. Kennedy, Dwight D. Eisenhower, Lyndon B. Johnson and Ronald W. Reagan. In each ceremony the caparisoned horse followed the caisson.

Continental Color Guard

The Continental Color Guard Team is a five-man unit and is comprised of two armed guards and three color ensigns who carry the National Color, the U.S. Army Color, and the Color of their parent unit, the 3rd U.S. Infantry Regiment, the Old Guard. The uniforms worn by the color team are replicas of the 1784 style infantry uniforms worn by The Old Guard's predecessor, the First American Regiment. Gen. George Washington approved the pattern of the uniform for wear by all Continental Army Infantry units in 1782. It consists of a blue coat faced with a red collar, cuffs, and lapels, white buttons and lining, long-fitting overalls, and a black cocked hat with cockade. A solemn part of any civic or military function, the presentation of the National Color assumes a special patriotic and historic significance when borne by the nation's foremost color team.

---

[55] Caparison: an ornamental covering (often a United States flag) spread over a horse's saddle or harness.

Army Drill Team

The U.S. Army Drill Team is a precision drill platoon with the primary mission of showcasing the U.S. Army both nationally and internationally through breathtaking routines with bayonet-tipped 1903 Springfield rifles. Standard U.S. Army Drill Team performances involve nineteen soldiers and are ten to fifteen minutes in length. Soldiers are selected for this elite unit after six months of rigorous and competitive drill practice. Trim military bearing, strength, and dexterity are mandatory prerequisites for qualification to the Drill Team.

K-9 Platoon

Another component of The Old Guard is the 947th Military Police Detachment, which contains the second largest Military Working Dog (MWD) Kennels in the Continental United States. This unit has assigned twenty-four MWDs with a variety of skills from Patrol Explosive Detection Dog, Patrol Narcotic Detection Dog, and Specialized Search Dog.

The soldiers who fall under this diverse detachment are the warriors behind the scene on many highly visible missions with their four-legged partners. These soldiers support missions for the president of the United States, vice president, and foreign visiting dignitaries. Missions range from working at Arlington National Cemetery, Camp David, the U.S. Capitol, the National Archives, the United Nations, and other places within the East Coast.

Army Fife and Drum Corps

During the American Revolution, the military used fifes, bugles, and drums in the heart of battle as the primary means of communication. Commanders used the shrillness of the fife, directionality of the bugle, and boom of the drum to relay orders to troops signaling precise tactical maneuvers, making those musicians the first, and only, signal corps of that time.

While fifes and drums earned their fame during the Revolutionary War, history records their presence as early as 1756, when they were used under the command of Benjamin Franklin, then a colonel in the Philadelphia militia. The sounds of the fife and drum were heard alongside his artillery regiment almost twenty years before the birth of the U.S. Army.

The fife traces its lineage to early fifteenth-century Switzerland, where mercenary armies used it. In American history, the fife was the key signal instrument used for light infantry units. During World War I, the German army was still using fifes as an effective means of communication in trench warfare—while enemy forces could cut cables, restricting conventional messaging, the sound of the fife would still carry on. In the past, the Army used the bugle for combat military operations, and today bugle calls regulate garrison life.

The martial drum is perhaps the most notable field instrument. Its roots date back to the time of Alexander the Great, when his army effectively used drums to move it across Eurasia. Ranging from advance to retreat and reveille in the morning to taps at night, these field instruments have proved invaluable on the battlefield and in the camp. Additionally, the fife and drum have played vital roles in maintaining *esprit de corps* and morale among soldiers on campaign.

The Fife and Drum Corps members wear uniforms patterned after field musicians of the First American Regiment of 1784. Further distinguishing this elite seventy-soldier organization are the unique instruments its members play. Soldiers perform on handmade, rope-tensioned drums, single-valve bugles, and ten-hole wooden fifes, giving The Corps a sound that is unmatched in both quality and style.

During the American Revolution, fifers and drummers had only basic musical knowledge and education. Today the men and women of the Corps have extensive musical training, ranging from a lifetime of fifing and drumming experience to advance degrees from the nation's top conservatories.

CHAPTER 22

It is generally inadvisable to eject directly over the area you just bombed.
United States Air Force Manual

OFF WE GO INTO THE WILD BLUE YONDER

Perhaps my (Lt. Stein's) proudest moment while serving in Vietnam occurred when returning back to the battlefield after a three-day pass to Hong Kong arranged by my first sergeant, Frank Moore. On the way back to base camp in An Khe, lack of aircraft availability caused me to stay overnight in Da Nang, a large Air Force, Marine, and Navy base located along the northern coast of Vietnam. I felt completely safe inside this substantial U.S. base, although Da Nang carried the nickname "Rocket City" for good reason. The Viet Cong and North Vietnamese regular army frequently launched Soviet 140 millimeter rockets into the airbase from positions within six miles of the runways.

Important air units stationed at Da Nang included the 366th Air Force fighter wing, *aka* the Gunfighters, and a huge Marine air wing consisting of several hundred aircraft and helicopters. At that time, Da Nang was described as the busiest airport in the world. The Air Force wing based at Da Nang flew only the tandem two-seat F-4C Phantoms, comprised of the 389th, 390th and 480th tactical fighter squadrons. (The Phantom had a top speed of over Mach 2.2 and had fifteen world records for in-flight performance, including an absolute speed record and an absolute altitude record.) Each fighter squadron had approximately twenty-five aircraft. While at Da Nang, pilots were frustrated that they were missing opportunities to shoot down enemy MIGs because the F-4C lacked a cannon and its missiles were ineffective at short range. Wing support personnel and air crews modified the mounting of an external 20-millimeter Gatling gun pod (containing 1,200 rounds of ammunition), which the Phantoms used in air-to-air combat, and in less than a month, the pilots scored four MIG kills. The gun pod innovation and the MIG kills that followed earned the 366th Gunfighters its nickname. During this period, the Gunfighters earned a Presidential Unit Citation for shooting down eleven enemy aircraft in North Vietnam in a six-week period.

That evening I went to the Da Nang Air Force Officers' Club, arriving early, about 1830 hours, and had a beer at the bar. I noticed a small stage with a drum set, microphones, and amplifiers; obviously a band would be playing. In front of the stage were twelve long tables marked "Reserved." Around 2000 hours the tables, bedecked with squadron-colored flowers, began to fill with pilots from the fighter squadrons. It was like watching over a hundred "Tom Cruises" file past me, resplendent with scarves and patches displaying their Gunfighter logos and colors; only these guys were the real deal. They looked hot in their aviator glasses, cocky and competitive, and they knew it! They deserved respect. Some of their squadron mates were spending that same night in NVA prisons.

I often wondered if Tom Moe was at the club that night. Captain Moe crashed only weeks later on January 16th, 1968, and was held for five years at the Hanoi Hilton before being released in 1973. In 1996 he wrote about his time as a prisoner of war in *Notre Dame Magazine*. A single paragraph from eight pages about his captivity follows:

> The body is first to give up. You cannot keep yourself from passing out, throwing up, screaming. I discovered that the more the body convulsed involuntarily, the more I could observe it as though it belonged to someone else. I found I could intellectualize pain, which allowed me to take a quantum leap in my tolerance of it. Sometimes, though, the problem was staying in touch with reality enough to keep alive. Detaching oneself too much has an insidious narcotic effect that invades one's reason and dulls normal danger signals. This is probably the way nature helps us die without being all tensed up.[56]

The prison, which was often referred to as the Hanoi Hilton, was officially named Hoa Lo Prison. (Hoa Lo refers to a potter's kiln, but loosely translated means "hell's hole" or "fiery furnace.") The prison's twenty-foot walls, topped with barbed wire and broken glass, made escape

---

[56] http://magazine.nd.edu/news/13873-pure-torture/, January 1996, online.

nearly impossible. Many Americans taken prisoner died from disease, injury or by execution, including another pilot from the 366th Gunfighters, 1st Lt. Lance Sijan, who was posthumously awarded the Medal of Honor for his leadership while a prisoner of war.

During the evening at the Officers' Club, I enjoyed listening to a six-piece Filipino band playing American rock and roll music including "Good Vibrations" (The Beach Boys), "You Can't Hurry Love" (The Supremes), "I'm a Believer" (The Monkees), "The Ballad of the Green Berets" (SSG Barry Sadler), and "Mustang Sally" (Wilson Pickett.). In 1965, the Animals released "We Gotta Get Out of This Place" and it became every soldier's Vietnam anthem.[57] It was the most requested song for American Forces Vietnam Network DJs to play. Every bad band in Vietnam had to play this song. I recall a lyrics passage going like this:

> We gotta get out of this place
> If it's the last thing we ever do.
> We gotta get out of this place
> Cause girl, there's a better life for me and you.

Another favorite song in 1966, Jefferson Airplane's "Give Me a Ticket for an Aeroplane," got a rewrite in Vietnam. The revised lyrics are:

> Give me a ticket for a 7-O Quick;
> Ain't got time for a hook or a slick.
> Lonely days are gone
> I'm a goin' home
> 'Cause Sam, he gave me my orders.

About 2200 hours, after everyone in the club was feeling good, the band broke into the Army's song, "The Army Goes Rolling Along," and about ten Army guys and I raised drinks to toast the United States Army. Then the thirty or so Marines burst into "From the Halls of Montezuma," singing loudly and were followed by about forty Navy Officers cheering,

---

[57] In 2006, a University of Wisconsin-Madison study of hundreds of Vietnam veterans found that "We Gotta Get Out of This Place" was the song most veterans identified with the war. Many veterans stated, "We had absolute unanimity, this song was the touchstone for all popular songs."
Bradley, Doug, and Craig Hansen Werner. *We Gotta Get Out of This Place: The Soundtrack of the Vietnam War*. Amherst: U of Massachusetts, 2015. Print.

"Anchors Aweigh." There was a deliberate fifteen-second pause and the highly anticipated chords of "Off We Go into the Wild Blue Yonder" blew the roof off the club. Pilots were standing on tables and chairs with a captain on the stage doing three forward summersaults and leading the song. High fives were exchanged along with hugs and pats on the back. I was so fortunate to be in that room seeing camaraderie I never witnessed before ... or since. I was proud to be an American.

Our Military Songs

In 1938, *Liberty Magazine* sponsored a contest for a spirited musical composition to become the official Army Air Corps song. Of 757 scores submitted, Robert Crawford's was selected by a committee of Air Force wives.

"Off We Go into the Wild Blue Yonder"

Off we go into the wild blue yonder,
Climbing high into the sun;
Here they come zooming to meet our thunder,
At 'em boys, Give 'er the gun! (Give 'er the gun now!)

Down we dive, spouting our flame from under,
Off with one helluva roar!
We live in fame or go down in flame. Hey!
Nothing'll stop the U.S. Air Force!

The Marine Corps Hymn can be traced back to 1805 when the Marine Corps flag bore the inscription *To the Shores of Tripoli*. Years later, after the Mexican War (1846-1848), the inscription was changed to read *From the Shores of Tripoli to the Halls of Montezuma*. In 1942, a verse was officially changed from "On the Land as on the Sea" to "In the Air, on Land and Sea." Since its first printing in 1918, the song's popularity has grown with great solidity, so that by 1930 The Marine Corps Hymn was familiar to almost everyone in the country. Check out the last two lines of the hymn. They're cool!

"From the Halls of Montezuma"

From the Halls of Montezuma to the shores of Tripoli
We fight our country's battles on the air, on land and sea

First to fight for right and freedom, and to keep our honor clean
We are proud to claim the title of United States Marines.

Our flag unfurled to ev'ry breeze from dawn to setting sun
We have fought in ev'ry clime and place where we could take a gun
In the snow of far off Northern lands and in sunny tropic scenes
You will find always on the job The United States Marines.

Here's health to you and to our Corps, which we are proud to serve
In many a strife we've fought for life, and never lost our nerve
If Army and Navy ever look on heaven's scenes
They will find the streets are guarded by the United States Marines.

In 1908, Army Brig. Gen. Edmund L. Gruber overheard a section chief call to drivers urging their horses forward, "Come on! Keep them rolling!" A year later Gruber and six young artillery lieutenants decided they needed a song for the field artillery. Gruber, whose relative, Franz Gruber composed "Silent Night," oversaw the creation of the melody. Gruber's composition was given to John Philip Sousa, who added a few beginning measures, and it became the Army's song. It became a blockbuster record during World War I, selling about 750,000 copies. Gruber heard of it and asked Sousa, "How about some money, since I wrote the song?" Embarrassed, the innocent Sousa made certain Gruber received his royalties.

"The Army Goes Rolling Along"

First to fight for the right,
And to build the Nation's might,
And the Army goes rolling along,
Proud of all we have done,
Fighting till the battle's won,
And the Army goes rolling along,

Then it's Hi! Hi! Hey!
The Army's on its way
Count off the cadence loud and strong!

For where e'er we go
You will always know that
The Army goes rolling along.

Valley Forge, Custer's ranks
San Juan Hill and Patton's tanks,
And the Army goes rolling along.
Minutemen from the start,
Always fighting from the heart,
And the Army goes rolling along.

Men in rags, men who froze,
Still that Army met its foes,
And the Army goes rolling along.
Faithful in God, then we're right,
And we'll fight with all our might,
And the Army goes rolling along.

Lt. Charles Zimmerman and midshipman Alfred Miles wrote "Anchors Aweigh" for the U.S. Navy in 1906. Over the years, changes were made to the lyrics. The below, written by Master Chief of the Navy, John Hagen, was released in 1997.

"Anchors Aweigh"

Stand Navy out to sea,
Fight our battle cry;
We'll never change our course,
So vicious foe steer shy-y-y-y.
Roll out the TNT, Anchors Aweigh.
Sail on to victory
And sink their bones to Davy Jones, hooray!

Anchors Aweigh, my boys,
Anchors Aweigh.
Farewell to foreign shores,
We sail at break of day-ay-ay-ay.
Through our last night ashore,
Drink to the foam,
Until we meet once more.
Here's wishing you a happy voyage home.

> Blue of the mighty deep:
> Gold of God's great sun.
> Let these our colors be
> Till all of time be done, done, done, done.
> On seven seas we learn
> Navy's stern call:
> Faith, courage, service true,
> With honor, over honor, over all.

The next morning, I caught a C-130 flying to An Khe with an onboard load of radar equipment. With the Air Force's touch of class, they provided me (the only passenger) a box lunch with a sizeable turkey sandwich made with delicious soft bread. As I quietly ate the meal, I reflected on the magical night I had the privilege to witness at the Da Nang Air Force Base Officers' Club.

CHAPTER 23

A strong woman is one who is able to smile like
she wasn't crying last night.

Author Unknown

Before reading this chapter, it is important for you to know that none of us wives had ever opened up to one another until after the following interviews with Charlene Blockinger had been completed. The years of keeping facts and emotions private had become routine way of life. We were stronger than we ever realized. We had to be to hold it all together. Now we have a special bond and are as eager to see one another each year as our men are.

Sharon Bohrer

AFTER ALL, WAR IS HELL, AND GRIEF IS COLLATERAL DAMAGE: REMINISCENCES FROM WIVES AND LOVED ONES IN THE STATES

The emotional repercussions of the Vietnam War played out in many ways in the lives of the men of E-Company, 4th Platoon, Long Range Patrol and in their loved ones. Woman entwined in the lives of these men—wives, fiancées, sweethearts, mothers, and sisters—found they were unprepared to deal with the emotional battle scars associated with the aftermath of war. The stories of their loves and lives offer insights that often pack an emotional punch.

Personal narratives make up the bulk of this chapter. As the women shared their stories with me, Charlene Blockinger, watching their expressions and listening to their words reminded me of the forceful, gushing waters of Niagara Falls—their torrent of memories, good and bad, spilling over into their personal reservoirs of commitment. They smiled when they spoke of their love, they cried when they spoke of their challenges—all against a backdrop of determination to achieve understanding and strength in their unions with these men.

The women who made this chapter possible are Cindy Ayers, Sharon Bohrer, Kathy Causey, Judy Hendrickson, Arlene Johnston, Mary Murphy,

Brenda Shankle, Pat Stein, and Ann Workman. Their deeply personal stories—and the trust with which these women shared their experiences—will forever remain a part of me. More importantly, it is my hope that these accounts are faithful to the spirit, facts, and intent of the contributors. I am indebted to the generosity and willingness to share their lives.

Thirty-eight years after President Nixon announced the war's end and "Peace with Honor," the men of the E-Company LRP declared a mission to find and help each other grapple with their experiences. At the same time, the women who love these soldiers also sought support in each other. In coming together, they finally give voice to their feelings of resentment, pride, anger, fear, loneliness, and love—a spectrum of emotions each had struggled with alone.

The annual E-Company LRP reunions began to take shape around 2004. As the wives gradually joined their husbands at these reunions and began to share their individual stories of life with a Vietnam soldier, a cohesive sisterhood of support slowly formed. The bulk of the interviews presented in this chapter were conducted at the 2011 reunion in Georgia.

The common denominator contained in many of the stories you are about to read is a disorder known as PTSD (Post Traumatic Stress Disorder) that can occur as a result of shell shock or combat stress. At the time soldiers were returning from Vietnam, little was known about the disorder, which presents itself in many forms—anger and irritability, loss of interest, feeling on edge, jumping at sudden noises. Nightmares return again and again, and you feel like your life is in danger—that you have no control over what is happening. "Even though I knew they were just fireworks on the 4th of July," states one person trying to describe this disorder, "they still sounded like incoming mortars. It took me right back to my deployment..."

Sharon Bohrer

For thirty years, Sharon and Ray did not talk about Vietnam:

We did not tell anybody that Ray had served there. It was almost an extension of the rigidness of the military when the men were instructed, 'Do not wear your uniform when you get home and don't tell anybody where you were,'" Sharon explains. So they went about their lives, not talking about it. But thirty years later they started to talk, and today Sharon is grateful. "Reuniting with these men has been the best thing that has ever happened for Ray because if you had met him in the 1980s and 90s, it was like something was always after him. He was never calm. Never seemed to be content with things the way they were."

Ann Workman

The more I've gotten to know each of the wives, I realize they all have story after story of mental anguish they tell about their relationship with their husbands," says Ann. "I often wondered if other couples went through the kinds of things we did, and how they were able to manage and raise a family. I attribute [my husband] Tommy's getting better to finding his buddies, being able to help them, talking on the phone, emailing, getting together, and seeing one another—being able to laugh and talk with one another and telling their stories. His detachment from them for all those years was lonely because they are bonded in a way that no one else can understand. I have friends who say, 'I don't think it's a good idea, that he's around that again—it's just not a good idea.' But I know it's good for him. It's good for all of them. Sharon, Ray's wife, will tell you the day that she came home from work and there was a message on the phone for Ray from Tommy, she came close to erasing it. She did not want Vietnam brought up again. All of the wives are different—Sharon is a schoolteacher, Judy is retired, Kathy is a dental hygienist—we all have different interests, and I love them like sisters.

Judy Hendrickson

I've made some good friends within this group, and it's been good for Milt," says Judy, referring to her husband. "He's gotten a lot better through talking with the guys. He's a bit more open. I didn't know what PTSD was. When he started meeting with these guys, they started talking about it. After we moved to Florida, the guys talked him into going to sessions for his PTSD. Oh, you have to know what's going on, and I didn't for too many years.

Brenda Shankle

Brenda recalls what happened when Tom and Randy first tracked Jerry down:

We were living in a rental house in Paris, Tennessee, while we were building our house. The phone rang one night and it was somebody I didn't know—Jerry was just astonished to be talking to Tommy, as they hadn't spoken in so many years. Soon after, they visited us in Paris and told Jerry, "You're missing out on something that is doing us a lot of good." They essentially said, "We want you to be part of us again." After that, Jerry did become a part of this group. It was good for him—one of the best things that could have happened, in fact. It was summer and I was teaching a summer class at night. I met them and then I went off to teach—Jerry stayed with them at the hotel and they talked until late into the night. Then, we got together the next day. Jerry's behavior changed after that meeting—he started taking medication for PTSD. He has found his military family. He leaves these gatherings feeling the reinforcement of support. When he attended his first reunion, that was the first time he met the wives. I didn't join him because I was teaching, but he felt a connection with the wives—they sort of adopted him. I'm starting to feel a real connection, too. I'm new, you know. I came into the group at a later time, as did Jerry. I believe he is one of the last ones the group found. Later, when Jerry was in some kind of depression, Regis Murphy came to see him. Since then, he's been in touch with Regis off and on—especially during bad times. It's good for them to be together and talk, but it also upsets them and resurfaces old memories. They feel very guilty to be alive. I wish I could have gotten help earlier, but where do you go? How do you convince somebody who says, "There is nothing wrong with me," that he needs some kind of help? No, it would have never happened had it not been for Tommy and Randy who cared enough about Jerry to find him.

Kathy Causey

Kathy has learned a lot from the other wives and can now see how her husband Ron's past behavior was connected to PTSD:

I don't recall when I heard the term *PTSD*, but when I first started learning about Ron and Vietnam it was with Tommy and Randy. I honestly think they saved Ron's life. At the time they first connected with Ron, he had recently lost his job due to downsizing and was having difficulty getting another job—he was depressed. They helped by telling him that he is not the only one. They also talked about the war. Ron was so pleased to hear from them initially. He got off the phone and said, "You aren't going to believe this" They came to visit. I thought I'd introduce myself, visit a bit, and then excuse myself to the bedroom to read a book or go somewhere. Instead, we stayed up all night talking and laughing. We had the best time, and I could see how good they were for Ron. Their first visit was very social and uplifting. I've just returned from Paris, France, from a trip with a few of the wives. I love the friendships that have formed through this group. The conversation I have with the wives helps me to understand. For instance, Ron doesn't like to be around crowds, and I now realize that is characteristic of these men.

Mary Murphy

The 2011 reunion was Mary's first time to meet the wives of Regis's Ranger buddies:

I didn't know if I wanted to participate in this interview, as I am just getting to know the wives, and we haven't talked much. I will tell you that Regis was one of the guys who formed this group. He did a lot of talking on the phone as he was diligent about tracking down the men of the 4th Platoon. Once he started getting in touch with them, it was up to them to reach back. Some of them he went to see—some visited us. I believe some of the guys weren't ready to see him or anybody else from the company, they just wanted to be left alone.

Pat Stein

I was only eighteen and minimally aware of the war when Bob left for Vietnam:

Before Bob's involvement, I didn't follow the war except for the "Hanoi Jane"' incidents and other front page items. What I do recall is the climate that overshadowed our home after Mother and Dad accompanied Bob from Minneapolis to Indianapolis, where he departed for Vietnam. They appeared very strong in front of Bob, wished him well, and then collapsed into each other's arms after he had boarded the plane. Although they didn't speak about it, and didn't show much emotion—remember, this was the '60s, and people didn't talk about their feelings—the sadness and nervousness of Bob's service infiltrated our life. My parents kept in close contact with another family from our town whose son was also serving. I recall the devastation when their son was killed two weeks before he was scheduled to return home on leave. The stress in our home increased after that. My younger brother, Jim, was only nine at the time. I remember my mother declaring, "Jim will never go to war—I'll send him to Canada first."

Lifelines to Home

Wives and sweethearts gave their men a lifeline to home. The women sent letters and care packages, though they never knew whether their loved ones would be alive to receive them. And when they received bundles of tattered and dirty correspondence—accumulated letters that their soldiers had written daily from the front—they could never be certain whether the writer was still alive as they read through them.

Sharon Bohrer

Sharon and Ray wrote every day:

He would write a line or two when he was on patrol and then eventually send a packet of letters. I was away at college living in a dorm. I would wait. I remember that just when you would think you would never hear from him again you would get a pack of letters. I would receive a package about every thirty days. You would just sit and read and read. Then, you would finish reading and realize that one was written just two weeks prior to when you got it. Ray, too, would get packages of my letters at a time because there wasn't the correspondence back and forth—no Internet access as there is today. One time, only once, he was somewhere where he could get a MARS radio hookup, and it was so exciting to actually hear his voice. You had to say "over" after every sentence, and then you realized that everyone in the room could hear you. Yes. That was the only time I heard his voice. He was gone thirteen months that time because he extended. Now with cell phones and Skype there are multiple ways to communicate every day, and I think about how wonderful that is.

But then, I think about the men who are serving today—they are seeing the daily problems of their wives and children. Is this instant knowledge age tearing at their minds and making it harder for them? Then, you did not talk about the bad things going on; instead, you just tried to boost their spirits.

Judy Hendrickson

Judy's first indication that Milt was in the hospital was when she received a clean letter. "If the envelope was clean, I knew, because the rest of them came with mud or dirt," she recalls. That dreaded call finally came. Judy and Milt had been married only six months when she got a call telling her that Milt had been killed. Judy, operating from an inner sense she could not explain, simply refused to believe Milt was dead. Weeks passed, then one day Judy got another call. "I'm still here," said her husband, to which she responded resolutely, "I knew it." The Army apparently discovered its mistake when the supposedly dead Milt requested cash for R&R. But the military offered no apology for what they had put Judy and Milt's family through.

Arlene Johnston
(Sgt. Bob Johnston's family call him by his middle name, Parker.)

Arlene, Parker's sister, recalls receiving a letter informing the family that Parker had been wounded in battle—unable to write a letter himself. This communication left the family dazed and uncertain, only able to speculate on the extent of the wounds, and in what condition they might find Parker upon his return home.

Confronted with a New Battle on the Homefront – PTSD

When the men finally returned, different battles emerged. The soldiers were often much different from the men who had left U.S. soil. They struggled with the effects of PTSD and the medical community's trial-and-error approach to controlling it. They seldom, if ever, talked about their experiences of war, and sometimes they did not speak at all for long stretches. They avoided crowds and were unsociable with friends and family; at restaurants they'd insist on sitting with their backs to a wall, keeping a wary eye on their surroundings. Through it all, they shouldered the responsibilities of husband, father, and wage earner.

Brenda Shankle

Brenda felt frustration, but she didn't attribute it to PTSD:

I knew Jerry had issues, and I guess in the back of my mind I knew they were related to the Vietnam War. After hearing the experiences of some of the other wives, I don't think I understood PTSD enough then. For Jerry, there was absolutely no transition from the battlefield to the home front, and that must have been the worst thing for him. He did not want to come home because he felt he was deserting the other men. He was sick with malaria when he left Vietnam, and somehow he lost all of his gear and wound up in a hospital. When he came home, he had no support. Our military let these men down—he needed help to transition. Things are better now. We go into a restaurant and I always let him choose where he sits as he doesn't want anyone behind him. I thought it was just him, but now I realize this is symptomatic of PTSD. Jerry had a tendency to be very vigilant, very territorial. When we were building our house somebody vandalized it—twice it was vandalized. We had a little RV out there, and we would use it to chill out. The RV was vandalized first, and Jerry went ballistic. I mean he wanted to set a booby trap. You know, blow somebody up, go to great lengths with very violent things. He felt violated. The violence in his response scared me. I tried to talk some sense into him. He wanted to sit outside with a gun and blow people away. We have guns all over the house. We have guns in drawers, we have one on the bedside table, in full view. We have guns everywhere. Now, I can't remember the last time Jerry has fired a gun, but he has this "don't mess with me" attitude. It's all just shocking to me. I have always been a pacifist. My father had no guns. He didn't believe in guns and now here I am living in an arsenal. Jerry bought me two or three guns and said, "This is your gun and we're going to do target practice." I know he's afraid for me.

Sharon Bohrer

Sharon learned very quickly that if she had to wake Ray up, she did it from across the room because he would wake up swinging:

There was a lot of anger and there was rage. The nightmares, you know, he would have terrible nightmares. We were married about a month when one night he was in the middle of an awful nightmare calling in gunships. I barely woke up in time, as he ended up on top of me choking me. I ended up hitting him and pushing him away as I felt myself beginning to black out. Everyday life was difficult. I never knew what the evenings would be like when Ray got home from working all day and going to school at night. Sometimes there would be a lot of anger, or rages, or he would just be very quiet. He was very volatile. From one day to the next, I never knew what his mood would be. Ray's family says I saved his life. You know, I was just doing what I thought I was supposed to be doing. We had some very difficult years. I was far away from home and we certainly did not have the money for me to go because at the time the military did not pay anything, and I did not have the wherewithal to leave. Besides, I had pride. I couldn't go back and say, "Maybe I made a mistake here," because I really didn't feel like I had. I loved Ray, I really did. It was a difficult life.

Judy Hendrickson

Judy didn't know for sure at the time, but in retrospect she's pretty certain Milt was suffering from PTSD. "Milt was a loner at home," Judy explains, "always hyper. I didn't know what PTSD was. I knew there was something. Then PTSD was identified, and that fit the situation. He would come home from work, drink beer, smoke cigarettes, and then go to bed. I think he was keeping it all in."

Mary Murphy

Mary's husband Regis was diagnosed with PTSD, and she says it played a big role in his job choice. "One of the main reasons he became a truck driver was to be by himself. When you drive a truck, you are alone a lot. You have contact with your dispatcher and receivers and shippers, but that is a minute part of it. The rest of the time you are in a truck and by yourself. That is why he did it. He is much better now. If he has nightmares he will tell me about them now. Before, he wouldn't. He would just get up and stay up for a little and then come back to bed and go to sleep when the episode had passed. I knew what was going on."

Ann Workman

Ann recalls the terrible nightmares—Tom waking up in the middle of the night in terror, drenched with sweat:

I didn't know what to do. Tommy didn't talk about Vietnam. It was all stuffed down inside, just really deep down in there. All of that was a real shock to me. We were very close—so connected that I could almost tell you what Tommy was thinking before he said anything. After about five years of marriage, there was a two- to three-year period when he became withdrawn. He would just go from the front yard to the back yard, and all day long would say only a few words to me. It was really hard. I don't recall the specifics, but at some point I ended up going to the VA doctor with him and explaining how I felt. Tommy was seriously depressed, but once he got some medication, he became himself again. He still takes sleeping pills every night—he cannot sleep without medication. It's terrible, sweat-dreams and nightmares. I think Tommy's PTSD got worse as he got older. I didn't know what PTSD was, so it's been a learning process. I did a lot of research, and have been with him for doctor's visits. He would say, "Do I really act like that?" "Yes, you do, you really do," I would confirm. "Are you sick?" I would ask. "Is there something wrong?" "Nothing is wrong, I'm fine," he would respond. This behavior went on for what seemed forever. He does not even remember those times. We would have people over for dinner or would be at someone else's house. Most of the time, he would be laughing, talking, and having a good time. Other times he would clam up and not say a word. We do not go where there are large crowds. He prefers smalls groups. If we go into a restaurant, he wants to be backed to the wall. He does not want anyone behind him. Once, we were standing in the yard talking with neighbors and a car a few streets over backfired. Tommy hit the ground. He gets angry when those kinds of things affect him—I think he's embarrassed.

Kathy Causey

According to Kathy, Ron's business required social skills, so he learned them. But sociability is not his basic nature:

When I learned more about PTSD, I became more understanding of why he did things or how he did things. For example, when he came back from Vietnam, he threw his medals away. Actually, he threw them in the sea before he left Vietnam. Later, his mother had a shadow box made and reordered all of the medals. At the time he said, "Thank you, Mother," and then he put the shadow box in the closet and that's where it stayed. I don't know where they are now. It's interesting, I don't know where they are. He just can't imagine why he came back when others did not. Why was he chosen to live? He feels guilt. He and I don't confront it directly, but the last time he was down he said something like, "What am I here for? Why do I exist?" I said, "Well, if the only thing that you did in your entire life was help to provide our grandchild, then that is important enough." He just grinned and then it was over, just like that.

Cindy Ayers

Cindy talks about her husband Del's inclination to pull away from people:

He retired from the police department and wouldn't have anything to do with his former colleagues. Then, he retired from Game and Fish and just cut off any contact, and he had friends in both places. He started staying outside all the time. If I wanted to go anywhere, I would have to go with my girlfriends because he didn't want to go anywhere. We've been married forty-one years now. I knew something was wrong long before we married, but I didn't know what PTSD was. I just knew he was withdrawing from everyone. He didn't even go to our youngest son's graduation; instead, he went fishing. You have a tendency to say, "Oh, Del. That's just the way he is." But I see other wives going through it, making excuses and coping. As a cop, he was wild. He worked undercover, and he was known as that crazy undercover guy—like the undercover guys you see on the TV. He took chances, and now I know after going through several sessions with a psychologist that he was trying to commit suicide by taking those chances; someone else would be blamed, and the kids and I would have been provided for. He had planned on working twenty-five years, but before that it started getting bad. He worked deep undercover in biker gangs. He had identification in four different names, complete with driver's licenses and credit cards. He had many different personas and would switch as the need arose. He was a loner, with nobody telling him what to do. He would sometimes work seven days a week for eleven hours a day. He had a snitch phone in the bedroom, and he was out at all hours of the night.

Tough Gals, Sources of Strength

The sweethearts, fiancées, wives, mothers, and sisters of the men of the LRP fought their own battles during the Vietnam War and its aftermath—a war that has carried through the lives of these men since their tours of duty, with an emotional finish line not even yet in sight. As courageous and strong as the men of the 4th Platoon were, the women in their lives turned out to be the source of their strength then and now, and the foundation on which the men rebuilt their lives. It was a role few of these women were prepared for, and it left them scarred in ways many have never acknowledged.

For their part, the women bravely forged ahead, trying to put the war behind them and build a normal life for their families. They dedicated their lives to sustaining both themselves and their men, and it would be years before many would come to fully understand the emotional toll the war had taken not just on their men, but on themselves. Even women who would meet and marry a veteran decades after the war ended would find that the conflict intruded like a third member of the relationship.

Ann Workman

"Tommy and I have been married for only ten years, but one way or another, we have all been affected by the Vietnam War's effects on our husbands. The other wives know—we talk. I have grown because of Tommy, and I believe I have been good for him. He will say to me, 'You're one of a kind. You can just mingle and have a good time. I, on the other hand, always feel that people are looking at me.' I am the one that does everything. I meet with people, arrange what we are going to do and how we are going to do it. I do all the ground work, and when it comes down to the final things I need, I ask Tommy to weigh in."

Brenda Shankle

Brenda and Jerry went to high school together. "Jerry dropped out of high school and joined the Army," Brenda recalls. "He never talked about any of the really bad stuff. He was not prepared to come back to the States. I was very careful not to say anything that would set him off. I tried to be diplomatic—it was very difficult. Most of the time he was fine, but there were other times. He was suspicious. He questioned where I was and who I was with. I laugh, because that would never be an issue now, since he's been on medication. My teaching saved me."

Judy Hendrickson

Judy met Milt through a guy she was dating:

We met in November, he gave me a ring in December. We got married in January. He went to Texas for medical training in February or March for three months, and then he went to Vietnam in June. Milt would be gone for nine months at a time—gone nine, home six. I'm easygoing, and I've always dealt with whatever I had to deal with. We didn't have kids until after he got home from Vietnam. I raised the kids. I've always dealt with everything—for Milt, for the kids. That's just the way it was. I roll with the punches unless I'm really pushed. Times were tough when Milt was overseas because you made no money in the service. When they went overseas, the Army reduced your income. I didn't have a support system around me because I tend not to reach out to people. Milt did not request base housing, so we were isolated. I got through it. I'm not much for asking for help. It's just the way I am. In retrospect, I don't think I would have done anything differently. The kids turned out well. I always thought of myself as namby-pamby, very shy. I was different back then, but I'm still quiet. I tried not to think about the danger Milt was in when he was away. Instead, I worked, I traveled and I took care of the kids. It takes a strong backbone to live with a service guy. You hear of a lot of divorces, so some people just can't handle it.

Sharon Bohrer

Sharon planned to go back to school to finish her master's degree in psychology after she and Ray were married. "I went to Pacific Lutheran University, enrolled, set up my classes—all I had to do was buy my books. I was ready for my semester to start when Ray came home with orders, so we went to Ft. Ord, California, instead."

Mary Murphy

"I was just there for Regis," Mary explains. "I didn't understand it, but if there was a time he wanted to talk I was there to listen, just listen. Sometimes it's just too difficult for me to talk about it."

Kathy Causey

"It was a number of years after Ron's return from Vietnam that we married, in 1980. I knew he had had malaria, but I didn't realize the emotional obstacles he was facing. He never talked about Vietnam, except for an occasional joke about something that had happened. After learning about PTSD, I realized he was sick. I didn't have a career. As a dental hygienist, I would work just here and there. As the children got older, I started doing my own things—fun things I wanted to do, since Ron didn't want to go anywhere. I was busy doing other things, very social—very busy."

Cindy Ayers

Del was home from Vietnam for over a year before Cindy met him and they began to build their life together. "Before the film *The Green Berets* was released, he would tell me funny stories about his time in Vietnam; after we saw the film together, he told me what really happened."

The repercussions of war surfaced in their lives in many ways over the years since they married. Cindy shared the story of Del's suspension and eventual retirement from the police force:

I asked Del what happened. At first, he didn't want to tell me. "They called me into the station," was how he began. You see, he had been working out of the station for two weeks, and he was scheduled to continue working from the station rather than on his own. The sergeant and lieutenant called him in and accused him of belching out loud in the squad room, saying that offended the lieutenant. "I had to apologize, and I would not do it," he told me. "Okay,' I said, 'I know there's more to the story." He went on: "They told me I'm antisocial, and I said I wasn't—I just didn't like them. They asked me why, and I told them they were both assholes. They asked for my gun, and I told them I didn't need it, that I hadn't carried a gun in seventeen years and if I wanted to kill them I would do it with my bare hands, right then and there. They sent me home." I said,

"Gee, I wonder why. I don't think you should go back. You can't do it—you can't work out of an office." So he retired. He never set foot back in the department and on his last official day he met someone in the lobby to give him his final check. He had been working undercover, so his hair and beard were long, the same as it is now, only bright red. That's the way he functioned.

No Flags Waved for Them

Loving a soldier is never easy, no matter the war. But the Vietnam War was different. Antiwar sentiment often divided families and communities. Sharon had a hard time finding a job when employers learned she was the wife of a vet. When Sharon told her parents her new boyfriend was shipping off to Vietnam, they told her to break up with him. Despite pressure from many sides, these women defended and supported their soldiers.

Sharon Bohrer

Sharon and Ray were married and had moved to Southern California—not a welcoming place for a Vietnam veteran—when Ray came back from his second tour:

We just had to move on because Ray was so disillusioned, and things were tough. We were treated badly by the general public. It was not a good time. We only had each other. We thought we had jobs waiting, but everything fell apart. We managed to get a furnished apartment. We had our wedding gifts. Ray finally got a job working in a door factory only because he had a cousin who was in management there. When I was interviewing, the interview would be going great. Then I was asked if I was married and what my husband did. The minute I said he was a Vietnam veteran I would be told, "Thank you for the interview. We will call you." The interviews would end abruptly. It was total discrimination. Ray, too, was faced with discrimination in his job search. "We don't need your kind," they'd say. "We have nothing for you." He became so discouraged that one day he said, "We're moving to Ft. Lewis. I want back in the Army." I said, "What? We didn't talk this over." He responded, "At least there I have some self-respect." The culture shock of coming back and the way they had to come back then was so cruel—I think that's what damaged them so much. I think that is what Vietnam did to a lot of people—broke their souls because the country was not behind them. They were doing what they thought was right. It was so unfair. I think that is why so many of them turned to drugs—because they were so demoralized by what was happening in the U.S. There was no transition. Ray was in a firefight only hours before he was put on a plane to fly back to San Francisco. The flights were timed so that they got into San Francisco at midnight so there would not be a lot of people around. There was no way of coming down from the terror of what they had experienced, returning to a country where you couldn't say you were over there fighting for freedom."

Brenda Shankle

I've always been antiwar. I thought it was a wrong war. If I'd had the guts, I would have been marching. I would have been protesting, but not to the point of mistreating them after they got back. That was wrong, and I guess I expected Jerry—from the experience he had—to have reached the conclusion that I've always held: that war is wrong and we need to go to any lengths to avoid it. Jerry's a thinking man—very, very intelligent and very deep. His belief is, "If they're going to be aggressive toward us, then what we need to do is go in and bomb the hell out of everybody." I'd say, "You're talking about children; you're talking about homes." "Well, sometimes, that has to be done," he'd reply. I'm appalled by all of that. It's a touchy topic, but lately he's not so much that way.

Mary Murphy

Mary kept informed about the war. "I knew what was going on. I knew a lot of the guys that were over there, and when they came back I was aware that some of them had some problems. The men that were around me at the time were in the National Guard, so I didn't have a direct association with the war, but I watched the news. I didn't agree with a lot of the things that were happening as far as when our guys would return home and the way they were treated."

Kathy Causey

Kathy describes herself as apolitical—unexposed to the climate that existed around the Vietnam War:

What I do remember about Vietnam were the reactions of my parents to the people who died. So many died in the war. My mother only cried once or twice in her life. For the most part, she could handle anything, but one day she was at work in Birmingham and got the news that our priest was killed in Vietnam. My mother was sitting at a restaurant by herself eating lunch when she heard the news—and she cried. Hearing that story from my mother was a depressing memory for me as a child, and is probably my most significant memory of Vietnam. Ron has always been loyal to the U.S., but has not always shown it. We didn't have a flag. When Ron was going through one of his worst depressions, it was around the bombing of the World Trade Center. His career was crumbling, the country was crumbling, and we did not even own a flag. I went to Walmart to get one and they didn't have any left. We have a flag now.

The Stories Have Changed, but the Memories Remain

Since the 4th Platoon's first reunion, annual get-togethers have become less about sharing war stories and more about catching up with old friends—life in retirement, plans for travel, what children and grandchildren are doing, updates on those who are not yet active in the group. But, eventually, talk returns to events that bonded the 4th Platoon together, stories of bravery, stupidity, hilarity, and camaraderie. The wives have heard the stories, many times over. Yet, the accounts of war never fail to stir emotions.

Judy Hendrickson

"We have a lot of fun now," Judy says. "I keep telling Milt he finally grew up when he hit fifty."

Brenda Shankle

Brenda enjoys talking about life in the present. "We have a really good life now, and that was not always the case."

Kathy Causey

Kathy believes the challenges she and Ron experienced have made their relationship even stronger. "I'm more understanding now. My knowing about Ron's history in Vietnam helped me. Every time Tom and Randy or Regis would visit they would say something like, 'You wouldn't believe what your husband did. You know, he was a hero—he did this or he did that.' I never knew what he did. I never knew about Vietnam. The more I learn, the better our relationship becomes."

Sharon Bohrer

Sharon often wonders whether she did the right things in trying to cope with the war and its aftermath. "Then," she says, "I look around and see that we are so blessed. I have so much respect for Ray. I talked about how difficult things were but, all along, Ray is the one who kept me going."

Ann Workman

"We have a wonderful life," Ann proclaims. "It couldn't be any better. Overall, I think that since Tommy has found his buddies—and continues to search for ones not yet found—it's been very therapeutic. It's been good for them to talk about their pain rather than keeping it inside."

The Price

Every soldier of the 4th Platoon needed help reestablishing his life when he returned home. The women profiled in this chapter provided help, love, and stability. But their sacrifices came at a price that has taken years to pay.

CHAPTER 24

War would end if the dead could return.

Stanley Baldwin

WHAT DID WE LEARN FROM THE VIETNAM EXPERIENCE?

Tom Workman

I brought Vietnam home with me; I live it, smell it, and think about it daily. I value the incredible bonds I still have with my men and platoon. I repress the difficult memories and think about the wonderful team I had the privilege to know. It's like 1968; the memories are still so very vivid.

- Darrell Presley, who was shot in the knee and hand; he's a wonderful soldier and we knew we could always count on him.
- Don Kinton is dead, but never forgotten; his last words were, "It's getting real grey," and finally, "I'll catch you later."
- Milt Hendrickson, who would always volunteer whenever we were short a man and walked point every patrol. After Vietnam, I was honored when Milt asked if he could consider himself part of my team.

I have many other brothers and sisters whom I love as much as possible, but almost five decades later, I love my team and platoon mates with that same love. Even today, I certainly would die for these men.

I entered the Army and requested Airborne. I didn't want to be the only Workman not showing up for the war. I had four brothers, all veterans. My two older brothers were in Vietnam, one in the Navy and the other with the 173rd Airborne Brigade. Later, my youngest brother was in the Marines and was at the Beirut Barracks bombing in Lebanon on October 23, 1983. Two hundred twenty Marines were killed on that day. It was the deadliest single-day death toll for the U.S. Marine Corps since WWII's Battle of Iwo Jima.

Our family had a tradition of military service and I didn't want to break the tradition. I tested well and was urged by the recruiter *not* to go into Airborne infantry. He said, "It's too dangerous." I said, "I'll take my chances." After I was assigned to a battalion in the 101st Airborne Division, the sergeant major wanted me to be his clerk. I said, "No, I want to be in the fight." He told me I'd probably get killed and I said, "I'll take my chances."

The war may have been wrong, but I value the American flag and I supported every minute of the war. I also support our troops in Afghanistan and Iraq, too. And just like us, they didn't start the war but do their duty with honor and discipline.

Bob Johnston

Our country had no idea what they were getting into. The Vietnamese had successfully fought the Japanese, Cambodians, and French plus the Chinese and others for centuries, and they had always triumphed in the end. What made the United States believe we could make a difference? Our politicians! They had it wrong and engraved more than 58,000 American names on the Wall. Was it worth it? Of course not!

I think it's no different than the United States inserting itself into the Muslim/Asian worlds today and the results will be the same. We did defeat the Japanese, but the goal back then was total victory, not fighting with one hand tied behind our back. Still, even though I was shot five times and spent a year recuperating in the States, I wouldn't trade that experience for anything. At that time, we all believed we were doing the right thing; in fact, it was a noble cause for us.

I loved the LRRPs (Long Range Reconnaissance Patrols) and believe I was nearly in the first LRRP Platoon organized in the 101st. I was a Washington, D.C. police officer when I enlisted and volunteered for the Airborne and Special Forces. After several LRRP deaths, a couple of slots opened up in 1965 and I was asked to join the LRRP Platoon. We wore a red diamond patch that distinguished our unit. There were four teams, and I was in Team Two.

On my second tour, I remember when a dusty Maj. Malone found me. I was walking and he was driving a Jeep at our fire base when he saw my red diamond patch and stopped. He told me about a new Long Range

Patrol Company being formed. He said, "Get in; if your paperwork checks out I'll put you in my company. You have to get through Recondo School and lead a team in the field without getting anyone killed." I talked to friends about the secret unit and then joined the next day. The major was the finest officer I had the privilege to serve. I loved our 4th Platoon Long Range Patrol.

On my third tour in Vietnam, I was selected to lead total security for Gen. Abrams, the four-star general commanding all Vietnam Allied forces. It was an incredible experience! I could select anyone in the country to be in my sixteen-man unit. Eighty percent of those I selected were Airborne and the rest were usually military police. I went wherever the general traveled, except to Thailand. He had a home there and went once each month to see his family living in Bangkok. Of course, I could have gone, but it was like vacation duty and I gave that opportunity to men in my unit.

I coordinated safe houses and escape plans. Surprisingly, the radios were PRC-25s or 77s just like those used by patrol teams in the field. Dignitary arrivals were endless and included the military, CIA, politicians, entertainers, and sports figures. I remember seeing Ann-Margret, Bob Hope, the prime minister of Australia, the football player Larry Csonka, the vice president of the United States, and the president of Vietnam.

Bob Stein

I learned not to trust my government because the facts they presented about the war were simply not true, and the lies were compounded by obstinate politicians who were unwilling to acknowledge their mistaken judgments. I recently spoke to a department chair of Asian history from a major university who told me that, even as a young man, he recognized there would be no domino effect of surrounding countries coming under the influence of communism, and that the United States would regret taking sides and its involvement in the regional conflict. History has proved the professor was right.

War brought many horrors, and unlike the *Bang! You're dead!* portrayals of death in movies, death usually came desperately, painfully, and slowly. While awaiting helicopter evacuation, medics and soldiers fought to keep their wounded friends alive using only bandages and morphine. They faced wounds that would severely challenge even the most sophisticated emergency room today, while at the same time trying to dodge enemy bullets.

    I observed various reactions to the most stressful conditions young men would experience in their entire lives. A memorable example took place during a combat air assault as Huey choppers flew to a landing zone that our intelligence believed was harboring enemy combatants. The four-man air crew plus the five or six men in each helicopter had just arrived in Vietnam and this was their first air assault. Some of the men prayed, some grinned (while pantomiming slashing their throat and pointing to the ground) and others stared blankly at nothing. We could see the artillery barrage on the LZ with a final white phosphorus round signaling that artillery fire was over. Almost immediately, the accompanying helicopter gunships began their rocket and machine gun fire on the LZ. Some of the men closed their eyes and began to shake, and just moments later the chopper door gunners began shooting two very loud M-60 machine guns at bushes or other vegetation hiding potential enemy.

    Just a couple of feet before touching the ground, the men pushed off the choppers' struts and formed two semicircles firing at any potential target. And then, just that fast, the choppers were gone. The firing stopped, and the only sound was coming from the brush fire set by the massive gunfire on the LZ. After a minute, radios began crackling and the mission began. These men had experienced extremely high stress without even a single enemy round being received as yet, and they still had twelve months before they rotated back to the States or out of the Army. Months later, these same soldiers would fly to another enemy LZ, and they'd be focused and looking at the maps showing them the geography most favorable when they dismounted. Then they'd be veterans, warriors whose lives could never be the same as they were before they deployed.

    Certainly, death and destruction were widespread. I am embarrassed to admit this, but I felt a primeval sense of satisfaction while holding the AK-47 of an NVA soldier who only minutes earlier was trying to kill me. I looked with satisfaction on his bullet-riddled body including two shots to his face.

War however, is not all terror, violence, and fear. Awesome bonding (unattainable by those not there) takes place with the backdrop of war. Nearly fifty years have passed, but we men and our families, still receive comfort, advice, and a sense of calm from each other. The genesis of our brotherhood was forged in Vietnam and is strong to this day.

Jerry Shankle

Lt. Stein called me with this question: "Jerry, what did you learn from the Vietnam experience?" He said the platoon's answers would be the final chapter in his book, *Ghost Warriors*. I thought about his question and answered, "Yes, I'll do it; give me a couple of days." I looked forward to answering since I think about my year in Vietnam at least two or three times every day, but now would be the first time to put my thoughts to pen. After almost fifty years, it's hard to say something. I started to write many times but each time I would just shut down; I couldn't do it. Finally, this is what came to me:

My family was patriotic. Everyone served—my dad, three brothers, and granddad were all in the service. I enlisted as soon as I was seventeen and attended basic training at Ft. Polk, Louisiana, with its support city, Leesville, commonly known by the troops as "Diseaseville." I still remember my drill instructor, Sgt. Gary Bartell. After that, I went on to AIT (Advanced Infantry Training) at Ft. Leonard Wood, Missouri and finished Jump School at Ft. Benning, Georgia.

My graduating class was sent to the 101st in Vietnam, with a few men going to the 82nd Airborne. The senior Jump School NCO, Sgt. Maj. Ligon, whom I feared more than any other man, read the orders to my assembled platoon, but left my name for last. Finally he said, "Shankle, you're staying with me." It turns out they wouldn't send me to 'Nam since I was still seventeen. I did a lot of unimportant chores for Sgt. Ligon until I was transferred to Ft. Bragg, North Carolina, where I joined the 82nd Airborne Ready Reaction Force and did intense training. Soon I was assigned to Ranger School back at Ft. Benning.

In Mountain School, I'd meet a Deuce-and-a-Half truck in blackout loaded with Ranger candidates going into the forest, and would serve as a forward guide leading patrols to their jump off points. I was always comfortable in the dark and in the forest. One day I remember acting as the aggressive force, sitting in a tree preparing to ambush Ranger patrols. I had an M-60 machine gun and put a C-ration can on its side as support for the ammunition belt so it would feed clean. I spotted a Ranger and rat-tat-tat "shot him dead." (All these candidates were from West Point, wild-eyed and tired!) The Ranger was so hungry that he took my C-ration can and I thought, "Damn, I *never* want to be a Ranger." Little did I know that soon I'd be one fighting in Vietnam.

Was it worth the war? No! No! It seems like whatever we do for the country we're trying to help doesn't last; it always reverts back to where it was. We see that happening in the Middle East (Afghanistan and Iraq). Worthless! We shouldn't fight again unless our country is united to win the war or unless our homeland is threatened.

I'm neither bitter nor sorry about the war. All of us went to do our job. We ended up not fighting for anything except for each other. I'm sorry I've not kept up with my Army brothers. When I do see them, I tell them, "If you ever need me, call and I'll be there." I mean it! I'm impressed with the men of the 4th Platoon and to this day feel safe with the guys and don't feel all by myself. Thanks, Steve Woodson, Sgt. Henry "Swifty" Swift, John Higgins, Paul Kuebler, Jim Brokaw, and many others. I haven't included here descriptions of the patrols and gunfights I experienced in my year in Vietnam. I'm just not up to it. I served as senior scout and eventually leader of Team 4-1.

I left Vietnam from Cam Ranh Bay after being sick for at least a week. I didn't report to a medical aid station since I wanted out on that flight home. I struggled clearing the processing center and then passed out in the door of the departure bus. I was in the base hospital with malaria and other respiratory problems for a week-and-a-half before they put me on a flight to Seattle.

I felt naked without a weapon and purchased a knife made in Denmark with a Hoffritz stainless steel blade and rosewood handle; I still have it today. Times have really changed. I bought that knife in the Seattle airport and then carried it on the plane and flew home with it. Northwest Orient

Airlines put me alone in first class for my last flight home. Sometimes I think about Vietnam and feel like an alien. Was it a dream or what?

Sam Pullara

I learned that the United States should never go to war for a draw. I learned it is immoral to send men to fight and die for any reason except absolute definable victory. I learned it is wrong to send men to fight and die for any conflict where there is not a formal declaration of war, thus engaging the entire country in the effort and not just a select group of young men. I learned that men should not go alone to war, but should go as part of a unit so they have around them men who will, from the first, value their life as they value their own. I learned that the Allies must be at least as committed to the effort as your country, and their soldiers should share the duty and danger as do the men of your country. I learned that without the support of the people and total support of the government for whom you are fighting, no war can be won, and should not even be fought.

On a personal note, I learned that the experience of war and responsibility given me and my success in fulfilling the duty such responsibility entailed was the most important determinant of the rest of my life. In addition, I learned that the men with whom I served were the best that my country had produced up to that time, and my pride in knowing them and my respect for their courage, professionalism, powerful sense of pride in the unit to which they belonged, and the love they had for each other is boundless. I learned that the men with whom I served were the best I had ever known, and are the best that I have known even up to the last quarter of my life. I've heard that wars bring out the worst in nations but the very best in the men who fight them. I heartily agree.

Steve Woodson

While I was in high school it seemed there was one of two ways of thinking about the war: You were either ready to join or you weren't. You were for it or against it. There was no middle ground. I knew when the Tonkin Gulf incident happened that I would join. My good friend Dennis wanted me to join the Marines with him, but I always wanted to be a paratrooper. I was slight of build and my recruiter tried to talk me out of it, but I wouldn't change my mind. At that time there was no tighter fraternity in the Army than the Airborne. It was great going to Jump School with the same guys that I had trained with in Airborne Infantry School at Ft. Gordon, Georgia. Then being assigned with a bunch of them to the same unit (173rd Airborne Brigade) was just as special.

As we all know, things don't always go as you plan. Upon our arrival in Vietnam we were informed that all of us were going to the 101st because so many casualties had hit the Screaming Eagles. My service in a rifle platoon with 1/327th (a Battalion of the 101st) ultimately gave me the opportunity to volunteer for E-Company, 20th Infantry, Long Range Patrol. I never served with an overall better group of guys. It was amazing how quickly this disparate group came together. Going to Recondo School with my team was a very good idea. It didn't take us long to work out the kinks.

I find it very hard to explain to others just what we as teams did. I will say this: I loved it. No one can imagine, for instance, the adrenalin rush flying into an LZ. Or that you're not only the hunter but the hunted. While with the 101st, I felt fairly safe because of the number of men around me, and in a Long Range Patrol team I felt the same, but for the opposite reason. Fewer men meant we could hide better and stay quieter.

I loved the country, the jungle, and the highland forests. I went to places I'm sure would be national parks in the U.S. There were stunning vistas and beautiful valleys that few men from larger units could have had the opportunity to see. The REMFs never saw the country as I did, and not only the flora and fauna, but the people, too. Considering their situation, they were very friendly. I'll never forget when we were at Plei do Lim Special Forces Camp and an old man in uniform came up to our team and said something in French. John Higgins, who'd learned French in school, replied. The old man ran off and soon returned to our team with a bottle of rice wine. He had not spoken French with anyone since the French army left Vietnam. We took turns toasting him with a drink. Little things like this are memories I cherish. For one evening we made an old soldier's life a little happier. Thanks to the wine, we were a little happier, as well.

There were a good bunch of guys in the platoon and I'm glad we stayed in touch. Has my Vietnam service made a difference in my life? Probably. Has it all been good? Certainly not. I will say I am very proud to have served. I show my appreciation to my fellow soldiers and my country by participating in local veteran organizations and ceremonies as a color guard member of the 82nd Airborne Association. It makes me feel better that Vietnam vets are finally being shown some appreciation.

What bothers me is the lack of recognition of the various LRP companies that preceded the name change to Ranger. Even in unit histories you would think we barely existed and did nothing. In Vietnam, being a LRP or LRRP was about the highest status one could have. Nobody messed with you because you had to be nuts to be one. To see guys in tiger fatigues or "cammies" meant they were doing something the line grunts didn't. We needed that psychological edge to survive because our missions were very demanding, mentally as well as physically. I'm proud to have served and proud of those with whom I served.

Jim Fisher

I think the most positive thing I learned was a sense of duty—duty to my fellow man if he was an ally, no matter if Korean, ARVN, Chinese, black, or white. I was a gunship pilot in my aviation company and we went when called to protect, extract, and resupply, often without knowing who we were helping, but knowing it was our duty.

I flew for the 281st Assault Helicopter Company, "The Intruders." The 281st was the first U.S. Army helicopter company organized and trained as a Special Operations Aviation unit in Vietnam. The Long Range Patrol Company would not have realized it at the time, but we flew training missions supporting their Recondo School. I had the privilege of extracting Chippergate 4-4 under fire. Fifty years later, that team told me I saved their lives. That still makes me proud.

My Vietnam experience was totally different from how I had lived my life until then, which was "what's good for me," not necessarily "what's right for everyone." I spent the next twenty-five years in the Army practicing taking care of others, which was my duty. It seems still to work out the best.

Oscar Caraway

I learned that old men should never send young men into a war that will not be fought to victory. I'm still bitter about it. I entered Vietnam as a seventeen-year-old after training for Special Forces at Ft. Bragg. I wanted to fight, that's why I joined the Army, so I volunteered for Vietnam and was immediately assigned to A-Company, "The Assassins," 1st of the 327th, 101st Airborne Division.

Just after turning eighteen, my nine-man squad was all killed or wounded except me, the last man standing. I quickly received a promotion to buck sergeant, I guess for being a survivor. Later our company was ambushed near Highway One with thirteen dead in addition to the wounded. It took us two days to find a small hilltop that we could secure and then cut trees down to allow Dust-Off Medevac choppers to land and extract our dead and wounded. I was assigned to hump one of the bodies—from the blood it looked like he had taken a couple of rounds into his chest. I didn't know his name. I carried him, I dragged him and slept next to him, putting a poncho over his body at night. The poncho was too short to cover him completely, and his mud-caked boots stuck out. Our company continued to exchange fire with unseen enemy. I still have nightmares.

Later our battalion had a battle with the NVA. Rumor had it that our battalion C.O. was getting pressure for exaggerating enemy body counts and he was angry. He ordered his companies in the field to collect the enemy dead and bring them to fire base Camp Eagle. After the two-day battle, choppers were sent out and we loaded forty-five shot-up NVA dead. Some of the bodies had lain in the field for two days in 100-degree heat. This was one of my worst experiences in the war.

I got out of the Army when I was only nineteen and had lots of positive opportunities. I never could take advantage of any of them. I spent most of my life floating around, drinking beer, getting into trouble and fights, and sleeping anywhere possible. Except for the last twenty years, I never used a Social Security card.

In 2006, Tom Workman found me and said the VA would help me. I said, "That would be great! It would be wonderful to get a new door for my trailer house because it gets so cold in the winter." Things are okay now. The VA assigned me to group therapy, but I got into a fight with several other vets (they were "posers"). I've been alone as a warrior my entire life, but I will never tolerate people lying to me. That's true even today. When it happens I still become outraged; I can attend VA anger management classes but only one-on-one with a therapist, not group therapy. According to the doctor, I have a bad case of PTSD. On balance, the VA is first class. They have helped me and made me proud to have served. I married my high school sweetheart, Sandra, when I was twenty, and as unbelievable as it sounds we're still married. She's wonderful and forgiving. We have had a good life together.

I want to say a word about Jim Brokaw. Jim and I joined the Army together, spent time in some Special Forces training at Ft. Bragg, and then we were off to Vietnam. Later he was a Long Range Patrol team leader and asked me to be his assistant team leader. On one of our first missions, we were both up on point and spotted two NVA on the trail. He motioned for me to go up one side of the trail and he took the other. We killed both enemy and kept their load-bearing equipment. One belt buckle had a hand-engraved star; I kept that as a souvenir of Vietnam and of Jim. He was the sheriff of Joy, Illinois, but he's dead now—died of cancer. Jim was a great soldier, a first-class friend, and I still miss him.

I left much of my life in 'Nam. It's still hard not to be a soldier. My final fifteen minutes of fame is a thank you to all my brothers-in-arms who helped me survive the war. I will always be your brother to whom all my Army combat missions and adventures are dedicated. I'm grateful for your service and strength. Thank you, "bros."

Don Williams

I believed in what we were trying to accomplish and I still do. If those who made the decisions in how we fought the war really wanted us to win, we could have done so. As I reflect on the results from a soldier's perspective, do I believe it was worth the sacrifice of more than fifty-eight-thousand who gave their lives? No, but we served our nation with honor and respect as any soldier would do.

Ray Bohrer

During my early time with the 4th Platoon I really believed that I was made for this job. As weird as it sounds, I absolutely loved combat: the adrenaline rush, the excitement, walking point, calling in gunships. After Don Kinton was killed, I changed a little. I was more cautious and death was suddenly a reality. I lost all trust in our government. In my heart I knew we were winning this war, and then they (our politicians) would call a truce. Of course, we were the only ones honoring the truce.

Going home was even worse. I was totally lost. I decided to surround myself in green, so I re-enlisted. I was angry; with what I didn't know. I drank a lot. Hell, PTSD wasn't even diagnosed back then. Even after my second tour, I decided to bury Vietnam for good. That lasted forty years and festered in my head. I now receive treatment from the VA. I now realize that life is really worth living. My wife, my daughters, and my grandchildren mean everything to me.

I now go to every reunion that E-Company and Charlie Rangers have. I realize how important true friends (brothers of combat) really are. I guess to sum this up, Vietnam screwed me up for over half my adult life, but with the help of reunions and a little from the VA, I'm looking forward to the rest of my life.

James Worth

I was lucky to walk away from Vietnam in April 1968 and from the Army in January 1969 in basically one piece. I'd been in more real, prolonged combat than was good for a teenager. It had taken its toll, and it did for years to come. The point was not lost on me that, despite prodigious effort and extensive volunteering for hazardous duty, I was walking away from the Vietnam War, and later my entire three-year military experience, with nothing at all to show for it. You could not have walked away from Vietnam with a more undistinguished official record than I did and still claim to have been in the war.

I did not fail to notice that I'd given all I had to try to save the Vietnamese from the other Vietnamese, and had gotten nothing in return for my pains but tattoos, scars, various diseases and syndromes, and a king-sized ration of shit. I'd learned I didn't like nor do well in a rigid, highly stratified caste system where all the freedoms, rewards, and privileges are at the top, and I'm at the bottom where all the risks, hardships, and dangers are. I made a mental note to never, *ever* again volunteer my way into a place where complete assholes (who cared nothing at all about me) had absolute control of my life (including the ability to send me into deadly situations every day, make me wash their dishes afterwards, and then throw me in jail if they didn't like the look on my face). I had not known it would be like this when I enlisted because if I had I wouldn't have enlisted, you betcha!

I'd never been in a system before (or since) which was so one-way. They demanded everything and gave back nothing. The light bulb had finally come on over my head. It took me long enough, but I finally got the concept that there was going to be nothing good for me in the end, and sure enough there wasn't. No medals, no stripes, no recognition, no useful skills learned—*nada*! Nobody was going to pat me on the back and say what a hero I was. My whole reward was that I got to walk away from a year in combat in two of the most hardcore units in the war. I knew for sure I'd just wasted three years of my life and that I was lucky enough just to be walking away.

And I'd volunteered for it all, another point that was not lost on me. I'd asked for it, that was the part that kept me awake at night feeling like a real sucker who got landed hook, line, and sinker. They had me at, "Ask what you can do for your country." I asked *not* what my country would do for me, which was a *big* mistake, and the entirely predictable happened. They didn't do anything for me. I'd lie awake at night thinking, *Fool!* I have been forever afterwards a whole lot more careful about what I volunteer to do. If my mom wouldn't like it, I don't do it.

The system did not value me or my contribution at all, and they went to great lengths to convince me they didn't. I ain't no Indian, but I can read signs well enough. One hundred percent of the evidence indicated that, and no evidence at all indicated otherwise. For example, telling me to take off the CIB I'd earned (and for decades afterward denying there was enough evidence to award it to me), even though they already had. How's that for a sign? Could you miss that?

I will never think America valued or appreciated my service at all. I have written, documented proof to back up that view, repeated over decades, too. It's nice to hear them being complimentary about my service now, but they should have said it when I needed to hear it; and they shouldn't have gone into such complete lying denial when I demanded they tell the truth about what I did.

When I got back to Ft. Bragg after Vietnam, I heard this, "You were a paratrooper/LRRP? Well, KP for you and then it's fall out for police call just like the others." They wanted to use us for grunt work right up to the very last day. That's why I volunteered to test parachutes; *anything's* better than being a grunt in war or peace. They acted like they owed us nothing, not even decent treatment, and when I left the feeling was mutual. The Army definitely taught me how to feel chewed up, spit out, and fucked over like never before or since. I was all done trying to get approval from people whose job it was to disapprove and who really enjoyed doing it.

I had volunteered to become a part of a system that had no civilian real-life equivalent; first in a shock troop with the 101st and then in the Long Range Patrol. I'd come to realize that the reason these were jobs no one else wanted was because they were truly awful jobs. Things like that may look good in the movies, but in real life they really, *really* suck.

There were no real useful transferable skills from those things I'd done. When I left I was as ignorant of life outside as when I went in, like I'd been sequestered. I had completely wasted those three years in terms of my own advancement, while the rest of my generation was getting ahead. I could take a .45 apart and put it back together in twenty-seven seconds, but I couldn't balance a checkbook and had never filled out a rental application. Considering what I'd spent the most time doing in the last three years on what the Army thought was very important, I could be a janitor, a ditch digger, a shoeshine boy—or a Mafia hit man. And that's where they left me. It's been a long, hard crawl from there up to the middle and no thanks at all to them.

I can't say Vietnam or my military experience improved me. I think it set back my development for years. While other people were learning skills and trades, I was spending my time getting my boots to a mirror shine. While other people were learning how to rent apartments, I was standing on my footlocker during shakedown inspections while my superiors rooted through my belongings leaving them arrogantly and contemptuously thrown around on the floor. (They did this whenever they felt like it, just because they could. We had zero rights in the situation.)

While other people were learning to cook and keep house, I was standing in line to eat chow off metal trays (if I wasn't eating out of cans I'd opened). While other guys were learning how to get along with women, I was learning that, if you want to get your money's worth, always jack off before you go in a whorehouse. And if someone shortchanges you, break his hands.

While the rest of my generation was learning how to get on in life, I'd wasted my late adolescence in barracks, bars, and whorehouses on three continents and a major isthmus, and that's when I wasn't sleeping on the ground in the rain and fighting a war. I'd seen three years of Army life, a year of war, and a lifetime of vices and I still wasn't old enough to drink or vote. I even had to have my older brother and friends buy beer for me. I didn't care for this situation at all, and I thought I had been very poorly served by the country I had been prepared to give my life for. I *still* think that. They didn't care about me at all; that was obvious and they meant it to be obvious.

When people watch a war movie, they ask themselves how they would react in those circumstances, but they don't realize that by the time they have gotten that far forward they would be someone else—another person. By the time you get there, experts will have torn your personality apart and remade you in their image, an image you may not like and that society for sure isn't going to like.

I'd learned a lot about myself; some things I wish I hadn't known — like the fact that I'd rather shoot someone in the back than in the front. I'd learned to put on the Great Stone Face: basically watching and taking part in the most murderous, gruesome and shocking things and still maintaining a blank, disinterested look like I was waiting for a crosstown bus. I'd learned to disassociate myself from the reality around me when it got too intense. *It don't mean nothin'.* Never give an enemy a break. Don't trust anyone. Cover your own ass because no one else will. Shoot first and shoot last. Don't volunteer for dangerous stuff, and if you do, don't cry because you're in danger.

What I really learned is that there are no rules except the ones *you* make up and make your own. Anything else is just restrictions you work around. Some of the other things I learned in The Great War to Save the Vietnamese from the Other Vietnamese are randomly:

- If you're in a war and someone asks, *"Who can type?"* for God's sake, *Raise your hand!* Go back and read that again and again! I cannot emphasize this enough!
- Going to war is its own reward. Don't expect anything more.
- Try not to be with people braver than you.
- The best rule of thumb in combat is: *Shoot at whoever's shooting at you.*
- When you can't think what to do, throw a grenade! (Oh boy, does this one work!)
- One of the hardest things to do in war is to *not* throw up.
- You never outgrow your need for ammo.
- There are no good choices in war, nor healthy ones, either.
- Never try to reform a corrupt country, especially if you're paying for it.
- I can still function pretty well even when I'm scared shitless, especially if my life depends on it. This may be what I went there to find out.
- Way down deep, I'm *really* shallow. This may also be what I went there to find out.
- Whatever else you do, don't make me really afraid of you: it's just not a lucky thing to do.
- There is no better example of the saying, *"The road to hell is paved with good intentions,"* than the Vietnam War. The Iraq and Afghan Wars would be second and third.
- The saying, "Pride and arrogance go before a fall" also works well.

- Never, and I mean *never* get into a war unless there's something in it for you, and I mean something besides the chance to *Save the World for Democracy*. Your best and most valiant efforts will go entirely unappreciated by everybody. Asking what you can do for your country and not what your country will do for you is a sucker's bet.

- I wish I had known it was my job to make sure I got the basic medals I was entitled to, that they were properly placed in my records in a timely fashion, and that my records truthfully accounted for what I did. If I had known that at the time, I would have paid a lot more attention to it and you can take that to the bank and cash checks on it. The level of corruption, incompetence, and indifference in the rear areas was astounding and very negatively impacted many people actually fighting the war, both then and in the future. Nothing was ever done about it, though it was a well-known open secret.

- Get everybody on the same page before debriefing. When you report your own activities, ignore your mistakes. *Always* give yourself the benefit of the doubt and *always* interpret everything in your favor. Don't kid yourself: everybody else is doing this, too. The world uses flaming martyrs to light its cigars.

- Never go to war against someone braver and more dedicated than you, who has a greater stake in it than you do, who's been fighting much longer than you, and who has uglier women. (This should be tops on the list, though it's certainly one of the most unlearned lessons of the Vietnam War.)

- Your enemy will be every bit as human as you are every time, and never let anyone tell you anything different! You can use that knowledge to further your interests or you can ignore it at your own peril. We kidded ourselves that the enemy didn't value life as much as we did. They valued life as much as we did, all right, they just didn't value *our* lives as much as we did. They were ready to spend more lives than we were to get what they wanted; that's why they won.

- Life is not fair; neither is war and neither is the military. Look out for yourself because no one else will. Keep your mouth shut and your face blank, if you know what's good for you.
- Never support a country with a secret police! This should be a no-brainer for Americans.
- Forget every war movie you ever saw. There's really no musical soundtrack in a war; you have to make your own.
- In a war 95% of the fighting is done by 5% or less of the people. Choose which percentage you want to be in very carefully, while sober, and after talking to your parents. (It's the same advice for getting a tattoo.)
- If you're actually caught up in a war, try to have as much fun as you can whenever you can. Always remember *this time* may be your last. Nobody else will set this up for you or even think about you in terms of this. The farther you are toward the rear, the easier this will be.
- The only good wars are the ones you survive.

Sometimes I would just be amazed at the fact that this *was* The Big Time, as *big time* as it ever gets. I made it as far forward as one could get in that war and still be in Vietnam. When you're out there so far you have to post teams midway to relay your messages, you do whatever you want. It's your war and when it's time to take it to the enemy, stuff it down his throat. No one's looking over your shoulder; you *are* the war!

I'll never forget the first people I killed. This was in the 101st in the Song Ve Valley (the site and time of the *Tiger Force Massacre*). One night on ambush, the trip flare went off and I pulled the trigger on the Claymore. It was horrendous: by the hellish light of the flare six people were dying in agony. I was awestruck, horrified—and I didn't know what to do.

The other guys sure did, though; they woke up pitching grenades. When we crept out by dawn's early light, six unarmed civilians were lying there dead. They'd been carrying a wounded man (he was later found dead, too). The squad leader told me and another guy to follow the blood trails into the bush and finish them off. He and I pushed in a ways and then decided we'd gone far enough; we sat down and had a smoke. I wasn't going in any further and I'm sorry if that's what lost the war.

I'll never forget the first man I shot in the back (this was also in the 101st). My radio had been shot up and I was working as a runner. I had just come from being personally mortared out in the paddies and my blood was up. I wanted to kill someone. I came around the corner of a hut and there he was facing the other way and holding an SKS (Soviet semi-automatic carbine rifle). I put a three-round burst in his back at twenty feet and down he went. I was elated! I ran up and kicked him. *Take that, Motherfucker!* I kicked him several times, then grabbed up the SKS and hauled ass. You bet I'd rather shoot someone in the back. If you want someone more heroic to fight for you, next time get Rambo.

I killed some enemy in hot blood and some in cold blood, but mostly it was just business. When you can sneak up on a sleeping man, pull the pin, and drop a grenade in his lap, stick your gun muzzle in his ear and pull the trigger, or slit his throat and it's *just business* to you, you are in a different reality than any you've ever known. You're in a different world where everything you've ever known before means nothing. When you're blowing apart dozens of men with artillery or air support and then slapping five and joking about it later, nothing is *ever* going to be the same after that. You haven't just crossed one of *life's brightest lines*, you've trampled it into the ground. You're where no one you know has ever been. You have walked right up to the *cliff of sanity and reason* and are looking far over the edge, far off into another world. You're high up on a peak all by yourself, death and destruction are all around you, and life and everything you ever knew as being good is very far away. This is what you have to find your own way back from all by yourself, because this is where they dump you out and leave you.

This is what the thousand-yard stare is all about:[58] you're looking into another world and the things of this world no longer matter. You are gone; you're different now and you always will be. And don't ever ask the

---

[58] The limp, blank, unfocused gaze of a battle-weary soldier; the despondent stare that reflects dissociation from trauma. The thousand-yard stare is thus often seen in cases of incipient post-traumatic stress disorder.

people who put you there for any help at all, because it'll only get worse. That's what I'd learned.

There I was: bad as I ever wanted to be and maybe worse, trusting in no one and believing in nothing, living only for the day and my vices, ready, willing, and able to kill anything that moved to get the job done and for my own survival. This was not an improvement on my former self.

And then when I got dumped out in the end with my walking papers, I knew it would be up to me to remake myself into something that society would accept. I had gotten so little in return for volunteering to serve my country. I just wanted to declare victory and start putting it all behind me, which was what the rest of the country did, too. I knew I was going to have to create a *new me*, starting from scratch, and I was anxious to get started. I was definitely not going to ask the same people who had been giving me the king-sized ration of shit for three years for help in any manner. I did not want them to know me or my problems, because to admit or display to them any kind of weakness or problem was counter to survival. They would only use it to screw me every time they got the chance. I knew by then that the U.S.A. had no loyalty to or concern for me at all. It was all about what they could get out of me before my enlistment was up.

This was not paranoia; it was prudent caution. This was still the time when they could and would commit you to a mental institution for life (for your own good, of course) and I was really sure they would happily do this to me if anybody ever knew the thoughts I was having. It was obvious to me by now that they would only do things to hurt and damage me for their purposes, nothing that would ever benefit me. I wanted nothing from them but my freedom, *which they owed me,* and I was definitely not going to tell them about any psychological quirks I might have picked up that they could use against me.

They had made me into what they wanted, and I was satisfactory at it, or so they finally admitted decades later after the Congressman made them, and now it was time to put it all behind me. Walking away from the Army with my honorable discharge was a great feeling. I really knew I'd earned it. I felt like I was walking away from a three-year jail sentence that I'd volunteered for, except I would have been a lot safer and more comfortable in jail, and treated better, too. Just let me out of this nuthouse and you'll never hear from me again, I promise, was what I was thinking. And they never did, either.

I berated myself for a long time for volunteering my way into that, but I finally came to value that experience highly for having survived it, and I came to love that teenaged LRP I'd been. He made a lot of bad choices, but he had a lot of moxie. He was as hardcore a teenager as you'd ever run across. He survived quite a few near fatal mistakes, walked through the fire and the rain, and acquitted himself honorably, if I do have to say so myself. He's not dead yet; I just keep him around for *Doomsday Defense. That*, he's really good at: he has good instincts and he's lucky, too. Like it says on one of my CIB orders: "For satisfactory performance under fire." It's not exactly, "Above and beyond the call of duty," but I guess it'll have to do. It's what I came to prove.

Ron Causey

I only served twenty months of active duty in the U.S. Army. Fourteen of those months were served in Vietnam, three months with the 101st Airborne, and the remainder with E-Company 20th Infantry LRP. What I experienced in Vietnam forty-eight years ago in one way or another has affected me every day of my life since. Sometimes good and sometimes not!

What have I learned from my experiences in Vietnam? I learned that it doesn't matter what a man's background is, where he grew up, his education, race or anything else—combat will change him forever. I learned that survival could be a blessing, but that it may also be a curse. I learned that the common bond I shared with my brothers-in-combat almost five decades ago remains ever so strong today.

John Wisheart

Arriving in Vietnam as an eighteen-year-old, I had no idea what I was getting into. I had orders for the 173rd Airborne but at the repo depot I volunteered for a new outfit that was forming (again not knowing what to expect). But it didn't take long to know I was in the best damn place and with the best soldiers of the Army. I had always been a loner, but not here—it takes a team to accomplish the mission. Relying on every man is a must. After almost forty years of not knowing where anyone was, we finally got together almost by accident. The bond is still strong if not stronger now than it was in 'Nam, if that is possible. I have tried to live that lifestyle my entire life and think that I have done so.

Del Ayers

Young men of courage find it easy to go to war when principle and country call. We who survived the nightmare find life after war difficult and a daily challenge. We honor our fallen by persevering and living our lives to the best of our ability, each in our own way. Living life using the many lessons learned from Vietnam is the purpose of bearing the sacrifice of our *forever young comrades* who gave their lives for their band of brothers.

As I walk past our black wall at the Vietnam Veterans Memorial, I stop at each panel to touch the name of a man I know. After my walk I step back to the apex and stand before each of the brave men and women to renew my promise to do the best I can to live the lessons my privilege of life has driven me to practice each day.

Joined together in 1967, this company of strangers qualified by training, experience, and commitment to a common goal are now inseparable by time, distance, and death. When we gather together in person or memory, I need not make Pvt. Ryan's request, "Tell me I am a good man."

Now retired from different walks of a life of service to community, the originals of E-Company LRP 20th Infantry Airborne, Vietnam 1967-1968 are a living legacy to our most important lesson of being personally responsible for being the best that we can be.

Honor, pride, perseverance, commitment, and duty have earned us quiet respect from those who knew us then and know us now. I lived this simple, but most important lesson alongside the bravest men I am humbled to call brothers. Living my life as those who could not, giving their ultimate sacrifice, knowing they would have been the best they could be, is a privilege I take seriously.

Darrell Presley

I thought being out in a five- or six-man Long Range Patrol was as dangerous as anything possible. However, I was wounded twice in two separate gunfights and both times I was a passenger riding in a truck. The first time was in a 100-truck convoy traveling to An Khe. We were ambushed and our truck flipped over, causing great confusion. We each had just three magazines and were without units or radios. Just as my truck started a turn, I was shot in the left knee. We returned fire but had to conserve ammunition. I was scared but soon things got squared away. We pushed the truck upright and drove another ten miles where there was a medic station at a fire base.

The second truck ride was another convoy and I was shot in the left hand. NVA or VC fired one RPG round but it whistled over our heads. This time we had only two magazines, as the ARVN was responsible for our security. The ARVNs never fired a shot. At the hospital the doctor patched up my hand and I was okay. I wanted to get back into the bush where it was safe!

I believed what we did was important to the war effort. We gathered intelligence and gave it to the brass. I remember using a Pen EE half-frame camera to take photos of the enemy; when we'd come off patrol and go back to camp, we'd turn in the camera. About a week later headquarters would return the camera with any personal snapshots. In the big picture as I think about it, the war doesn't seem worth the effort we all gave.

Milt Hendrickson

Even to this day, my reflections on the Vietnam War cause anger and disgust for the very government and country we fought for and served. I believe that the soldiers, marines, airmen, sailors, and men from the Coast Guard didn't lose the war. We won the battles on the ground, water, and air; it was the politicians and the peace movement with their lack of support that brought on this shameful defeat.

How can someone find respect for those who either went to another country or burned their draft cards, and called those who served baby-killers and murderers? Yes, I have very little respect for that generation except for those who did not shy away from their duty to serve their country, and yes, I am speaking of my generation, the Baby Boomers.

I served three-and-a-half tours in Vietnam, two with the Army Special Operations units and one with the Naval Advisory Group and half year with a special Naval Detachment during the Easter Offensive. Each time I came home to a different country, one I did not recognize. I also found that I could not adjust to civilian life, and found it hard to work beside people who either protested or talked trash about those who served. Having that attitude, I can be thankful that because of my dislike of civilians, I stayed in the military for twenty-four years. And yes, like many other Vietnam veterans, for me there is not a day that goes by without thinking about the war.

Frank Moore

The Vietnam experience was tough, but if I ever had the choice of the war to fight, I'd choose Vietnam over Korea. The weather in 'Nam was hot, sometimes unbearable, but nothing as oppressive as the brutal and heartless winters of Korea. I was with the First Marine Division for their breakout from the Chosin Reservoir. Besides fighting waves of Chinese Communist troops, the cotton socks we wore trapped moisture and cold next to the skin. This guaranteed frostbite.

Both wars came up zero for me. We obeyed our orders, I did my job, and am proud of my service, but our government didn't understand the cultures of either country. We were in over our heads. Coming out of WWII and just achieving total victory over Germany and Japan, our government believed all wars would end the same with great American victories. Sadly, they were proven wrong—more than 58,000 young men died in Vietnam and 33,000 in Korea. It was not worth it. We need to understand the consequences of conflicts and the finality they bring to so many before we make a national commitment to start combat.

Phil Mayer

I served two tours of duty with the infantry in Vietnam as a rifle platoon leader, Long Range Patrol (LRP) Platoon leader and infantry company commander spanning parts of 1967, '68, '69, and '70. My exposure to ground combat during both tours was probably about the same as most infantry officers serving in similar assignments during the same time period. By far and away, the first half of my first tour as a rifle platoon leader in the 3rd Battalion/8th Infantry, 4th Infantry Division was physically the most demanding. Combat operations were conducted primarily in the mountainous areas of the Central Highlands, an area characterized by rugged, steep terrain, dense jungle consisting of double/triple canopy tall trees affording minimal sunlight during the day and extreme temperatures—hot and humid during the day and chilling cold at night.

Battling the elements on a daily basis was every bit as debilitating as engaging the enemy of North Vietnamese army regulars who were totally committed, highly professional, and well-prepared. They were elusive, tenacious, and usually determined where and when our battle engagements would commence and end. It was not unusual for infantry line units in search of the enemy to move slowly, single file, through nearly impenetrable jungle behind a point element, with one soldier using a machete to hack a path through dense vegetation. Most of the time less than one thousand meters forward movement was realized by nightfall, after which the unit would set up in a defensive perimeter, prepare fighting positions, and set out Claymore anti-personnel mines.

In addition, each rifle platoon would usually deploy a two- or three-man listening/observation post at a predesignated location thirty or forty meters outside the defensive perimeter. Squad-size ambushes (four to five men) were frequently deployed along trail systems indicating recent enemy use. The average strength of most rifle platoons in the field was twenty to twenty-five men. Most infantrymen carried fifty to seventy pounds of load-bearing equipment that included ammunition, food, water, grenades, C-4 plastic explosive, and individual weapons, usually an M-16 rifle, M-79 grenade launcher, or an M-60 machine gun. About six weeks after arriving in-country at a healthy 215 pounds, I was down to an even more healthy 170 pounds. It was not uncommon for some of the smaller guys to go from 150 pounds upon arrival to 120 pounds in six or eight weeks.

My first respite since arriving for duty as a rifle platoon leader in the 4th Infantry Division came around September 1967. I was instructed to report to IFFV Headquarters in Nha Trang, a beautiful city situated on the central coast of Vietnam, where I would be interviewed for a new corps-level, "all volunteer" long range patrol/reconnaissance company that was being formed and trained to conduct long range patrol and reconnaissance missions throughout the II Corps tactical area of operation. Little did I know that I would embark on one of the most exciting and interesting assignments of my military career.

After shuttling by helicopter back to my battalion's rear area in Camp Enari, I was given twelve hours to clean up and prepare for the hour and a half helicopter flight to Nha Trang, departing at first light the next morning. I couldn't believe the physical transformation that had taken place on my body during the last 120 days. Not only had I shed forty-five pounds, but my face was gaunt and my hands and arms were covered with the open, running sores known as jungle rot. The sores began as cuts from the razor-sharp elephant grass, but they wouldn't heal because of the dampness brought on by the torrential rains endemic of the rainy season in the Central Highlands.

At Nha Trang I met up with 1st Lt. Bob Stein, who had been recently awarded the Silver Star for his heroic actions during the Battle of Vien Thien (3) on 21 June 1967 while serving with the 1st Air Cavalry Division. Both Bob and I were interviewed by Maj. Dandridge "Mike" Malone, who would serve as E/20th Inf. LRP, (Airborne) 1st Company commander.

Shortly thereafter, Bob and I learned we had both been selected to serve as patrol platoon leaders. Of four LRP platoon leaders, we were the only two not Ranger qualified. Even the communications platoon leader was Ranger qualified, as were most of the platoon sergeants and a handful of squad leaders.

In looking back, I can say without hesitation that Maj. Malone was the most dynamic and charismatic leader with whom I had the privilege of serving in a military career of more than twenty years. He had been designated a Patterson Award winner (Top Officer Candidate School Graduate of Year) and an Honor Graduate from Ranger School. In addition, he served as Detachment OIC of the Florida Ranger Camp and on the faculty and staff at West Point where he taught psychology and leadership.[59]

I was indeed blessed and honored to have been given the opportunity to serve with some of the bravest and most courageous soldiers I ever met, especially the team leaders and members of Company E, 20th Infantry (LRP/Airborne). The first two corps-level LRP units were organized in response to the nature of the war in Vietnam. Confronted by an enemy adept at using terrain to mask movement, thereby leaving friendly forces blind to their intention, it was only natural these units would be created with the capability to monitor and disrupt deep within enemy-held territory. It was dangerous and specialized work, usually conducted by close-knit teams of five or six lightly equipped but well-armed volunteers operating beyond artillery support in difficult terrain. Their mission to gather information, target acquisition, and conduct ambushes and occasional prisoner snatches were vital to denying North Vietnamese/Viet Cong initiatives.

My tour of duty with E/20th Inf (LRP/Abn) ended around the latter part of June 1968. Most of the high points were described in an earlier portion of this book. My return to the States was with somewhat of a heavy heart. My marriage to my first wife was on shaky ground and to tell the truth, I missed the excitement and the camaraderie of serving with such an elite group of brave soldiers. In a way, I was addicted to the adrenalin rush of being involved with a variety of challenging and interesting missions. That being said, I was not too excited about reporting to my next assignment as an assistant professor of military science at Georgia Military College in Milledgeville, Georgia. After about six months I became bored and volunteered for a second Vietnam tour of duty. About six months later I was on my way.

Needless to say, my hasty departure did not result in rave reviews on my efficiency report after only one year into my assignment. Upon arrival

---

[59] Shortly after leading our unit through its recruitment, organization, training, and activation, Maj. Malone was promoted to lieutenant colonel and given command of the 3rd/8th Infantry Battalion in the 4th Infantry Division where he served with distinction Upon completion of his tour in Vietnam, Malone was selected to attend the prestigious Army War College.

in-country, I was assigned as a company commander of Delta Company 1/508th Infantry, 3rd Brigade, 82nd Airborne Division. After about four months the brigade rotated back to the U.S. and I reported to 3rd Brigade, 101st Airborne Division, where I served as a company commander until my departure in June 1970. I had achieved my goal to serve as a rifle company commander in combat.

Upon my return to the States following my second tour of duty in Vietnam, my exposure to the antiwar movement prevalent at the time was minimal. After a brief period of leave with my parents and wife, who were residing on a military installation (China Lake Naval Ordinance Test Station) in Ridgecrest, California, I reported to Ft. Benning, Georgia to attend Ranger School prior to attending the Advanced Armor Officer Course at Ft. Knox, Kentucky. By this time, my first wife and I had decided to divorce; thus a rewriting of the old adage, "Distance apart does not necessarily make the heart grow fonder." One of the reasons for volunteering for Ranger School was to take my mind off our divorce. It wasn't long before I started to think I might have made a mistake attending Ranger School, especially at this stage of my career. I then briefly considered the possibility of coming up with an honorable way of exiting the course (such as breaking an ankle or leg) in lieu of quitting. In the end, I stuck it out to graduation (honor graduate) and was glad that I did.

In retrospect, I failed to recognize the source of the symptoms I was experiencing following my second tour in Vietnam. These were characterized by frequent periods of depression, sadness, and anxiety, followed by episodes of anger, aggression, and defiance of authority. It wasn't until after my retirement from the Army, that I realized my behaviors were symptoms of something I had never heard of called Post Traumatic Stress Disorder (PTSD). I avoided seeking psychiatric/mental health treatment while on active duty for fear of causing irreparable damage to my military career. Little did I know that the damage had already been done.

From a career standpoint, my second tour in Vietnam was quite rewarding; twelve months of command time in U.S. units—nine months with two different rifle companies and three months commanding the 3rd Brigade Headquarters Company in the 101st Airborne Division. My time with the two rifle companies, addressed in an earlier portion of this chapter, was challenging, high stress, dangerous, and at times exhilarating.

For more than forty years I have experienced frequent sleep interruption caused by nightmares followed by anxiety attacks. To this day, I still experience occasional episodes of deep depression and sadness characterized by feelings of hopelessness. I still relive vivid memories of the dozens of brave young men who died right before my eyes. Most of their deaths were not instant nor without excruciating pain. To witness their last gasps for breath as they lay choking on their own blood is something that will stay with me forever. I have yet to come up with any meaningful justification for our involvement in the internal political and military conflict with which our country became embroiled in countries like Vietnam, Iraq, and Afghanistan. There was hardly any likelihood that any of these countries would invade the United States or become a threat to our way of life.

As I grow older, I find myself harboring a deep resentment and burning anger when I think about the thousands of young men who were cut down before their time. Most were barely into their twenties and would never experience marriage, starting a family, or becoming a parent. It is especially galling when the orchestrators of the Vietnam debacle (Robert McNamara and Henry Kissinger) publish egocentric memoirs, openly admitting their policy blunders and strategic planning errors regarding the extent of our nation's involvement and the number of troops committed to the open-ended Vietnam conflict, without a definitive plan for victory and lacking our nation's backing and support.

More than anything else, the Vietnam War convinced me that our elected representatives (politicians) who drag us into these needless conflicts, are by-and-large clueless concerning the horrendous cost to those who do the actual fighting in such misguided endeavors. More than 58,000 made the ultimate sacrifice. In talking to the families and loved ones of these individuals, I can honestly say that the pain and heartache never go away.

In September 2012, at a B-Company 3/187, 101st Airborne Division Reunion in Washington, D.C., we hosted the family of one of our young sergeant squad leaders who was killed in action in February 1970. Family members of the deceased in attendance were his mother, wife, sister, and a lifelong friend from high school (former USMC infantryman, RVN WIA, now a pastor). While visiting the Vietnam Veterans Memorial (The Wall), his mother, a gracious eighty-eight-year-old from Atlanta, Georgia was looking at the upper portion of The Wall, straining to see her son's name. Noticing this, a memorial guide brought a ladder over and offered to help her climb to where she could see it. She did not hesitate to proceed up the ladder with the assistance of the guide to steady her upward ascent. Upon reaching eye level with her son's name, she kissed her fingers and lightly touched the name. As she descended the ladder, we could see tears forming in her eyes. Upon reaching the ground, she apologized for her loss of composure. She then said something I will never forget:

"You know, there is not a day that goes by that I don't think about my son Larry. I will grieve his death until my life ends."

Sgt. Larry Harrison left behind a wife and seven-month-old son. It is our politicians and elected government officials who should be apologizing to Mrs. Harrison for drafting her son to make the ultimate sacrifice for such a futile cause. Unfortunately, the young men who serve in combat maneuver units, where the rubber meets the road, all too often end up being used by our government policy makers and strategic planners as collateral damage tokens wagered in a high-stakes poker game. One need only to review the history of the battle of Hamburger Hill, May 11-20, 1969.

"You may not be able to read this. I am writing in a hurry.
I see death going up the hill."
Extract from a GI's letter home.
Dong Ap Bia (Hamburger Hill) May, 1969

In less than ten days of fighting, troopers of the 101st Airborne Division lost seventy killed and suffered 372 wounded. Approximately 633 NVA were killed. Although Hamburger Hill was eventually taken after ten days of bitter fighting, the victory turned into a political defeat for the American public that was incensed by what was perceived to be a waste of the lives of young GIs who had died to secure a hill that was abandoned in less than three weeks. Later the movie *Hamburger Hill* depicted this battle.

After retiring from the Army in November 1982, I decided to use up my VA educational benefits by enrolling at the local community college in Sierra Vista, Arizona. After one year in Cochise County Community College taking business courses, I applied for and was accepted into the University of Arizona master's degree program specializing in career counseling. While in graduate school, my second wife, the mother of my son, decided to divorce. As was the case with my first wife, we seemed to grow apart from one another. At times, I thought maybe there was some connection between my tours in Vietnam and the failure of two marriages. I'm now on my third marriage, but am not absolutely convinced there is a correlation to my time in Vietnam.

About five years ago, Bob Stein introduced me to the E/20th Infantry (LRP) association. I started attending the reunions and found that I really enjoyed the incredible bond with other members. It filled what had been a painful void in my life. I began reconnecting with old friends and accessing various veteran resources, which helped me better understand the impact Vietnam had on my life. Prior to that, I had never been a joiner of typical military organizations such as the American Legion, Disabled American Veterans, Veterans of Foreign Wars, and the World Wide Ranger Association. Attending the reunions are now a high part of my life. Tom Bragg and I remained in contact off and on throughout my time on active duty. He was a best man at my marriage to my second wife. Also, Bob Stein and I remained in contact over the years. Both of these individuals fill a special place in my life and are like brothers. I consider the other E/20th Infantry (LRP) members as long-lost brothers and value the friendship of every one of them.

Men,

As the decades passed, all too often our Vietnam War experience continued to invade our relationships, reactions, and everyday reality. My hope is your good memories and our friendships provide some comfort and compensation. After reading *Ghost Warriors* in the twenty-first century, I trust you will continue to take great pride in both your personal contributions and in what our company accomplished.

I am very proud of you.

Bob Stein

Appendix I: History of E-Company (LRP) 20th Infantry IFFV and C-Company (RGR) 75th Infantry IFFV[60]

On 25 September 1967, Company-E (Long Range Patrol), 20th Infantry (Airborne) was activated and assigned to I Field Force Vietnam, commanded by Lt. Gen. William B. Rosson. The unit was originally formed in Phan Rang by procuring combat veterans from the 1st Brigade (LRRP), 101st Airborne Division, along with personnel who were scheduled to join the Military Police Brigade. Additional assets were also drawn from the replacement detachments.

Company-E was originally commanded by Maj. Dandridge M. Malone. The unit was to provide long range reconnaissance, surveillance, target acquisition and special type missions on a corp level basis. In addition, the company had the capacity to operate as a platoon-size force and conduct regular recon-in-force missions. They were known as Typhoon Patrollers, taken from the code word *Typhoon* favored by I Field Force headquarters.

On 15 October 1967, Company-E was placed under operational control of the 4th Infantry Division and was relocated to the Division's base camp at Camp Enari in the western Pleiku province. The company trained through December and phased its four platoons through ten-day preparatory courses, followed by sequential attendance at the MACV Recondo School in Nha Trang, which was run by Special Forces cadre, at two week intervals. Each Platoon concluded their training with a one-week field training exercise outside the Special Forces camp at Plei Do Mi in the Central Highlands. The first platoon completed its program on 1 December and the entire company was declared combat operational on 23 December 1967.

Company-E was organized for 230 men, broken down into four platoons of seven six-man teams each. A headquarters section handled all the administration and logistics and a communications platoon was responsible for the vital radio contact with the teams. Although the

---

[60] This detailed history is from suasponte.com.

company was designed to field two active platoons while the other two platoons trained and prepared for further missions on a rotating basis, it wasn't long before every platoon was tasked with their own mission at the same time.

Each platoon consisted of a platoon leader (2nd Lt.), a platoon sergeant (SFC), the seven teams and communications support as required. Active platoons were deployed to mission support sites, such as Special Forces camps and forward fire bases. Each team was structured for a team leader (SSG, SGT), an assistant team leader (SGT, SPC), a radio operator (SPC, PFC), and three scouts (SPC, PFC) and was designated by platoon and team number within the platoon. Second platoon, team 1 would be Team 2-1. As time went by and personnel were rotated out, for a variety of reasons it was not uncommon for a team to consist of five men or less and to be led by a specialist (E-4). Also due to limited available resources it was not uncommon for a platoon to deploy with only three six-man recon teams. This did not keep the teams from completing any assigned mission, and after training together as a team the men were capable of handling each others duties and positions regardless of their rank. On some occasions, two or more teams would be combined (two-teamer) for specific missions such as a reaction force, prisoner snatch, or downed aircraft search/recovery (SAR).

In January 1969 the Army reorganized the 75th Infantry under the combat arms regimental system as the parent regiment for the various infantry patrol companies. On 1 February, Company-C (Ranger), 75th Infantry, was officially activated by incorporating the Company-E "Typhoon Patrollers" into the new outfit. The Rangers were known as "Charlie Rangers" in conformity with C in the ICAO phonetic alphabet. Company-C continued to operate under control of I Field Force and was based at An Khe. From 4 to 22 February 1969, three platoons rendered reconnaissance support for the Republic of Korea 9th Division in the Ha Roi region and two platoons supported the Phu Bon province advisory campaign along the northern provincial boundary from 26 February to 8 March. During the first part of the year, teams also pulled recon-security duty along the ambush prone section of Highway 19 between An Khe and the Mang Yang pass.

During March 1969, Lt. Gen. Charles A. Corcoran assumed command of I Field Force and an enhancement of Ranger capability was begun. Company-C constructed a basic and refresher training facility at An Khe and conducted a three-week course for all non-recondo-graduate individuals during April. The company then used the course for new volunteers before going to the MACV Recondo School. In late April, Company-C shifted support to the 173rd Airborne Brigade's Operation WASHINGTON GREEN in northern Binh Dinh Province. Company-C assisted Company-N by conducting surveillance of enemy infiltration routes that passed through the western mountains of the province toward the heavily populated coastline.

Most Company-C assets remained in Binh Dinh Province in a screening role, but at the end of April one platoon was dispatched for one week in the Ia Drang Valley near the Cambodian border. This was followed by two platoons being kept with the ROK Capital Division on diversionary and surveillance operations through mid July.

On 21 July the company received an entirely new assignment. Company-C was attached to Task Force South in the southernmost I Field Force territory operating against Viet Cong strongholds along the boundary II and III Corps Tactical Zones. The company, now under the command of Maj. Bill V. Holt, served as the combat patrol arm of Task Force South until March 1970.

The Rangers operated in an ideal reconnaissance setting that contained vast wilderness operational areas, largely without population or allied troop density. Flexible patrol arrangements were combined with imaginative methods of team insertion, radio deception, and nocturnal employment. Numerous ambush situations led by Company-C to anticipate an opportunity to use Stay-Behind infiltration techniques. As one team was being extracted, another team already on the chopper would infiltrate at the same time on a Stay Behind mission. The tactic was to be very successful. The company operated in eight day operational cycles and used every ninth day for "recurring refresher training". The teams rehearsed basic patrolling techniques varying from night ambush to boat infiltration. Ranger proficiency flourished under these conditions, and MACV expressed singular satisfaction with Company-C's results. The Viet Cong had taken advantage of the "no man's land" of Binh Thuan and Binh Tuy Provinces straddling the allied II and III corp tactical zones to reinforce their Military Region Six headquarters. Company-C performed a monthly average of twenty-seven patrols despite inclement weather in this region and amassed a wealth of military intelligence.

On 1 February 1970 the company was split when two platoons moved into Tuyen Duc Province and then rejoined on 6 March. Numerous team sightings in the Binh Thuan area led to operation HANCOCK MACE. Company-C was moved to Pleiku city on 29 March 1970, and placed under operational control of the aerial 7th Squadron of the 7th Cavalry where they conducted thirty-two patrols in the far western border areas of the Central Highlands.

On 19 April the company was attached to the separate 3rd Battalion, 506th Infantry and relocated to An Khe, where it was targeted against the 95th NVA Regiment in the Mang Yang Pass area of Binh Dinh Province. The rapid deployments into Pleiku and An Khe provided insufficient time for teams to gain sufficient information about new terrain and enemy situations prior to insertion and they sometimes lacked current charts and aerial photographs. Company-C effectiveness was hindered by poor logistical response, supply and equipment shortages, and transient relations with multiple commands. These difficulties were worsened by commanders who were unfamiliar with Ranger employment. Thus, the Rangers performed routine pathfinder work and guarded unit flanks as well as performing recon missions.

On 4 May 1970 the company was opconned to the 4th Infantry Division. The following day Operation BINH TAY I, the invasion of Cambodia's Ratanaktri Province, was initiated. Although Ranger fighting episodes in the BINH TAY I operation were often fierce and sometimes adverse, the operation left Company-C with thirty patrol observations of enemy personnel, five NVA killed, and fifteen weapon captured. On 24 May 1970 Company-C was pulled out of Cambodia and released from 4th Infantry Division control. Four days later they were rushed to Dalat to recon an NVA thrust toward the city. Their recon produced only seven sightings but an enemy cache was discovered containing 2,350 pounds of hospital supplies, and 50 pounds of equipment. They remained in Dalat less than a month before being sent back to rejoin Task Force South at Phan Thiet. May, June and July of 1970 were described by the new commander of Company-C, Maj. Donald L. Hudson, as involving a dizzying pattern of operations. The company operated in Binh Thuan, Lam Dong, Tuyen Duc, Pleiku, and Binh Dinh Provinces during this time. Twenty-seven days were devoted to company movements with sixty-five days of tactical operations, each move necessitating adjustment with novel terrain, unfamiliar aviation resources, and fresh superior commands.

On 26 July 1970 Company-C was transported by cargo aircraft to Landing Zone English outside Bong Son and was returned to the jurisdiction of the 173rd Airborne. The company supported operation WASHINGTON GREEN in coastal Binh Dinh Province with small unit ambushes, limited raids, and pathfinder assistance for heliborne operations.

During August, "Charlie Rangers" attempted to locate and destroy the troublesome Viet Cong, Khan Hoa provincial battalion, but were deterred by Korean Army jurisdictional claims. The mission became secondary when the 173rd discovered a large communist headquarters complex at secret base 226 in the Central Highlands and on 17 August the 2nd Brigade of the 4th Infantry Division moved into the region and Company-C was attached for reconnaissance.

In mid-November 1970 Company-C was attached to the 17th Aviation Group, and it remained under either aviation or 173rd Airborne Brigade control for most of the remaining duration of its Vietnam service. Following the inactivation of I Field Force at the end of April 1971, Company-C was reassigned to the Second Regional Assistance Command, and on 15 August was reduced to a brigade strength Ranger company of three officers and sixty-nine enlisted men. The I Field Force rangers were notified of pending disbandment as part of Increment IX (Keystone Oriole-Charlie) of the Army redeployment from Vietnam. Company-C (Airborne Ranger), 75th Infantry commenced final stand-down on 15 October 1971 and was reduced to zero strength by 24 October. On 25 October 1971 Company-C was officially inactivated.

APPENDIX II: RECONDO SCHOOL, E-20 4TH PLATOON LRP ROSTER

1st Lt. Bob Stein and SFC Harold H. Crowe

Team 4-1	Team 4-5
S. Sgt. Henry L. Swift	Sgt. Terrence L. Stolzman
Sgt. James K. Brokaw	SPC4 Peter G. Nebe
SPC4 Jerry W. Shankle	PFC George L. Carter
PFC Steven O. Woodson	PFC Larry D. Clark
PFC Paul M. Kuebler	PFC Michael Peace
PFC John P. Higgins	PFC Matthew Shealey
Team 4-2	**Team 4-6**
Sgt. Robert L. Malone	Sgt. Charles W. Samuelson
Sgt. Thornton P. Mills	Sgt. Ralph R. Sedgwick
PFC Joseph A. Brinthaupt	PFC Juergen A. Besecke
SPC4 Milton D. Hendrickson	PFC James E. Perry
PFC Richard A. McKenzie	PFC Richard Spears
SPC4 William B. Rosenberg	SPC4 James G. Worth
Team 4-3	**Team 4-7**
S. Sgt. James Nobles	Sgt. James E. Clay
Sgt. Thomas D. Workman	Sgt. George Hutchison
SPC4 Donald R. Kinton	SPC4 David T. Thomas
SPC4 Raymond F. Bohrer	PFC Robert L. Townsel
PFC Richard A. Gosnell	PFC Ronald D. Causey
PFC James T. Smith	PFC Herman M. Dunklebarger
Team 4-4	
Sgt. Robert P. Johnston	
Sgt. Charles N. Haney	
PFC Delbert L. Ayers	
SPC4 Lieuan W. Hansen	
PFC Norman D. Grubb	
PFC Charles E. Curtis	

Appendix III: Long Range Patrol and Rangers of the Vietnam Era Killed in Action

David Bruce Tucker – MAJ – October 1, 1967 – E-20-LRP
Calvin Arthur Greene – 1LT – December 19, 1967 – E-20-LRP
Patrick Lee Henshaw – SGT – December 19, 1967 – E-20-LRP
John Richard Strohmaier – SGT – March 12, 1968 – E-20-LRP
Donald Ray Kinton – SP/4 – March 25, 1968 – E-20-LRP
David Allen Parker – SSG – April 6, 1968 – E-20-LRP
Edward Gilbert Lee – SGT – May 13, 1968 – E-20-LRP
Frederick William Weidner – SGT – May 20, 1968 – E-20-LRP
Emory Morel Smith – SSG – June 13, 1968 – E-20-LRP
Eric Stuart Gold – SGT – January 5, 1969 – E-20-LRP
Paul Robert Jordan – SGT – January 24, 1969 – E-20-LRP
Elton Ray Venable – SGT – February 19, 1969 – E-20/C-75
Ronald William Cardona – SSG – July 6, 1969 – C-75-RGR
Frank Daniel Walthers – CPL – August 1, 1969 – C-75-RGR
Harold David Williams – SSG – August 1, 1969 – C-75-RGR
William Russell Squier Jr. – SSG – September 13, 1969 – C-75-RGR
Keith Mason Parr – SGT – October 26, 1969 – C-75-RGR
Walter Guy Burkhart – CPL – November 11, 1969 – C-75-RGR
Rex Marcel Sherman – CPL – November 19, 1969 – C-75-RGR
Richard Gary Buccille – SP/4 – December 20, 1969 – E-20/C-75
William Joseph Murphy – SGT – February 16, 1970 – C-75-RGR
Steen Bruce Foster – SSG – May 14, 1970 – C-75-RGR
James Lee Loisel – CPL – May 14, 1970 – C-75-RGR
Michael Edward Kiscaden – SSG – July 1, 1970 – C-75-RGR
Hilburn M. Burdette Jr. – SGT – July 12, 1970 – C-75-RGR
John William Rucker – SGT – December 14, 1970 – C-75-RGR
Edward Earl Scott Jr. – CPL – February 22, 1971 – C-75-RGR
Kevin Garner Thorne – SP/4 – February 27, 1971 – C-75-RGR
Gordon Keith Spearman Jr. – SSG – March 10, 1971 – C-75-RGR
Loyd Eugene Robinson – SP/4 – June 11, 1971 – C-75-RGR
Jimmy Lyn Dunagan – SGT – January 21, 1972 – C-75-RGR

Names provided by: Bob Smyers, Chaplain 75th Ranger Regiment Association

APPENDIX IV: FIRST BRIGADE, 101ST AIRBORNE DIVISION

Original orders transferring soldiers to E-Company
20th Infantry (Long Range Patrol)

```
             1ST BRIGADE 101ST AIRBORNE DIVISION * 3
                      APO San Francisco 96347
                                                              bh
SPECIAL ORDERS                                        18 October 1967
NUMBER    291                    EXTRACT

    18. TC 254. RSG dir as indic this sta. NTI. Fol data appl to all
indiv unless otherwise indic.
    Rel fr: As indic  Asg to: Co E 20th Inf (Long Range Patrol) APO 96350
    Rept date: 20 Oct 67  Lv data: NA  EDCSA: 20 Oct 67  Sp instr: NA

FNI HHC 1st Bn (Abn) 327th Inf
SAMUELSON, CHARLES W RA13868076 SP5 E5
SEDGWICK, RALPH R II RA19818617 SGT E5

FNI Co A 1st Bn (Abn) 327th Inf
CLAY, JAMES E RA15736647 SGT E5

FNI Co C 1st Bn (Abn) 327th Inf
BRINTHAUPT, JOSEPH A RA12744351 PFC E3

FNI HHC 2d Bn (Abn) 327th Inf
STOCK, WALTER DAVID RA13655450 SSG E6
STRANGE, RODERT R RA19685238 SSG E6

FNI Co A 2d Bn (Abn) 327th Inf
TOWNSEL, ROBERT LEWIS RA12867493 PFC E3
HUTCHISON, GEORGE W RA14883347 SP4 E4
SNELL, LAWRENCE R RA15409541 SSG E6
KINTON, DONALD R RA17730656 SP4 E4

FNI Co B 2d Bn (Abn) 327th Inf
CAUSEY, RONALD D US53842078 PFC E3
AMITY, JOHN F JR RA19842855 SP4 E4
DUNKLEBARGER, HERMAN M RA13894541 PFC E3
WISE, EDDIE L RA53343618 SSG E6
GOSNELL, RICHARD A US56425901 PFC E3

FNI Co C 2d Bn (Abn) 327th Inf
HIGGINS, JOHN RA11810518 PFC E3
HANSEN, LIEUAN W RA19866112 SP4 E4
HENDRICKSON, MILTON D RA19863357 SP4 E4

FNI Co A 2d Bn (Abn) 502d Inf
PEACE, MICHAEL E US56690855 PVT E2
ROSENBERG, WILLIAM B RA16867901 PFC E3

FNI Co C 2d Bn (Abn) 502d Inf
RUIZ-GUERRERO, GASTON P RA12756939 SP4 E4
```

Para 18 SO 291 HQ 1st Bde 101st Abn Div APO SF 96347   18 Oct 67

FNI 1st Plat (FASC) Co D 501st Sig
JONES, ORRIE RA12607675 SGT E5
WATKINS, CHARLES W RA16829352 PFC E3
CHARITY, CHARLES H II RA12762548 SP4 E4

FNI Sup Det 501st Sup Co Spt Bn
THOMAS, DAVID T RA17722003 SP4 E4

FNI HHD Spt Bn
SWIFT, HENRY L JR RA15197753 SSG E6

FNI Fwd Spt Det Co A (Grd)(Maint) 801st Maint Spt Bn
PUCKETT, ARCHIE D RA16604229 SP5 E5

FNI Det 1 Admin Sec 101st Admin Co Spt Bn
BOHRER, RAYMOND F RA19863079 SP4 E4
SHAFFER, ROBERT J RA13863169 PFC E3
DIBARTOLO, PETER RA12679147 SP4 E4
MULLANE, HENRY V US56585628 PVT E2
ZOLLO, JAMES A US52721812 PFC E3
SMITH, LEONARD RA14960073 PFC E3

FOR THE COMMANDER:

OFFICIAL: E. M. STRONG
                                         MAJ, AGC
                                         Adjutant General

DAVID A KORFONA
CPT, AGC
Assistant AG

DISTRIBUTION:
D - plus
2 - Co E 20th Inf (LRRP) APO 96350

Appendix V: Army Orders for Combat Infantry Badge

Incomplete List

HEADQUARTERS
INFANTRY DIVISION
APO San Francisco 96262

SPECIAL ORDERS
NUMBER 347   EXTRACT   13 December 1969

151 TC 322. UP AR 672-5-1 fol indiv this sta are awarded COMBAT
INFANTRYMAN BADGE: Unit as indicated.

FIRST AWARD

Co E (LRP), 20th Inf (Abn)

Name	Service No.	Rank	MOS
MALONE, DANDRIDGE M.	071832	LTC	72162
PARKER, JOSEPH S.	05326626	1LT	71542
DRINKER, RONALD V.	RA16600421	SFC E7	11B4P
BRAGG, THOMAS A.	RA24751511	SSG E6	11B4P
BARBER, GEORGE I.	RA17595728	SSG E6	11B4P
NOBLES, JAMES F.	RA18684234	SSG E6	11B4P
RUDOLPHO, SANTIAGO	RA18401226	SSG E6	11B4P
STRANGE, ROBERT R.	RA19685238	SSG E6	11F4P
YARBROUGH, JEFFREE	RA53340514	SSG E6	11B4P
CLAY, JAMES F.	RA15738643	SGT E5	11B4P
ELLIS, GEORGE M.	RA13847964	SGT E5	11B4P
HICKS, LEON JR	RA18743979	SGT E5	11B4P
MALONE, ROBERT L.	RA14953623	SGT E5	11C4P
MILLER, DONALD D.	RA28790151	SGT E5	11B4P
ROSS, PATSY L.	RA52514937	SSG E6	11F4P
BROKAW, JAMES K.	RA16838312	SGT E5	11B4P
HANEY, CHARLES N.	RA16873074	SGT E5	11B4P
LEE, EDWARD G.	RA21347833	SGT E5	11B4P
OGDEN, JAMES R.	RA18749367	SGT E5	11B4P
ROTH, ROBERT C.	RA19841536	SGT E5	11B4P
SMITH, EMORY M.	RA14912180	SGT E5	11B4P
WORKMAN, THOMAS De	RA14922521	SGT E5	11B4P
MILES, JAMES W.	RA18748196	SP4 E4	11B2P
ROLLINS, CALVIN F.	RA18768979	SP4 E4	11B2F
VALDAYS, WILLIAM G.	RA18684497	SGT E5	11F4P
WATKINS, LAWRENCE	RA15738881	SGT E5	11F4F
WILLIAMS, ORVILL C.	RA18950644	SP4 E4	11B2P
KOONS, GEORGE B.	RA16838364	SP4 E4	11B2P
MC NEILL, ALAN M.	US55876078	SP4 E4	11B2F
MILLER, MARK A.	RA18773330	SP4 E4	11B2F
STEPHENS, ALEXANDER	RA15757591	SP4 E4	11B2F
THOMAS, DAVID T.	RA17722003	SP4 E4	11B2F
AYERS, DELBERT L.	RA19883019	SP4 E4	11B2F
CORRIGAN, THOMAS F.	US51977904	PFC E3	11B1F
CURTIS, CHARLES E.	US54401842	SP4 E4	11B2F
CODERLY, MICHAEL D.	RA18751081	SP4 E4	11B2F
GOSNELL, RICHARD A.	US56425901	SP4 E4	11B2F
HESTER, STEVEN K.	RA15806667	PFC E3	11B1F
HOPKINS, DAVID	US52751316	PFC E3	11B1F

321

ACKNOWLEDGEMENTS

The author is indebted to many contributors and collaborators:

The men of E-Company, 20th Infantry, Long Range Patrol (Airborne).

The wives and family members who shared in their soldier's experience, and made unique and valuable contributions to this book.

Pilots Don Williams and Jim Fisher for providing insight into the Vietnam air war.

The Pritzker Military Museum and Library

Abbey Benoit

Joey Welsh

Johnny Chau, re:creative

Alexander Echevarria, Attorney at Law

Len and Carolyn Goss, goodeditors.com

David Hansen, CPA

Naomi Miali

Michael and Elise Stein

Pat Stein

Randy Vaughn, DDS

Dr. Erik B. Villard, U.S. Army Center of Military History

B.J. and Hillary Wall

Patrick and Meredith Watkins

My wonderful wife, Virginia, for transferring her job skills from a corporate desk to our kitchen table. I'm grateful that she helped me wrap-up this seven-year project lest my copy require delivery to Arlington National Cemetery!

ABOUT THE AUTHOR

Lt. Bob Stein considered himself a good soldier. He didn't think of himself as a warrior, but he would become one. After graduating from the University of Minnesota, he volunteered for the Army in 1965 thinking he would be garrisoned in Germany for a chance to see Europe on the government's dime. Vietnam was not in his vocabulary.

In 1967 Stein arrived at Pleiku Air Base in South Vietnam and was assigned to the First Cavalry Division as a platoon leader in the Fifth Cavalry Regiment (B-1-5). During the next twelve months, he was in frequent combat, and sometimes daily gunfights, surrounded by exceptional warriors fighting veterans of the North Vietnamese army.

In the battle of Vien Thien (3) on June 21, 1967, his cavalry company clashed with the 7th Battalion, 18th NVA Regiment.

Lieutenant Bob Stein is awarded the Silver Star by Major General John J. Tolson, 1st Cavalry Division Commanding General, for actions at the battle of Vien Thien (3), June 21, 1967.

Stein was the only lieutenant in the field since the other three lieutenants and most senior non-commissioned officers were dead or seriously wounded. Two men of his company were awarded the Congressional Medal of Honor for their actions on that day. Stein received the Silver Star.

In November he was selected as the 4th Platoon's leader for a new Long Range Patrol Company being formed in-country principally with battle-hardened combatants volunteering from the 101st Airborne Division. He participated in a night combat jump, rowed a raft from a Navy riverine patrol boat that inserted a Special Forces team, and was at Camp Enari in the Central Highlands on January 30, 1968 for the massive Tet Offensive.

His platoon's seven six-man teams usually patrolled along the Cambodian border and provided intelligence as they reported enemy movements on the Ho Chi Minh resupply route from North Vietnam. About half of those patrols ended in gunfights requiring extraction under fire. Normally Stein was found in the Command and Control helicopter inserting and recovering his brave men from deep inside the enemies' domain.

Army Ranger units had been disbanded in 1959, and his teams' successes as well as those of another Long Range Patrol Company and Long Range Reconnaissance Patrol units, prompted the Army to reflag them on February 1, 1969 creating today's Army Rangers. Following his stint in the Army, Stein worked for the Marriott Corporation for thirty-three years and retired in 2007.